CHINA SAILOR

THE SHOOTING OF WHALES

CHINA SAILOR
THE SHOOTING OF WHALES

a novel

Franklin Lafayette King

tP
Texture Press
2016

This book is a work of fiction. Names, characters, businesses, organizations, places, events, and incidents either are the product of the author's imagination or are used in a fictitious manner. Any resemblance to actual persons, living or dead, events, or locales is entirely coincidental.

Copyright © 2016 Franklin Lafayette King

All rights reserved.

Published in the United States by
Texture Press
1108 Westbrooke Terrace
Norman, OK 73072

For ordering information,
visit the Texture Press website at
www.texturepress.org

Cover painting:
Franklin Lafayette King

Book design: Arlene Ang

ISBN-13: 978-1-945784-00-2
ISBN-10: 1-945784-00-8

No part of this publication may be reproduced, stored in a retrieval system, or transmitted in any form, or by any means, electronic, mechanical, photocopying, recording, or otherwise without either the prior written permission of the publisher or the copyright holder. This book may not be lent, hired out, resold or otherwise disposed of by way of trade in any form of binding or cover other than that in which it is published without the prior consent of the publisher.

Dedicated to Donna Chan

TABLE OF CONTENTS

Chapter 1: Pier Echo 13

Chapter 2: Night in Heaven and Hell 16

Chapter 3: Paula's War 32

Chapter 4: Sea of Change 38

Chapter 5: Turning of the Wheel 68

Chapter 6: Battle of the Movie Projector 82

Chapter 7: Doubt Is a Visitor 89

Chapter 8: To Dream 94

Chapter 9: Bridge Watch 116

Chapter 10: Sign of the Crab 132

Chapter 11: Sailor's Prayer 138

Chapter 12: Among the Clouds 167

Chapter 13: Combinations 178

Chapter 14: Aiding the Affluent 191

Chapter 15: The Searcher 203

Chapter 16: Never Again, or at Least Until Tomorrow 210

Chapter 17: Lost Horizons 223

Chapter 18: Ascension 232

Chapter 19: Repulse Bay 236

Chapter 20: Tiger Balm Garden 258

Chapter 21: Moment of Regret 285

Chapter 22: The Enemy Is Exhaustion 293

THE SHOOTING OF WHALES *

To lift, to pause, to fall once more.
Resurrection afloat upon the Western Sea.
Gray prow slices into the waves.
Ship of the line designed to pursue then kill.

Beasts whose spray does fill the salt-smitten gale.
Death by presidential decree is made.
A blood offering of atonement sought.
Shooting of whales the order demands.

Flash of light in the black tropic night.
Shells fall upon the sea; shooting stars of man's design.
A scent of well-burned soot.
Spent powder stings my flesh anew.

Viewed in a curio shop where dreams are sold.
Rice paper windows and bamboo floor.
China sailor upon a shelf does stand.
Porcelain sailor, a prisoner of glass.

Like that required by mortal man,
I take the figure in my hand.
To stare upon myself in stark relief.
Bellbottom trousers and Dixie Cup.

I cannot resist, but caress the altar's gift.
In moist hands the image now held.
Through my fingers it slips then falls.
Porcelain shards of shrapnel burst upon the floor.

The shell well-struck; the harpoon set.
Blood and brine to the black sky hurled!
The belly of the whale to the sea is cast.
Feast for sharks, officiated by the servant of man.

* Referring to the Gulf of Tonkin incident that propelled the United States and other nations into the Vietnam War, President Lyndon B. Johnson commented in 1965, "For all I know, our Navy was shooting at whales out there."

THE SHOOTING OF WHALES

US DESTROYER BEATS OFF ATTTACK BY 3 RED
VIETNAMESE TORPEDO BOATS
—*The Sun*, August 1964

Why do wars start? I do not know. I only know that my own war started the night of August 2, 1964 as I slept in a small farmhouse in Texas. It was a typical night, dry lightning coming from the east. A gentle wind blew from the cotton fields; moonlight lit the gardenia bush by the front porch, its odor slowly drifting through the open windows of my room.

Thousands of miles away on a gulf unknown to me, a destroyer was engaging North Vietnamese Navy torpedo boats. In my youth, I did not know the significance of that night on my life or the lives of the millions of others that were to follow and of the birth of the drug culture—the illegitimate child of conflict.

CHAPTER ONE

Pier Echo

It had been fifty years since Professor John Yorktown's last visit in the Los Angeles area. The convention was typical. His speech that morning had been memorized and borrowed from one of his early scholarly articles. He no longer bothered to use PowerPoints, but instead hurriedly recited the speech, his eyes seldom making contact with the audience.

He spent lunch eating, not a salad as his doctor had ordered for his high blood pressure and life-threatening cholesterol, but a steak with well-salted french fries to celebrate the end of the event that he had not particularly enjoyed. He had attended many such professional meetings, drunk from silver-colored ice pitchers, and strained to see under the dim lights of the conference hall. He was very happy to be free of the meeting's agenda. As evening approached and with the knowledge that his flight back to Dallas would be after midnight, he asked the taxi driver to take him to

Terminal Island.

"What's at Terminal Island?" asked the driver in a thick Middle Eastern accent.

"I shipped out of there over fifty years ago. I would like to see what it looks like today."

Upon joining the Navy, John had been assigned to the USS *Yorktown*, homeported in Long Beach. He had just reported aboard the ship when he was transferred to the tin can USS *Hyman* (DD 715). John said, "If I remember correctly, Yorktown used to tie up at Pier Echo."

"Me, I don't know what is Pier Echo?" the driver replied loudly, staring at his ride from the rearview mirror.

The trip through Long Beach was faster than John remembered. Terminal Island soon appeared before him. In the 1960s, the small island had supported numerous oil derricks as well as discarded beer cans and other refuse thrown from the city buses that sailors boarded for the short ride to Long Beach.

He remembered the sailors exchanging their bellbottoms for civvies in one of the city's many locker clubs. What they could not change were the crew cuts and tattoos that marked them as members of a distinctive and ancient profession. Men tanned not only by the sun, but from the whiskey they consumed as they traveled the great oceans of the world.

Many things had changed in the island, but not the arid landscape and salt-water smell. John found himself approaching the deteriorating concrete pilings where *Yorktown* had moored during the Vietnam War. The once polluted and oil-slick water was now clear and the bottom, once veiled by overboard discharge, yielded a variety of sea life to the inquisitive visitor. Small crabs could be seen crawling along the bottom while starfish sat waiting for what the shallows of the harbor provided.

John asked the driver to return for him in two hours for he wanted to be alone with his thoughts. He was soon accompanied by the sounds of seagulls resting upon the pilings of a deserted and decaying pier. He looked towards the western sun as it quickly became veiled by the sea fog that draped Catalina and the other Channel Islands. His thoughts, reluctant at first, took him from *Yorktown* and Pier Echo to the destroyer *Hyman*.

CHAPTER TWO

Night in Heaven and Hell

FIGHT-IF-WE-MUST RESOLUTION BACKED
—*Pacific Stars and Stripes*, August 8, 1964

The Navy-chartered 727 touched down at 1500 at Tachikawa Airfield just outside of Yokohama. It bounced twice before settling down. The brakes were applied hard as the engines roared in reverse, casting the passengers forcefully forward. The passengers were young, just boys, some bound directly for Vietnam and others for the various military bases along the way: Yokosuka, Naha, and Subic Bay.

"Ensign, you can release the armrest now unless you plan on taking it with you," said the chief petty officer sitting next to John. "Not used to flying?" he asked with a smile.

John looked at him. "Yes, chief, that's just about correct.

Anything above the height of my Dad's barn results in a prayer of deliverance." He knew that he was a boot ensign with only a first class midshipman cruise under his belt. In addition, this was only the second flight that he had ever been on. Until now he had always been able to drive, take a bus, or a train in order to avoid flying.

John was of average height with blond hair and blue eyes. Nothing spectacular but okay—at least a few girls at the University of Texas thought so. He owned a homemade sailboat that he kept on Lake Travis near Austin. He did not have any difficulty in getting dates for a crew since sailing was a sport that the coed community was more than willing to participate in. In addition, he could afford the free wind and sun.

"Sir, that won't last long. I mean your fear of flying. Soon you'll get used to everything. And I mean *everything*," the chief said with a smile.

A mix of Army, Marine, and Navy people debarked from the aircraft into the night spotlighted by the bright lights of the military airfield. John was nervous, not necessarily because of the flight but the uncertainty of what lay ahead. He had volunteered for any duty west of the 180th meridian that divided the world in half. He had wanted a swift boat in Vietnam, instead he was now assigned to a destroyer homeported in Yokosuka, Japan. He was lucky. Any career officer would have given his ass for a tin can since it was the pathway for a line officer to advance quickly up the chain of command.

The debarked passengers, who were destined for shipboard assignments, were quickly loaded onto a bus that, upon leaving the military installation, sped through the dimly lit streets of Yokohama on its way to the Yokosuka Naval Base. The feel of the air, the abundant shop lights, and myriad odors of Japan were very different from those of Austin, Texas. The smell of pollution was strong and the streets were crowded with people who spoke rapidly in a harsh but musical language that John had never heard before.

He was temporarily assigned to NAVCOMSTAYOKO while awaiting his future ship's return from the gun line off the coast of South Vietnam. The *Hyman*, like the other three squadron destroyers were World War II Gearing-class tin cans of DESRON 9. They were assigned to gunfire support, plane guarding carriers, and search-and-rescue missions in the Gulf of Tonkin.

In the month-long wait ahead, John was to report daily to the COMSTA that had little for him to do. No command looked forward to receiving transient officers. Much of his time was spent reading manuals and drinking coffee. Strong coffee that was served black since sugar and cream containers sat empty on the Formica tops of the COMSTA and BOQ lounges.

After work hours, John sat in the BOQ surrounded by out-of-date journals like *Readers Digest*, *Navy Times*, and *Naval Proceedings*. *Playboy*, the magazine that he really wanted to read, was missing from the lounge. That helped explain why he found himself sitting alone in the temporary wooden building. Loneliness was something he had not prepared for.

A Lieutenant Junior Grade or LTJG, in what appeared to be perfect physical condition, trim waist, and straight gig line, came in to use the telephone. After calling a friend, he hung up and spoke to John.

"Ensign, I bet you're one bored son of a bitch. Last night I saw you sitting in the same place. What the hell are you doing? Saving yourself for marriage?"

At first, John thought it would be in his best interest to act professional. "Yah, I just like to sit here and read *Naval Proceedings*."

The LTJG and John could not help but laugh at his awkward reply, obviously intended to impress senior officers. Both of them knew that LTJG was certainly not a high rank.

"Real career type. Yah, I bet. Have you gone to Thieves Alley?"

"What for?" John replied innocently. "I'll buy my suits in Hong Kong. I hear it is cheaper there."

"The Alley is where you find the China sailors that don't read professional journals."

"Okay, maybe I'll give it a try. Another night here and I will qualify for priesthood." John laughed uncomfortably.

"Just go out the main gate, cross the street, and step right in. Can't miss it. Try not to drown in a benjo ditch."

That evening, twenty-one-year-old John Yorktown put on Old Spice and walked to the base entrance. Before him was a street lined with bars, their lights flashing like fingers inviting him to enter. Grand Sukura, Stand Bar Yokosuka, and Bar Texas were just the first few marquees he saw. Loud American music could be heard seeking freedom from dark, smoky interiors that smelled of alcohol, cigarettes, and urine. In the center of the Alley were vendors selling unlabeled meat on sticks and other snacks that always included pasty rice. Profanity greeted him at every entryway into which he peered. Occasionally, he would step over vomit discharged by a drunken sailor that had preceded him.

After several false starts, John finally walked into Bar Texas. Women of all ages and various body types swarmed around him. It was too dark to determine their attractiveness. Two ladies grabbed his arms and led him to a booth. After a heated conversation in which they spoke only Japanese, the alpha girl was alone with John.

"Buy me lady cocktail!" she shouted above the jukebox's music.

"What?" said John, having difficulty understanding her request.

"Buy me lady cocktail!"

"What for?" asked John innocently.

"You boot ensign. I call you Cherry Boy Eddie."

"Well, thank you. I've been commissioned for two months and have been to sea as a midshipman aboard the *Ranger*. Before this, I was briefly assigned to the *Yorktown*. I am hardly the boot you think I am."

Ignoring his very limited accomplishments, the alpha girl shouted above the loud sound of the music, "You virgin when you come to Japan? You still cherry boy?"

"I've had a few dates. No woman has said that she was disappointed," he said uneasily.

The hostess smiled at him, then glanced at her companion. "I haven't had a virgin before."

"Well, I don't think you're going to 'have me' either." John laughed.

"Cherry Boy Eddie, we'll see about that. Now you order me a lady cocktail!"

Despite her insistent request, John rose from the booth and walked out into the street. Thieves Ally was filled with sailors who had drunk too much and who were invariably escorted by bar girls who managed to support them as they walked. The staggering sailors were led to taxis and taken to either the home of the hostess or to the nearby Fukasuka Hotel.

John continued to walk down the street, looking at the sailors and their dates. He felt like he was a part of the flotsam that flowed through the alleyway. Soon he saw a bar called Heaven and Hell. As he walked past, he noticed that the music was quieter, more to his taste. As he entered the dark interior lit by small wattage lamps, a record player was uttering The Vibration's version of the Wes Farrell and Burt Russell song, "Hang on Sloopy."

"God, how I love that song," he whispered to himself.

There at a table sat a beautiful Japanese woman on her own, smoking a long Virginia Slims cigarette. Her classic features reminded John of the paintings from the Tokugawa period that he had studied in various art museums while attending a study abroad program in Paris. Her hair, unlike the traditional style, was cut with bangs that emphasized her dark black eyes.

She did not appear to notice him while being partially hidden behind the spiraling motion of her cigarette smoke. Her maturity appealed to him. Unlike the other hostesses, she appeared not be interested in John as he approached her table. "May I buy you a drink?" he asked.

"You American officer?" she asked in unfaltering English. "If you are, you may buy me a lady cocktail."

At first John thought her veil of sophistication had lifted. She was as ambitious as the other women he had just encountered in Thieves Alley. While tempted to walk past her, he was also immediately attracted to her. Her short hair, white blouse, and tight black skirt appealed to him. She did not wear the gaudy jewelry characteristic of the others he had just seen. Thick cigarette smoke continued to ooze from deep within her lungs.

He lowered himself onto the hard wooden bench seat and looked towards her. "I am not going to ask you why you became a hostess. I know that no question of such magnitude can be answered in a single conversation or in the length it takes to consume a lady cocktail."

She did not reply. The music changed as a new LP dropped on the turntable. Nancy Sinatra's "These Boots are Made for Walkin'" blared throughout the small bar.

"What is your name?" he shouted to her.

"Misa," she replied, blowing her cigarette smoke away from John.

"Misa what?" he asked in an attempt to make conversation.

"Misa Murakami," she replied.

"Would you leave the bar with me tonight?" John asked.

"You can buy me out, but I don't think you have enough money," she replied with a smile.

"Try me," replied John.

"It will cost you 10,000 yen plus taxi fare to my house," she said, looking into his eyes.

"Okay, I can do that if I don't have to buy you any more

drinks for 350 yen a piece."

"You can't sit with me if you don't buy me drinks."

"I tell you what, I'll come back for you when the bars close. Just remember that a Navy curfew is in effect. I have to be off the streets between 0100 and 0400."

She did not reply. Looking away, she exhaled a thick cloud that curled above her head and pointed towards the door of the bar. John said no more. He rose and reentered the loud street.

He stood in the middle of the Alley looking at passersby. Submariners walked unsteadily towards Submarine Alley, the most frequented place for the silent service. Occasionally a merchant sailor would walk past him as well—always alone and with a quick pace.

John entered a small Japanese restaurant and sat by himself. The waitress did not speak English. He looked around and ordered by pointing to what another customer was eating that he thought he might enjoy.

After a brief moment, she returned with a green tea float. To John it was the best treat he had ever tasted, much better than a Texas Dairy Queen float. By the rear wall of the restaurant was a small electric-powered waterfall that provided just the right amount of ambient sound to the otherwise barren wooden structure, creating an artificial mood of relaxation.

As he sat there, two off-duty hostesses entered the bar, looked around, and walked to his table. Without being invited, the larger of the two sat down next to him followed by her much thinner associate who sat across from them.

"American officer? Merchant Marine officer?" the larger one

asked, covering her giggle with her hand.

"Your first guess is correct," John replied with a smile.

"What your name?"

"John Yorktown," he reluctantly replied.

"You off the *Yorktown*?" she asked, knowing that sailors off of a newly arrived ship had more money to spend than a crew that had been in port for several days.

He laughed, realizing that his last name was the same as the USS *Yorktown* (CVS-10) that had just arrived in port. He had earlier reported aboard her prior to being transferred to the *Hyman*. It was apparent to him that all capital ships were being deployed to the Far East. When a carrier docked along with her escorts, thousands of sailors were released to enter Thieves Alley. Inevitably, the price of lady drinks soared, making it almost impossible for an enlisted homeport swabbie to go on the beach. Only those in a long-lasting relationship were able to enjoy Thieves Alley.

When he did not immediately reply, she said in a teasing manner, "You been in port too long. You probably broke."

John did not know how to reply. He had spent very little from his less than three hundred a month paycheck. He knew if she thought he had more money, her persistence might just pay off.

"No thanks, ladies, I already have a date for the evening," he said with a smile.

"You no-good butterfly! You belong in an officers' bar."

Officers' bars were to be avoided. What ensign wanted to try to outbid an admiral? Besides the Old Man might be in the room next to you. In addition, the women were older and much less attractive than in the enlisted bars where the hostesses could relieve an eighteen-year-old swabbie of his money quicker than she could a married officer who took pride in not having to pay for sex with a stranger. No way would a boot ensign go into an officers' bar, no way.

"You no tell me what ship you off of?" she said once more, attempting to see how much money he truly possessed.

"Sorry, ma'am, I can't talk about what ship I am assigned to. Navy regs, you know." John felt proud of himself since he had been well taught in Communications Officer School not to betray ship movements. It was believed that hostesses could provide such information to the enemy.

"I don't think you are officer material," she said, rubbing John's leg. "I am going to call you G.I. Joe. I give you good special, G.I. Joe."

"I'm sorry, but I'm not bargain hunting. Whatever special you have in mind, I don't need it. The Navy sees to all of my special needs," John said seriously.

She started laughing. "You must be off the Queer Barge. You sure no hot ensign."

John had no idea what she was referring to by "special." The two young ladies could not control their laughter at his reply. Since he had refused their offer, they got up, holding on to one another and trying to control their amusement. John sat in a state of confusion, not understanding what was so funny.

He remained alone as though an off-limits zone had been declared around him. No other lady approached him even though he was the main topic of conversation on the periphery of the bar.

He looked towards the bartender. "I'll have a tall beer. Make it the tallest one you have." If he could make it last, he would not have to buy another one.

John realized that he was going to have to nurse the beer until Misa got off work at 0100. If the beer were short, he would drink it too fast. The bartender brought him an Asahi. In fact, it was two Asahi beers poured into an extra tall glass, the kind you would put flowers in. The end product was that he had been charged twice for a single beer. Awkwardly he nursed the flower vase, waiting for the time to meet Misa.

Time passed very slowly. He remembered a curio shop at the entrance to the alley. Along with other small, dimly lit, unpainted buildings, it formed the collective gatehouse of the alley. He left the bar and strolled back down the alleyway and entered the shop. The windows were made of rice paper and the floor was of bamboo. The strong smell of incense filled the damp, cold air. Upon a shelf a music box played the soft tones of "Sayonara".

"What you want, American sailor?" asked a harsh voice from behind the display.

"Just looking, ma'am," he said in his strong Texas accent, unable to see the speaker. There was no response to his statement.

As he looked at the small display of objects, he noticed a porcelain sailor, the image of an enlisted man in fine China. He picked up the object and held it in his hand, noticing the detail and expression of obedience painted on the prisoner of glass.

Suddenly, for some strange reason, his hand relaxed and he dropped the object to the floor where it broke into shards of sharp glass.

"You pay! You pay!" shouted the voice.

John reached into his wallet and put one thousand yen on the wooden counter top.

"Now you go! You go!"

He stood just outside Heaven and Hell observing his Timex as the hour approached. In the distance, he could see two shore patrol officers strolling towards him, their sticks swinging. One twirled his baton while the other struck his palm with his black wooden mallet. John knew that if Misa did not emerge shortly, he would be arrested for curfew violation. Then, the door to the bar swung open. Misa emerged smiling.

"You nice man. You waited for me."

He followed her obediently to the curb where she hailed a speeding taxi. Once seated in the back seat, she instructed the driver to proceed. A lengthy conversation ensued between Misa and the driver. It was apparent to John that she and the driver knew one another. Then she lit another Virginia Slims cigarette, exhaled, and looked at John.

"You English major?"

"No, Geography major," John replied. "But I took four years of English electives. I love to read and to think that I got credit for doing what I enjoy."

"Oh, okay. You read Shakespeare?" she asked.

"Yes, I did," he replied, wondering about the real intent behind her question.

Through the darkened back roads of Yokosuka, the taxi traveled swiftly until it stopped in front of a dark one-story wooden house on the edge of a benjo ditch. Outside the cab window, John could hear the waters of the open sewer flowing past on its journey to Tokyo Wan. The moonlight, the sound of the flowing waters, and the dim lights hidden behind rice paper windows created an image of harmonious beauty. The scent was a cacophony of odors whose sources were not to be revealed by lantern light.

She led him to her front door. "You wait here. I go inside for just a moment. Then we go sit in park."

John could not imagine what kind of evening lay ahead. It was well past curfew. If the shore patrol saw him, his night would be over and he would be placed on report and then sent back to the COMSTA.

Misa reemerged from the door, then closed it and took his hand. Her grip was very warm in the chilly air of the port city, a former naval base used by the Imperial Japanese Navy during World War II. In the night, the snows of Fujiyama glistened like polished silver.

They walked a short distance to a dimly lit park. It was a small oasis from the city with beautifully trained trees that created various sculptures.

They sat down on a night-moistened wooden park bench. Misa looked at him still holding his hand. "Have you read the *Great Books of the Western World?*"

John replied, "My uncle has the collection in his house. When I visited him, I would occasionally take a book home with me. I can't claim to have read all of the ones I borrowed."

"I have read all of them in English," Misa said.

"Why?" asked John.

"I only want to date officers. They smart men. They want to talk about books. I am not a dumb bar girl."

"Well, some officers are smart and may have read the *Great Books of the Western World*, not so sure about the rest."

"You gamble?" she asked in a nonchalant manner.

"That is a strange question," replied John.

"I bet you twenty-five American dollars that I know more about English literature than you do," she said boastfully.

"It wouldn't take much for you to win that bet. To be honest, for pleasure I have read Hemingway, Faulkner, and Steinbeck, but not much more. Didn't have the time," replied John. It occurred to him that she was smarter than he thought. She was challenging his ego in order to get him to bet money on something she was an expert on. *I can just see a senior officer taking up the bet, thinking that no Japanese bar girl could know more about English literature than he does*, thought John.

Still, John fell victim to his own pride. "Okay, I can play the game. Can I pick the category?"

"Of course," she replied with a smile.

"Okay, ask me some trivia about Ernest Hemingway." John had read several of his novels and some current articles on him in *Look* and *Life Magazine*.

"Okay. I will start with an easy question that any officer who reads should know. What was the last book that Hemingway almost completed before killing himself?"

"Misa, you know what? I have no earthly idea," he replied,

shaken by his lack of immediate recall.

"*The Garden of Eden,*" she replied.

John decided he might as well concede to losing the bet. "Normally, I would not pay until I had the chance to check the answer. For some reason, I think you are correct. You are probably always correct." John fumbled with his wallet and paid her 10,000 yen. "Is that enough?"

"Yes, close enough, American officer." She rose and led him to a taxi. "I see you tomorrow?" she asked.

"Yes," replied John. He had expected far more of the evening, but he was in a strange land and with an even stranger woman.

In his youthful naivety, John was attracted to her. She already knew more about life and its value than he did. What he could not understand after moving in with her later was the fact that she would not have sex with him. It was true that they slept together, but that was it—they just slept. Then, one day the truth was revealed.

"John, you need to move out of house for four days," Misa said.

At first he was offended but reasoned that they were spending too much time together. He was about to propose to her even though they had known each other for only three weeks. Maybe a few days apart would help him sort things out. He knew he had to be rational.

As he gathered his things into his duffle bag, he happened to open the wrong drawer of the vanity. There staring him in the face was an 11" x 12" picture of a master chief petty officer. "Who the hell is this ugly brute? Your father?" he asked sarcastically.

"No, he my other lover. We are engaged," she replied.

"Your other lover? Engaged?" John shouted in amazement.

"Yah, he much better lover than you. He off the *Okie City*, big cruiser. He got lot of money. He not as smart as you but he better man. He promised to read the *Great Books of the Western World*."

"Like shit he will," said John in frustration. Then it dawned on him, *Oklahoma City* had just arrived in port. As he turned towards her, she pushed him aside and placed the chief's picture on top of the vanity.

"So, you have been doing port and starboard all along. Damn, I should have seen this coming."

CHAPTER THREE

Paula's War

MARCHERS ARRIVE AT CAPITOL
—*Los Angeles Times,* March 25, 1965

The snow was beginning to descend the slopes of the sacred mountain. Soon the persimmon trees would be changing their colors. In the tropics, nothing changed but the direction of the wind, a wind that brought the monsoons to Southeast Asia.

While reading the message traffic in the communications shack, John noticed a CONFIDENTIAL message from the local NAVCOMSTA asking for a communications officer with top-secret clearance to act as a courier to CONUS. It would be a three-day assignment and would not count towards his annual leave.

John asked for permission to volunteer. It had been three long weeks since his arrival in the Far East, and he was anxious to reestablish his relationship with Paula Andrews, a second-year nursing student at the University of Texas. Before his departure, they had discussed the possibility of marriage. They frequently exchanged letters, each more passionate than the previous one. He had even bought an engagement ring in Yoko, financed by the Navy Federal Credit Union, just in case they became more serious in their relationship.

The plane left the Tachikawa Air Force Base with a nervous John on board. He had previously wired money to Paula so she could join him in San Francisco. Since it was only for an overnight stay, missing classes would not be a problem for her, or at least he hoped so. John was unable to contact her ahead of time since his calls had not been returned. It was a leap of faith on his part that she would join him on such short notice.

In John's possession was a leather satchel handcuffed to his left wrist. It bore an official seal to show if it had been tampered with since his receipt of it. Upon his arrival in Alameda, he reported to the NAVCOMSTA and the handcuff was removed. Then he was briefed by a petty officer.

"Sir, you need to check into the housing unit you've been assigned to. You are not to wear a uniform when you are off base. If anyone approaches you inquiring about the nature of your mission, you are to gain as much descriptive information as you can regarding the person and log it. There will be a curfew in place that requires that you be off the streets between 0100 and 0400 hours. The arrival and departure times of all guests at your lodging must be promptly reported," the PO1 said while looking at John's newly awarded ribbon, as Boats would later say, just for showing up. "Don't forget that your departure is scheduled for the day after tomorrow. You are to arrive at the NAVCOMSTA four hours before departure time for additional courier duties on your return to NAVCOMSTAYOKO."

The petty officer looked at him once more after checking his medical file. "I see your VD lecture is up-to-date."

"Thank you, that is good to know," replied John.

A young chief arrived just as John's briefing was being completed.

"Sir, don't forget that the military is not popular here. We are treated like an occupying force."

John sat in his room awaiting a visit from Paula or at least a call. Then the phone rang.

"John, this is Paula. How have you been?"

"Great, just having a fantastic time. I can't believe I'm actually hearing your voice. It has been such a long time. How are you doing? I thought you would be here by now"

"John, there's something I need to tell you." Paula paused. "I am engaged."

"What do you mean, engaged? That can't be!" he shouted into the phone.

"John, there is no future for us. I got so lonely while you were away. Besides, what value is the war you are fighting? America has changed. The message is love and not war. Peace!"

"Peace, hell!" he replied. "You mean I've been gone less than a month and American has changed?"

John's hand was trembling as he put the receiver back onto the cradle of the phone. He called for a cab to pick him up.

"Where to?" asked the driver.

John replied, "I have already been to hell; let's try heaven. On second thought, the San Francisco Bay Hotel will have to do—the one with a view of the Golden Gate Bridge. I had a drink or two with a friend on the rooftop bar before I flew to Japan. Good memories."

As John emerged from the cab, the driver said after receiving the fare, "Be careful. I don't mean when you're overseas, but here." With those words, he sped off.

John entered the ornate lobby and was soon sitting at the rooftop bar alone. The fog slowly arrived and hid the harbor navigation lights. After he ordered a rum and Coke, an older man joined him at the bar.

"How are things going?" asked John.

"Not so well!" the stranger replied after ordering a whiskey sour.

"Health or finances?" asked John.

"I retired from the Navy about two months ago. I'm Chief Warrant Officer Key. You look like a military man yourself, short hair and all."

"You're right. I'm Ensign Yorktown," John said, looking down at his drink.

"That was the name of the first ship I was assigned to after Pearl Harbor. I am talking about the *Yorktown* that went down at Midway."

"I salute your bravery. That was a fierce battle that turned the tide of war." They saluted one another with their now empty glasses. "You mentioned things are not going so well."

"Yes, sir, that is true. Everything is changing. When I came home from World War II, I was treated like a hero. People stopped me on the streets when I wore my uniform and thanked me. Today I couldn't wear my uniform to my own funeral if I wanted anyone to attend."

John was taken back by his comments. "It wasn't that way when I left Texas. What changed?" he asked.

"Students and Hollywood! That's what changed everything. You mentioned you're from Texas. Things don't change as quickly there as they do in California."

"You mean war movies?" asked John.

"Hell no, movie stars and other assholes. Wealthy spoiled brats, that's what they are. Jane Fonda is one of the worst of them all. She's even saying great things about our enemies, the Viet Cong and Ho Chi Minh. It didn't take any time for the students with their beards and pot smoke to join in. Now we have the movements, kidnappings, murders. Racial unrest is everywhere. Shit happening every day. People have replaced their minds with TV commentary."

"Pot smoking? The only things I have seen in Asia are sailors drinking whiskey, beer, and Akadama wine."

"Weed didn't exist here until everything I've been telling you about happened. You want my advice: go back to Asia. There you know what you are fighting for. Here, not even the politicians seem to know."

John looked out the windows of the bar. The fog was now

completing its journey through the Golden Gate Bridge. He looked at his watch and realized he needed to get back to Alameda before the curfew. If he arrived at the gate past 0100, he would be on report.

"Warrant, take care of yourself," he said with a smile.

John took the cab back to his lodging and waited for dawn and for the receipt of another leather satchel and handcuff. He was ready to return to Yoko and the war that he too questioned. He didn't want to think about the politicians, Hollywood, or the students who had a cause even if they did not clearly understand what it was they marched for or against.

"Yeah, just like that James Dean movie, *Rebel Without a Cause*," he said to himself.

After returning to Japan, John learned that his own ship was in Taiwan and that he needed to leave immediately for Kaohsiung. From there, *Hyman* was scheduled to go to Hong Kong where she was to serve briefly as Station Ship, Hong Kong; a tin can representative of the United States Navy.

After a year on a destroyer, he reasoned that he could get a swift boat. John felt he had to see action. He knew there might not be another war for years. But in youth, dreams change just as quickly as California culture. The protest movements were beginning to gather momentum, and the disillusionment of the war had already sat in among the young.

CHAPTER FOUR

Sea of Change

CONGRESS BACKS PRESIDENTS ON SOUTHEAST
ASIA MOVES; KHANH SETS STAGE OF SIEGE
—*The New York Times*, August 8, 1964

Vietnam—a word of beauty like stripes worn by the tiger. It waited for the young in the underbrush, the stench of the river. They were the game herded by the politicians; their patriotism fed by films and books. Soldiers, sailors, marines too soon caught in the net of the jungle hunt. Their original sin was being born, to be punished by one year in hell; only one year if they were lucky enough to live. But then they did not know this, this fact of war.

The *Hyman* was a small destroyer manned by teenagers and officers in their early twenties. Aboard, they carried a nuclear weapon, enough to start World War III. Two officers and the Old Man were all that was needed to release it. They had avoided the jungle and the stench of the river, yet they too were to engage an enemy that dwelt deep within themselves.

After boarding the ship, John was assigned to share a stateroom with Tom Fuller. He was a native of Chicago and a graduate of the University of Illinois. He was nice-looking with curly brown black hair. Despite his tan skin, his light blue eyes attested to his Celtic heritage.

  John inwardly knew he was as fortunate as Tom. His patriotic feelings and juvenile desire for combat quickly matured in the cinema of his youth. The reality of the small ship tied to a Kaohsiung industrial pier brought him to a new sense of what was about to occur.

Soon the word was passed for the ship to prepare to get underway. Tom, who had previously welcomed him aboard, vanished as he ran up the port ladder to the bridge where he was to assume the position of underway OOD. John walked to the wardroom to get out of the way of those hurrying to their various stations. After not finding any hot coffee in the wardroom, John proceeded onto the main deck. A strong wind was blowing, absorbing the odors of the harbor. The smells of soot, diesel, and dead fish were quickly inhaled by anyone venturing onto the weather deck.

John and Tom were both officers, short timers ordered to a destroyer homeported in faraway Yokosuka, Japan.

No grunt's sweat for us. No, sir. Just do your time and go home. There was only one holy commandment if you wanted to live: Do not volunteer. Never, never volunteer. Do I want jungle rot or a destroyer? John thought as he looked seaward, the distant shore of Taiwan now growing faint in the frothy, windswept wake.

Taiwan was slowly being veiled by an evening fog and its own pollution. As John viewed Kaohsiung from the port railing, his homesickness increased as the land grew smaller. It was a desire for home, a longing to touch his father's fields; to hold earth in his hands as his father had done before him; to smell plowed fields that possessed the promise of life in the warm spring air of the Blackland Prairie of Texas.

John had joined the Navy out of his love for the ocean. Even though in youth he had been far removed from the sea, he harbored an instinctual desire to sail upon the oceans of the world. Having also been brought up in the patriotism of the Eisenhower era, he felt it was his duty to serve without questioning the purpose of that bondage.

He had not been noticed at the University of Texas. His failure to be popular was a direct result of his lack of money and his childhood naivety fostered by the conformity demanded by the work schedule of a cotton farm. His broad smile and blue eyes did attract some coeds who too quickly learned that he could not afford a MGA and had failed in his bid to be a member of a popular fraternity. The only option open to him was to join NROTC. For him and other likeminded young men from poorer families, it became a type of fraternity isolated from the wealthier students.

The aroma of coffee ended his nostalgia as Boats, the all-knowing boatswain mate on every ship, came alongside the rail upon which he was leaning. He was in his late twenties, smoked, and drank whatever alcohol was available. Boats was wiry thin with heavily tattooed arms and chest. He wore a crew cut under the Dixie Cup that partially shielded his sea-weathered face.

"Missing land already I bet." He leaned close to John, careful to keep his coffee to his lee side. "We ain't even out of sight of land and I already miss the company of a woman." The creases in the darkly tanned face of Boats grew deeper as the sun swept across his reefed features. "A female and a steak are what I really need. Wouldn't object to a tall beer either."

"Yah, you bet, Boats. Nothing I'd rather have more." What a lie! John was ready for the sea with all of its loneliness and close confinement. Money had gone too quickly for him in port. He felt disillusioned by Paula and Misa ever since he had found out about their lovers.

He could do little for personal entertainment aside from looking for misplaced *Playboys* that arrived and departed the wardroom regularly during their passage to Hong Kong. He soon found out that entertainment was not part of the plan of the day for the crew of a wartime destroyer.

Boats shouted against the wind as the *Hyman* changed course, "The truth is, Mr. Yorktown, I'm broke. There ain't a swabbie on this ship that will loan me a dime. I can't even collect on the suckers that I lent money to out of my personal slush fund. They ain't got a penny. Spent every cent on women and Tiger Beer."

Since there were no prostitutes or Tiger Beer available for Boats at sea, he felt righteous. He gave the impression that he had not coordinated the expeditions to the brothels that surrounded the harbor. Even John, on his first night in Keelung, had been sucker enough to follow him to Mother Wong's Bar.

Mother Wong was an expert on Boats. She was a small woman with a strong cigarette breath. Her hair was dark black and fixed in a bun. Her hairstyle was most unusual for a woman whose occupation was to sucker sailors into buying watered-down cocktails. Her classic beauty, however, was diminished by her rapid conversation that increased in pitch as she spoke. Even though barely thirty-five, she seemed much older.

Mother Wong knew how to get Boats to spend everything he possessed plus what others would lend him. He always referred to her as "The Smart One." The madam was no ordinary prostitute. She was the proprietor of one of the largest and most successful houses in the Far East and charged accordingly.

Looking at the ocean was making John hungry. With the galley upwind from him, the odors of a bakery filled the air.

"Boats, right now you can have your hookers, I just want something to eat."

"Mr. Yorktown, you sure ain't no China sailor. Not yet, that is."

Out of a nearby hatchway, Tom emerged. Tom was the bull ensign on board having outranked John by a year. After graduating from the University of Illinois, he had decided to pursue a law degree. The military, however, saw little need for more lawyers. His ambition had landed him upon the shoal waters of the draft. Even though it would have been easy, he was too honest to fake a physical disqualification.

"Hey Tom, what's happening?"

"John, I guess you heard about the stiff we picked up?"

"No, what do you mean?"

"Well, we have to jettison this retired chief quartermaster at the 100 fathom curve. He had lived in the Orient since retiring."

"Are you kidding me? You mean someone wants to be buried out here?" John said as he looked at the slate-colored swells that rolled under a cloudy gray sky.

"Hell yes. One of the bennies of the service is burial at sea. I guess his family figured this was cheaper than shipping his ass stateside to Oklahoma. It seems like the old fart married a Chinese woman and retired in Kaohsiung. I guess she just flat wore him out along with cartons of cigarettes and Early Times."

"Sir," Boats interrupted, "you mean we have to slow down and jettison his ass on our way to Hong Kong?"

"I sure do," replied Tom. "Now don't worry Boats, the CO will kick her in the butt once we are through, and we will make Hong Kong on time."

"I participated in a burial at sea once," Boats informed the two young ensigns, "and let me tell you something, once you see one, you sure don't want no sailors dropping your ass over the sides."

"What happened, Boats?" John inquired.

"Well, sir, this first class requested his remains to be scattered at sea from a destroyer. He was an old tin can sailor out of

Diego who had spent most of his life on these rusting mothers. We picked him up, that is, his ashes, his wife, and two brothers in Yokosuka for the burial. He was deployed at the time, you see."

Boats continued after lighting another smoke, "Boy were they soused; looked like they'd been drinking steadily since the bad news and maybe even before that. Being part of the burial party, I helped them on board for the trip. I even held the first class while the messenger of the watch took the widow and the others to the chow hall for some coffee. By the time we were at the 100 fathom curve, the swells were big and the wind was high. We all gathered on the fantail just the same and made an effort not to barf because of the sea state. It was my job to cast his last remains into the brine while taps sounded, and then we were to have a gun salute—just like the book says."

Boats looked very serious as he continued, "The OOD brought her into the wind and slowed down just enough to give her steerage. Then the widow handed me the jar, and I opened the lid and threw him. Well, about that time the ship yawed and created a back suction on Mount 52. And damn if the first class didn't blow into both my face and the grieving widow's. There we were coughing, spitting, trying to get the first class out of our mouths and eyes. In the meantime his teeth and bone splinters fell on the deck. Well, after the widow had wiped him off her dress and gone back to the wardroom for more coffee, me and another sailor hosed the first class through the scuttles. You might say we gave him a saltwater send off."

From the 1MC came the traditional command: "All hands, prepare to bury the dead."

The officers and crew in the uniform of the day gathered on the ASROC deck. The E9 had been placed in a large wooden casket that Boats said must have contained two fat-ass chiefs.

"Hey Tom, with a wooden casket, how does it sink?" asked John, speaking above the mechanical roar of the revolving radar.

"How do you think it sinks, dumb ass?" Tom smiled. "They bore holes in her and weigh her down with spent brass shell casings. She goes down like a rock."

"Oh," replied John.

The CO read a short Bible verse. Then the coffin tenders raised the old salt and let him go over the side as taps sounded. The chief hit with a loud splash and vanished, then suddenly resurfaced like a sounding sub and bobbled.

"Shit, a floater!" passed from Boats' lips.

The gun salute was held up because the cue was for him to be below the surface. As the chief rode the swells, the ship's company, except for the burial detail, broke formation and manned the railings to watch. It was apparent that no one knew what to do.

Boats shouted the solution above the mix of sounds, "Let's either ram the fucker or man the 50 caliber. I knew of one asshole that washed up on Virginia Beach. They said he surfed ashore."

Tom looked towards Boats. "Hey Boats, I heard you told the new fellow in deck that the undertaker put the chief in his dress blues and fixed him in a saluting position." Just then a larger than average swell covered the coffin. It rose once more, turned turtle, then dove beneath the froth-covered swell. The volleys were not fired together but instead sounded as echoes.

"Yorktown, let's chow down," said Tom.

"I'll try to eat, but I'm not real hungry," John replied.

The wardroom was silent while they waited for the Captain to arrive. As was customary, officers could only sit down once the Old Man, who just turned 36, had seated himself at the table. Tradition dictated that officers should never discuss politics, religion, or sex in the wardroom. This last fact explained the absence of any enthusiastic discussions. Religion and politics lost any sense of relevancy to men at sea.

The Captain entered the hatchway and sank into his chair at the head of the table, relieving his legs from their burden of weight. He wore a pallid complexion that Boats attributed to lack of Irish whiskey. The more senior officers, lieutenants, and JGs then sat down according to rank, careful not to appear clumsy. This was especially difficult since the destroyer was taking heavy rolls. Ensigns had to wait until all the other officers were seated before grabbing an empty space as far from the Captain's chair as possible.

There was an unbridgeable gulf between senior and junior officers in the wardroom. The senior officers spoke about how much they loved their mission. Despite the saying that sailors belong on ships and ships belong at sea, the junior officers whispered about getting short and how, if they could it to all do over again, they would be wearing flowers in Canada. A rack in a split-window VW bus would have seemed perfect to anyone under 25.

While they waited to be served, the Filipino stewards busily attended to the table where each dish tasted as if catered from their home island.

John leaned towards Tom. "I feel like I'm eating in a foreign restaurant. Rice at every meal is going too far. What I could use now is a big Dixie Burger with cheese, fries, and a tall Coke."

"Boot! I might have known that a Dairy Queen was the height of your ambition in eating." Tom drew closer to John and said in a confidential manner, "What are you going to do when we get to Hong Kong? I bet you'll spend every cent you have or can borrow from Boat's slush fund. You've been hanging around him for advice, and he can give it. When I first came aboard this pig-iron mother, I followed that asshole ashore in Yokosuka. He claimed to know all the girls in town, and they would give us cut-rate prices on everything."

Tom continued to whisper, "We're not supposed to talk about this in the wardroom so keep your reactions under control. Let me tell you what happened. First of all, Boats decided we needed a hot sea bath so we flagged down a taxi and told the driver what we wanted. I don't know if he really understood what we said. Every time we told him something in English like, 'Now they have to be really pretty and know how to give, you know, a special,' he would answer in Japanese. Oddly enough, I would find myself replying, 'Yah, that's right and big breasts won't hurt either.' He must have driven us around for fifteen or twenty minutes. What I remember most is my listening for the next click of the meter.

"He finally hit the brake in front of a dark, windowless wooden structure that looked like a den's interior—nothing painted, just natural wood. We thanked the driver and richly rewarded him for his knowledge of hot sea baths and big-breasted women. Boats and I then quickly entered the building after noticing that the only sign was in Japanese. The entrance hall was lit with what appeared to be a single 40-watt red light. As my eyes adjusted to the electrical gloom, I noticed a very old Japanese woman sitting behind a counter. 'Hey Boats,' I said, 'she might be of historical interest since I understand that Japan has living art treasures.' Boats was not interested in art. 'Fuck it,' he replied. 'I hope she ain't the one that gives you head."

Tom continued, "The mamasan stared at us intently, which made me very uneasy. I had the urge to tell her that my intentions were honest, and that all I wanted was to get clean. Finally she spoke to the shadows that yielded two very small, young women who giggled as they approached.

"Without so much as a how-much-you-pay, they led us to what resembled a destroyer boiler room. When they opened the door to the bath, steam gushed into the passageway. There was a tub that looked like a child's wading pool and three or four small benches. The tub was covered by a wooden lid. When they pulled the slats back, it was a cauldron of steam and boiling water.

"I said, 'Hey Boats, this must be a Japanese P.E. Department. Some sexy evening. Looks like all we're going to get out of this is a scalding.' Undiscouraged, Boats leaned towards one of the small girls and began to talk in lower Alabama Japanese. The more he spoke, the more she giggled. Shit, I don't think she understood a word he was saying. I barely understood the Alabama lingo myself."

Tom continued in a confidential manner, "They helped us

undress, placing our clothes, watches, and billfolds inside two wire baskets they kept with them. Soon they left us sitting on the hard wooden seats in the hot, humid heat.

"When breathing became almost impossible, I leaned towards Boats. 'I hate to mention this, but it seems like your two friends have been gone long enough. It is hotter than hell in here.'

"'Mr. Fuller,' Boats replied, 'am I supposed to know how long those two girls have been gone? There's no damn chronometer on the bulkhead. What bothers me is that in all this heat, it's hard enough to raise my arm much less my utensil.'

"'Boats, I'm ready for a beer and a steak,' I confided. 'I kind of figured out you just have a thing for bathing. I can get this much excitement back in the shower stall of the pig-iron mother. I'm gonna go out there and find those two hookers and ask for my clothes back.' I peered down the totally darkened passageway. The air felt chill as though hours had passed without disturbing it with a blower motor.

"Suddenly, the front door flew open and blinding light hit me smack in the face.

"'Stand still! Shore patrol!' someone shouted.

"'Hey wait, what's going on?' I pleaded.

"'Put your hands against the bulkhead and tell your buddy the bath is all over!'

"I said to Boats, 'Hey buddy, get your ass out here. It's the shore patrol.' That launched Boats out of the steam buck naked.

"Boats pleaded, 'What's going on here? Me and Mr. Fuller were just getting a hot sea bath. Ain't nothin' illegal about that.'

"One of the burley assholes replied, 'You're both under

arrest. First, you're in an out-of-bounds location. Secondly, the owner of this place called in and reported that when she came by after closing hours to see if she had locked the door, she heard some talking going on in the rear. She said she was scared shitless since she was probably being robbed. Now get your clothes on!'

"I couldn't contain my temper any longer. 'I'm an officer and I expect you to take our word that we were here to get a hot sea bath.'

"'Sir, you don't look a damn thing like an officer to me,' the first class shore patrol said as he grinned at his companion."

"Tom, you mean you got arrested?" asked John.

"Sure did. Not only arrested but confined to the ship for one week. I also had to pay the Japanese court fees and a fifty-dollar fine. It might have been worse had the old woman not dropped the burglary charges. What pisses me off is that she has my University of Illinois graduation ring, the picture of my girl, and my I.D."

During Tom's account of his pilgrimage to the bath, John felt nervous. This was his first month on board, and he felt that he should be telling the senior officers how much he was learning and what a challenging situation he was in. Instead, he ate as fast as was polite, knowing that at any moment the Captain might ask him to explain the difference between "deviation" and "variation". The twitching in his stomach indicated, as reliably as Pavlov's dogs, that he had no earthly idea what "deviation" and "variation" were even though the names haunted him from his navigation class at the University of Texas.

John excused himself from the table with the intention of finding *Dutton's Nautical Navigation*. In college he had owned a used copy of *Dutton's*, but didn't bring it aboard. Instead he intended to read the *Hyman*'s edition that held the shipboard record for remaining untouched for the longest time.

The food was good and thoughts of a few moments on the donated wardroom couch with a cup of coffee and *Dutton's* in hand seemed almost enjoyable. Seated also on the couch was Chief Warrant Officer Sjurset (the 'j' was silent according to Tom). Tom had warned John about CWO Sjurset. The chief warrant believed in extraterrestrial visitations. The Pyramids of Egypt were frequently his launching pad.

As John burned his tongue on the coffee and glanced at the end table for *Dutton's*, he could feel CWO Sjurset staring at him. He was overweight and wore a crew cut while his stomach reminded John of a ship that had hogged.

"The pyramids! Have you ever thought about them?" his voice was loud and serious. John sensed it was not a joking matter.

"Not lately, I haven't," responded John. *Oh my lord*, thought John. Tom had warned him that he could go on for hours about such crap.

"Well, think about it. How do you suppose they got there, huh? You can't tell me they just happened. No sir, something strange went on there. How did those fuckers move all them rocks? Some of them weighed forty tons, and they had to move them over sixty miles through the sand. Have you ever been stuck on the beach? Now you tell me how they did that?"

John responded shyly, "I think they pulled them?"

The chief warrant didn't really want him to supply any answers. This was more like one of those college lectures where the professor did not want any response from the class but felt compelled to ask anyway.

"Shit! They pulled them? Like hell they did! You know there weren't any small stores to supply those deck apes back then. Yah! How did they supply 'em? I'll tell you how they supplied them. They had manna. You know what manna is? No, I bet not! It's space food!" Sjurset leaned back and cupped his hands over a cigarette as if he were lighting one on the weather deck even though the wardroom was without sufficient ventilation.

"Let me tell you how they moved them rocks. They had an anti-gravity device on board. Those forty-ton mothers didn't weigh nothin' when they put that gear on line. That explains why they didn't have to form burying details and shit like that."

"What has that got to do with burying details?" John asked.

"Well, that's cause they didn't have a lot of them dying on 'em or making sick call because the bastards didn't have to work. You see, what I want to know is where all the deck apes' bodies are if they died pulling those rocks? They ain't any bodies except for the mummies and a lot of them are up there in Philly on exhibit. I seen them myself."

The CWO's tone became even more serious. "I'm going to prove my point that space men did the yard work. You see, if you were pulling a forty-ton rock on straight logs in sand, that's one thing, but what if you had a crooked log? I'll go one further; they didn't have no trees to get logs from, and if they had trees, you can't tell me they found that many straight logs. Shit, there ain't that many damn trees in the desert no how." He leaned back and coughed on his cigarette and swallowed more coffee, then stared at

John like a scholar who had made a sterling point and was awaiting the response of his doctoral-level student.

"Well, sir," responded John out of respect for the CWO's years of experience and service, "you definitely have got some good points, and I am going to read about the pyramids. In fact, I'm going to do some reading right now."

John felt relieved to be released from the confinement of the wardroom. The night's salt-filled air smelled good to him while the large swells buoyed a full China moon. The constant sound of the waves breaking, sliced by the bow, soothed him. The phosphorescent trail of fish, brushstroked the surface of the sea.

Tom followed John to the weather deck. He had returned for a fresh cup of coffee after having journeyed to his stateroom.

"So, you got the pyramid lecture. I bet you were also scared about being questioned by the Old Man. He always interrogates junior officers on *Dutton's*. He even asked me to define 'compass error' during my first breakfast on board. Shit, it about scared me to death. Seniors appear to know it all, but they're humans just like us. They even pretend to be holy around us JGs and ensigns but every one of them is shackin' in Yoko. There ain't a saint on board this mother."

"You mean the CO is shackin' too?" John asked innocently.

"Hell yes. He goes with a schoolteacher in Yoko. Man, a real loser."

"Tom, wait a minute, he's got a wedding ring on," John said in disbelief.

"Yorktown, I don't know if you're even officer material. The motto of those Yoko teachers is 'We Service the Fleet' and they live up to it. Now about the Old Man being married, his wife's in D.C. keepin' the kids. I guess you can say he's a geographic bachelor. The skipper told me that not having sex for a full deployment keeps her as tight as a virgin. I wonder what happens when a sailor gets back home and she is looser than when he left? Most of their wives are taking care of more than just the kids I might add. You know, WestPac widows often make the Hags and Hogs call at the 'O' Club. Well, anyway, the Old Man found this teacher in the Yoko 'O' Club. What you would call a lot of pork on the huff. I bet she was real tight."

"What about the XO?" inquired John.

"Oh, you mean Pebbles?" Tom smiled.

"Is that what you call LCDR Stone?" asked John.

"Yah, well, he found himself a whore to shack with from one of those two-bit bars for officers off the main gate in Yoko, real Thieves Ally material. She is short, fat, and old; probably someone's grandmother. Lord, you can't tell the age of Japanese hostesses. Maybe he's got a parent fixation; that's what Boats figures it is."

"Well, Tom, what about you? What kind of arrangement do you have?" inquired John with a laugh.

"Yorktown, I'm no fool. I don't pay any hostess money to go home with me. I found a more traditional honey in one of those stand bars right outside the main gate, Stand Bar Marakin."

John asked, "How did you meet her? I heard back in the States that in Japan things can be real formal. You know, her mother should introduce you. However, Boats told me it's not as traditional as they taught us in school. He said everything changed when the war ended. Of course, I learned a few things after staying with Misa.

I keep forgetting it's been twenty years since Japan surrendered."

Tom replied, "Boot, you have a lot to learn. Money is money, and I don't care if you are in Yokohama, Abilene, or TJ; a pro knows how to drain you for all you have. Now that honey of mine started out telling me about her dying mother, how she sent her younger brother to college, and how she was saving her dough so she could open a tailor shop. You know what the truth is? She's a war orphan. Yah! No brothers, no sisters. The only person who lives with her on occasion is an old fart off *St. Paul,* one of those big-ass cruiser sailors. The first night I went home with her, I noticed a man's picture in a drawer that she had left half-open. She said it was nobody. Well, I opened that drawer wider. It was an 8" x 10" glossy picture of the asshole. He had even signed it: *Truly and eternally yours, Morris.*"

Tom laughed as he spoke. "It turns out that the big-butt chief and I stand port-and-starboard together now. When *St. Paul* is in port, we are out; and when we are in, *St. Paul* is out. It always works that way. You see, most of these girls can shack it with two sailors at one time and more than likely the two will never meet or even know that the other one exists. Hell, some of them even marry two fellows; doubles the income."

"Listen, Tom, I heard the same story in Yokosuka from my own girl. The only difference is that the ship was *Okie City*. I can't believe we both found the picture of some asshole." John paused. "You said she didn't cost you anything. How did you work that out?"

"Well, I've got an unbeatable approach. I carry my best C&W records with me when I leave the ship. Then I just place them on top of the bar when I order my beer. These girls love

C&W. Before long, they are eyeing my records; mainly Hank Snow types."

Tom continued, "So after a little while, I'd suggest we go to her place and listen to them. They all have record players and nine times out of ten, they go. Yah, Sakura Sally. That's how I got in her pants." Tom looked towards a veiled moon as though contemplating his lost horizon. John was silent for a moment in reverence to his thoughts.

"You say, C&W records? How did you figure that one out? No, don't tell me it was Boats," John said as he too looked at the moon rising from the haze.

"It is beautiful out here tonight," Tom said quietly. "It's like my dad told me. This is a time you only get to experience once. He said it was both a sad and beautiful time for him; a continuous mixture of two emotions. You know, it sounds simple but he was right. In a few years, it will all be gone. He was out here during the Big War. Tropical nights; air smelling of orchids and a woman's powder. What a time and place to have a beautiful woman. Oh shit, Yorktown, do you have any *Playboys* to look at? The ones hidden in the wardroom are as worn out as the yellow pages; that is, if you can find one. They are like flotsam; one day an issue washes up on the wardroom couch, and the next day it is gone."

"No, Tom," replied John. "If I ever have a son and he is fool enough to join the Navy, I am going to buy him 200 back issues of *Playboy*."

"I think senior officers go to bed with a copy of *Jane's Fighting Ships* or some shit like that," Tom added with a smile.

Suddenly, one of the third class quartermasters approached

John. "Mr. Yorktown, I have to talk to you privately."

Tom looked towards Abato. "I guess you're going to tell us you're pregnant."

The last person John wanted to talk to was Abato. "Let it wait until tomorrow," John uttered hesitantly, unsure of his position. Abato was short and stocky. The type of person that one immediately dislikes but cannot explain why.

Just as quickly as John had spoken to Abato, another form appeared from the shadows: Boats.

Abato spoke with more conviction. "No, sir, this can't wait. I have got to talk with you now."

"Okay, come to my stateroom."

Boats stayed in the shadows talking to Tom, whom he had captured. John and Abato entered through a metal hatchway into a world of semi-darkness and machinery noise. The strong scent of rubber and electrical circuits emanated from the blower motors. The staterooms they passed were dark since many of the senior officers had, as they would say "pulled a good one" in port. The curtains to the darkened rooms swayed to the rhythmic motion of the tin can as she rolled in the Pacific swells.

John stumbled into his shared stateroom after tripping over a pair of trousers that had been left on the deck. *My bunkmate must have pulled a better one than I thought.* A strong odor of vomit and alcohol floated into the stateroom from the nearby head.

"Mr. Yorktown, what I am about to tell you, you ain't goin' to believe nor like. It's about Mr. Passmore, the supply officer. He's a homo!" Abato said in a loud whisper.

"Come on, Abato," John replied. "You're hung over. Think

about it for a while, then come back and tell me the truth."

"No, sir, it's the truth. I'm going to the Captain about it just as soon as I finish here. It's against Navy regs."

A stunned silence filled John. He could not speak a word. Paul and he had become friends during the few days they had known one another. They had pulled liberty together in Taipei and Kaohsiung. He was known to be one of the hardest working officers on the ship and certainly one of the most respected. Some of the men had told John about his having a girlfriend in Yokosuka.

John spoke sternly to Abato. "Well, what happened?"

"Me, Mr. Passmore, and Boats went on liberty together." It was apparent to John that Boats had to play a role in this somehow.

Abato continued, "I figured Boats knew where the action was, and Mr. Passmore would probably buy more than his share of the drinks. So, I believed it would be profitable for me to go with them. Hell, I didn't know he was a damn fairy." Abato paused to allow John a few moments to grasp the import of his charge. Also, he wanted to make sure that John understood he was innocent of any but the noblest actions required of a U.S. Navy career petty officer.

"We went to Mother Wong's," Abato continued. "You know, the old madam that gave Boats the clap. Well, we all got drunk pretty quick. Mr. Passmore kept buying and hell, Boats is a well when it comes to booze. After a while we were all drunker than a seaman deuce. I had to go to the head so many times I figured I had turned to piss."

John could not contain his anger any longer. "Damn it, Abato! Get to the point, if there is one. I want to catch some sleep before the mid-watch and you're telling me about having to urinate in Taiwan."

"I'm sorry, sir. So it gets to be about three in the morning, and we decide that no launches are running back to the ship. 'Might as well stay at Mother Wong's,' Boats says. You know, sir, he'll do anything to get to Mother. Hell, sir, you ought to see the rooms Mother Wong rents by the hour."

Abato looked at the deck and then directly at John. "Well, anyway, Mr. Passmore went along with it, too. Boats and Mother went off to a room together. I guess to give him a new case of the clap. So me and Mr. Passmore went to a room. There was only this one rack so I told him that since he was an officer, I figured he was entitled to it. You know how rank is. If I had wanted the rack, he would have brought it up when we got to sea. I'd catch hell later on, I know that. So he takes the bunk, and I hit the deck. Well about 0400, after I'm sound asleep, I feel this person getting under the cover with me on the deck. Back in Tennessee, I would have thought it was one of those damn coon dogs we had. Here it just scares the shit out of me. I jumped up and landed a good one on the bastard. Yeah, right in the jaw."

"Maybe Mr. Passmore was drunk and didn't know what he was doing?"

"Shit!" Abato replied.

"'Did he touch you?" John asked. "You know what I mean."

"Hell yes, Mr. Yorktown. Why do you think I knocked the piss out of him?"

"Okay, Abato, but wait here thirty minutes. I want to talk to Mr. Passmore about this. He has the right to answer the accusation before we bring this up with the Captain."

John walked rapidly through the dark swaying passageway. He thought about what he was going to say but everything flew out of his mind as he pulled aside the curtain to Passmore's stateroom.

"Paul? You in there?" he asked quietly, almost out of respect. John felt the emotions that a priest must experience when he summoned a condemned man. The prospects of talking Abato out of reporting Paul were nil, and John knew it. Abato now had a cause. This would elevate him far above the other sailors. Not even Boats had ever been propositioned by an officer.

Paul answered softly, "Yeah. Come in, John, and cut the overhead on." He was lying in his rack, apparently hung over like the rest of the crew. He was still wearing his silver bars. The odds were that he wouldn't remember what had occurred at Mother Wong's, at least John hoped he wouldn't. Paul's only chance was either to claim it never happened or to say he was so drunk he thought Abato was a woman. *Oh hell,* John thought, *I guess even I can't bear the thought of Abato, under any circumstances, being mistaken for a woman. He is uglier than shit. Surely Paul has better taste in carnal pleasures than him.*

John hesitated and then said, "Paul, it's Abato. He says you tried to get in bed with him. I guess it means he's accusing you of being a homosexual."

Paul stared at John as though shaken by the allegation coming from a friend. It was then that John noticed the large bruise on his jaw.

After a short silence, Paul said in a broken voice," Johnny, it's true. I need help."

"My god, Paul! Think this over. Lie if you have to. No one

will believe you tried to screw a fart like Abato. Not even Mother Wong would want to wake up and find him in bed with her. I've seen hostesses run for the hatch when he walks into a bar."

Paul sat up and placed his feet on the metal deck and rested his head in his hands. Even the slightest hint of defense was not present. He seemed resigned to his fate. It was apparent to John that he could not reprieve the sentence Paul had already decided he deserved.

"Paul, I have to report you," John said weakly. "If I don't, Abato will make it worse for both of us. He's determined to take it to the Captain."

"It has to be, Johnny. It can't be helped. I don't belong here," Paul said, his eyes filling with moisture.

"I'm sorry, Paul. I really am." It was strange how inappropriate his words were. How little they really expressed what John felt deep within.

John returned to his stateroom and asked Abato to accompany him to the XO. Abato led the way walking with the conviction of an early Christian martyr who had to meet his responsibilities regardless of the cost. After all, the Uniform Code of Military Justice required Abato to report the offense. It seemed unbelievable to John that Abato would be on the side of justice and Paul the accused, the one found guilty of an unforgiveable sin.

John, with Abato standing just behind him in the shadows of the corridor's red night light, reported the accusation to the executive officer who looked dismayed and thanked them both for telling him. Probably Pebbles' only thoughts that night dealt with all of the paperwork he would now have to do. It was Saturday night, and like all of the ship's company not on watch, he had planned on sleeping through most of Sunday morning. As John and Abato left, they heard him fumbling through his bookshelf looking for the printed instructions stated in the regs.

The accuser and John located the Captain reading a novel in his at-sea stateroom, a small cabin just aft of the bridge. The Captain, a lean man with chiseled features and narrow eyes, was known as a CO that could not sleep. Regardless of the hour, he was always awake, frequently relighting a pipe that refused to remain lit. The crew liked to joke that he was high on matches.

The Captain peered at them with an aggravated expression; his eyes but narrow slits. After all, it was late and he did not care to see anyone. The only time a captain at sea desired to be bothered during the mid-watch was in case a course had to be changed, a maneuver executed, a shoal was sounded, or a collision was imminent.

"Captain, sir," John said weakly, "Abato wishes to report an offense of a critical nature."

"Yes, sir," Abato said loudly. "I want to report an offense on my person."

Well, I be damned, John thought. *He's trying to put his accusation in legal terms.*

"Captain, Mr. Passmore attempted to make a homosexual advance on my person."

A long pause then occurred so the Captain could grasp the import of his accusation. The Captain and Abato stared at one another in silence.

"Sit down, Abato." The Captain forced a courteous smile as

he continued, "Mr. Yorktown, will you please close the door?"

The loud mechanical noises of the ship prevented anyone on the bridge from overhearing the discussion. Only the most foolish sailor would dare to listen through the voice tube that provided a direct audio path between the Captain's stateroom and the wheelhouse.

"Now explain what happened," the CO said with restrained distaste. The Captain had obviously planned on spending his evening reading a worn paperback copy of *Lady Chatterley's Lover* that lay partially concealed on his desktop. For a brief moment John wished he too had a copy.

"Well, sir, you see, me, Boats and Mr. Passmore planned on pulling a drunk together at Mother Wong's. Well, I figured Boats knew the place and could get things cheaper there, and Mr. Passmore could get me out of trouble if I decided to start a fight with a jarhead."

"Abato," the Captain said with reproach, "do you know that Mother Wong's is off-limits?" Fear ran through Abato and John.

"No, sir," Abato said weakly. "I sure didn't. I never would have gone there if I had known."

The lying little bastard, John thought. *He should have been flattered that Paul wanted to try something with him.*

"No, sir," Abato continued his defense, "I never intended to go off-limits."

Liar. The word flashed in John's mind again.

"Go on!" the Captain spoke with growing agitation.

"Well, Captain," Abato stuttered, "Mr. Passmore and me had to share a room. It seems like Mother Wong's was doing a better business than usual. There was a lot of sailors there. I guess they were just like me. Didn't know it was off-limits."

"Get on with it," the Captain's cheeks seemed to reach for his eyebrows with exasperation.

"Yes, sir. Well, Passmore, I mean Mr. Passmore, got the rack as was only fitting since he's an officer, and I ended up on a tatami mat on the deck. There weren't any women with us. I can't stand those bar girls anyway. I just about fell asleep when he started fooling around with me," Abato said, followed by a long pause.

The Captain leaned towards Abato. "What do you mean 'foolin' around?'"

"Sir," Abato confided, "I feel disrespectful talking about an officer. I woke up when I felt someone kissing me on the mouth and grabbing Luther. At first I thought it was some whore, then I realized it was Mr. Passmore. It made me madder than hell. I ain't no damn homosexual."

"Mr. Yorktown, get me Mr. Passmore—and I mean now!" the Captain said.

When John found Paul, he was already fully dressed. They didn't looked at one other until John spoke.

"Paul, the Captain wants to see you."

They walked slowly together towards the Captain's at-sea cabin. With each step, his friend's life was being irrevocably changed.

As they entered the CO's cabin, John could feel the stare that the skipper gave Paul; a stare as tangible as one grabbing another in anger.

"Mr. Passmore," the Captain said, "a very serious charge has been leveled against you. I assume Mr. Yorktown has already informed you. I can only hope, for your sake and for the sake of the Navy, it is not true. I need not tell you the consequences of such an accusation should it be proven."

"Yes, sir," Paul acknowledged respectfully.

The Captain stared at Paul and corrected his myopic vision with a prolonged squint. "Are the charges true?"

On this question rested a friend's future. John thought he had to lie for there was no way Paul could admit the truth when facts were seen in black or white, not in shades of gray.

"Yes, sir," Paul said without any sign of emotion in his voice; his eyes alone were the conduits of his emotions.

"That's all, Mr. Passmore. Mr. Yorktown, Abato, return to your duties. I trust, Abato, that you will keep this matter confidential."

"Yes, sir. You can be assured of that," Abato said, his patriotism showing. They all knew he was lying. As soon as Abato left the Captain's stateroom, he hurried towards the forecastle where Boats was leaning against the rail. Abato, at a time like this, would need the wisdom and experience of Boats to guide him and to share his new sense of importance.

The executive officer approached John from the darkness of the passageway. "Mr. Yorktown, here's a message I want you to encrypt offline. Send it out tonight."

In crypto John read the message:

```
SECRET — OFFICER'S EYES ONLY

LTJG Paul Passmore suspected of violating
```

```
UCMJ article ...
Because of the sensitiveness of this
violation and the difficulty involved in
keeping this information from the crew, I
request transfer of LTJG Passmore to the
USS Kitty Hawk upon arrival Hong Kong.
Transfer to CONUS to be arranged.
```

After sending the message, John wanted some fresh air. The ocean was grooved by long smooth swells yet there was not a breath of wind except for the breeze created by the ship's passage. John leaned on the rail and thought about home and the people he knew. He didn't want to think about Paul or anything in his immediate world. A large bird, silhouetted by the twilight, flew nearby and carried his eyes to the fantail. There stood Paul looking towards the sea's horizon now awakening in the vivid predawn colors of a Matisse.

He approached Paul, without looking at him. "I'm sorry. I guess you already know about Hong Kong." Paul said nothing. "You were brave—braver than I could have been. Why did you confess when you could have lied? The Captain didn't want you to tell the truth. Think of the god-awful number of messages he now has to send. You must really believe in something to pay so high a cost for being honest."

Paul turned and faced John. "No, you are wrong. If I believed in anything, I would have lied. You tell the truth when there is nothing to lose. I had already lost, and I'm not talking about now. There is little sympathy or understanding in the Navy and in the world for what I am."

"Paul, I don't know what to make of all this. Abato survives and thrives in this environment and you are destroyed; not him. Look at Frisbee still sitting up there on the radar platform." Paul looked towards the platform that was illuminated with spotlights as the work detail labored to restore operational capability to the radar—a system that had unexpectedly been fried by an electrical surge. "The Captain told him to stay aboard and ensure that the radar was repaired in Taiwan. Well, you know Frisbee, he had to get some. So he not only goes ashore without permission but the fool spends the night. I saw him at a bar called Saddle-Me-Up, sitting with some old hostess. I guess she's the hog he shacked with. Anyway, yesterday morning I heard the Captain tell him to stay on the top of the platform until the gear is fixed. In other words, he was to directly supervise the work. That was nearly twelve hours ago. I guess they can't find the part or something like that. They brought some chow up to him earlier. He hasn't moved in a while, but I hear him curse his chief every now and then for working too slow. He survives just like Abato. All Frisbee wants is whiskey, a woman, and to avoid work. I can't believe he's been made an officer. Shows how desperate President Johnson is to kick some ass."

"I had to face this, John. It's no good hiding the truth."

Both officers stared into the wake of the ship that reflected the colors of the dawn—beautiful, primitive, and yet welcoming.

"I guess our home is the sea, after all," Paul continued quietly. "I feel close to the ocean. Man defaces the earth but not the sea. He can't destroy her. She provides a reference point; a place to begin again."

CHAPTER FIVE

Turning of the Wheel

VIET CRISIS GROWS
—*Los Angeles Times*, March 25, 1965

Estes, the petty officer of the watch, approached John. "Sir, we just received a secret message in Com. I wanted to route it to you first before showing it to the OOD. Shit, man, what a fuck!"

John looked at the clipboard illuminated by the red light of Estes' flashlight.

> *You are to proceed immediately to rendezvous point 18° 00' N, 107° 00' E.* Hyman *to participate in Sea Dragon operations. You are to replace the* Hamner *on station. Happy Hunting!*

Before showing the message to the CO, John asked Tom, "What the hell is Sea Dragon?"

Tom replied, "From having read the message traffic before you came aboard, it is a duel fest between small boys and North Vietnamese gun emplacements somewhere around Vinh, North Vietnam. It is not exactly R&R. More the John Wayne type of things. Why are you asking?"

"Well, Estes just arrived with a message from COMDESRON 9. We're being sent there."

"Did the message mention the *Hamner*? She was assigned to Sea Dragon ops."

"Yes, it did. It seems like we are her replacement."

"*Hamner* was not to be relieved for a couple of weeks. Something must have gone wrong."

"I'll ask the chief to check last night's message board to see if she is referenced," said John, referring to Chief Rogers, the Communications Department Chief Petty Officer.

John knocked on the cabin door of the Old Man. "Sir, we just received a message from COMDESRON 9." In the red light of the commanding officer's stateroom, he handed the message to the Captain who had been resting his head on the fold-down desk.

The CO read the message silently. "Mr. Yorktown, have the messenger of the watch bring us some black coffee. I think we are all going to need it."

Before long the CO was on the deck, calling for the executive officer and the OPS boss. The bridge was alive with activity as a new course and speed were plotted for the rendezvous point. A review of the message traffic revealed that *Hamner* had been hit twice by shore batteries. Luckily, there was only one casualty. It was fortunate for the *Hamner* that one shell had struck a metal frame on its way to the boiler room. Had it entered the boiler room, there would have been mass casualties.

Tom was handed the new course and speed. "Come right to new course 187. Speed 17 knots."

The helmsman spun the wheel as another sailor rang up the knots. The *Hyman* responded immediately to the wheel. The increase in speed was felt in the vibrations of the ship. The used coffee cups vibrated across the tabletops.

The bridge was void of conversation except for whispers of disbelief. Even Boats was silent as the course changed. Then, in hushed tones, someone said, "Fuck this man's Navy." It was a feeling shared by each member of the watch.

Soon the colors of the sky changed with the anticipation of dawn. The beauty of the sea was revealed in varying shades of pastels. The light of the quarter moon was quickly dimmed by the awakening sun. The sea, like a desert, was void of all clouds, only the mist of the low horizon bore the colors of the morning rays.

Even though the bridge team had been awake prior to four, they mustered at their various assigned places. Soon Boats appeared in the passageway.

"What good is a fucking paycheck if you're not allowed to spend it?"

"Are you asking me?" questioned John. "I haven't been paid yet." John moved closer to Boats. "What is the scuttlebutt?"

"Well, they're saying that we'll be on station for a couple of weeks unless we are hit by a damn North Vietnamese shore battery or a damn boiler goes down. Either way, it's not good since a hit or a down boiler can land us in Olongapo."

"Where?" asked John.

"Olongapo," replied Boats. He'd forgotten that John was not a China sailor. "Well, it's in the Philippines. Most of it off-limits since the gangs and communists enjoy a macho sport like shooting sailors. I admit I had some good times there. There's a bar in Olongapo where you can buy baby ducks to feed to alligators." He paused. "I like my time ashore to be on liberty and not repairing some goddamn piece of equipment. On the bright side, if we get hit really bad, then we'll be sent stateside for a long overdue FRAM job. This old fucker was scheduled for one last year. Now that I'm thinking clearly, maybe Sea Dragon isn't such a bad idea after all. I have this broad up in Portland who ain't half bad-looking."

"Well, Boats, I don't share your sentiments, but I admit that you're one hell of an optimist. Any way you look at it, you win."

"How do I win if we just get stuck on Sea Dragon for two weeks and nothing happens to the ship?"

"Well, you get to save all the money you would have spent on liberty. You can then afford to party until you drop or get robbed."

"Mr. Yorktown, you're making sense today!"

Two days later, the *Hyman* arrived on station. The *Hamner* had already departed the area on her way to the Philippines. China sailors knew what lay ahead: no sleep. Between UNREPs and H&I fire and shore bombardments, the ship would remain at General Quarters most of the time. The only way to stay awake was to drink coffee and then more coffee.

The Gulf of Tonkin was a fresco of clouds and junks. There was no motion upon the surface of the sea. Only a few clouds hugged an invisible coast. John had seen more movement on his father's pond.

The shrill sound of the bosun's pipe was soon heard. "Now hear this, now hear this, the ship will go to General Quarters at 1400." The two hours of work in the communication shack passed quickly.

The loud sound of the bosun's pipe was heard again blaring throughout the ship: "General Quarters! General Quarters! All hands man your battle stations. Secure all watertight bulkheads and hatches. Now hear this, General Quarters, General Quarters. The smoking lamp is out throughout the ship." The call to battle continued to ring loudly throughout the ship. Immediately flak jackets, life jackets, and steel helmets were handed out to the bridge team.

As John left the communications shack, he stared at the land that suddenly appeared off the starboard bow. The white sandy beaches and green canopy of palms made North Vietnam look more like a tourist destination than a nation at war.

"This is the Captain speaking. It is my intention to close the beach to 25,000 yards. Mounts fifty-one and fifty-two will engage."

John, as the communication officer, was assigned to the bridge. His task was to have the conn during all battle engagements.

"This is Mr. Fuller, Mr. Yorktown has the conn," Tom shouted loudly.

"This is Mr. Yorktown, I have the conn," replied John less forcefully.

As they approached the rendezvous point, suddenly the bridge phone rang. "This is Cactus, I'm receiving counter battery. Repeat, I am receiving counter battery."

"Captain, I have just received a message from *Port Royale*, they too are receiving counter battery," John shouted to the skipper who had just sat down in the captain's starboard wing chair. Everyone on the bridge knew immediately what that meant. *Port Royale*, an Australian destroyer, was being fired upon by the batteries that guarded the port of Vinh. The North Vietnamese weapons, the D122s and D130s, were similar to the *Hyman's* 5-inch guns with an equally effective range of 30,000 yards and were of the same caliber. The North Vietnamese batteries and the *Hyman's* guns were radar controlled. If a battle was to ensue, the ship would have to close the beach. To most observers when the weaponry is equal, the advantage falls to shore-based artillery.

The Captain looked towards John, and then activated the squawk box so that the entire crew could hear him. "This is the Captain speaking. The ship we are to accompany is now receiving counter battery. We'll be working with *Port Royale* until she is relieved. *Hyman* will remain at General Quarters."

The Captain looked at John. "Mr. Yorktown, increase our speed to 27 knots." The Captain knew he was fast approaching the maximum speed at which the WWII-era ship could perform without risking possible damage to the turbines. The *Hyman* vibrated with the surge of speed; the hull moaned as spray lifted flying fish upon the bow.

Upon arrival at the rendezvous point, the rig for a highline transfer was put into place. An exchange of messages and greetings was required. John held the small satchel that was to carry the operations instructions in one hand and held on to the haze-gray metal railing of the small chair with the other.

The two ships came alongside one another. As he sat in the chair, sailors on the ships began to pull on the ropes meant to carry him to the Australian destroyer that they were to partner with while on Sea Dragon. Once aboard, John was escorted to the wardroom.

"Welcome aboard, Yank. Good to see you. The other small boy didn't fair too well. She is headed to Subic for repairs. Care for a cup of Java while on board?"

"No sir," replied John, looking at the small number of officers congregated in the wardroom, each wearing shorts and unstarched uniform shirts with their ranks embroidered on soft shoulder boards. What struck him was how much older they were than the crew of *Hyman*. He thought it must take a hell of a lot of time to make rank in the Australian Navy. After exchanging greetings and messages, he bid his farewells to the crew and was once more highlined to the *Hyman* with the top-secret messages held tightly in his leather satchel.

Once the two ships parted and the highline rig was secured, the *Hyman* resumed the normal watch routine, everyone having been relieved of their General Quarters stations. For reasons unknown to John, it was too late in the afternoon to engage the enemy that lay but a few miles off the starboard side of the ship. As usual the day had turned into a "hurry up and wait" situation.

"Now hear this," the Captain said, "the ship expects to rendezvous with USS *Ashtabula* (AO-51) at 2000 hours to take on black oil. *Hyman* will then rendezvous with USS *Mauna Kea* (AE-22) for ammunition and mail at 0200. Tomorrow at 2200 we will rendezvous with USS *John Brown* for ship stores. At 0100 day after tomorrow, we will engage in H&I fire south of the DMZ." He paused. "General Quarters will sound tomorrow at 0600."

John who had the 2000 watch looked at Tom. "When do we sleep?"

"What a dumbass question. There's no sleeping in this man's Navy. Be thankful you didn't have to show the movie before coming on watch. Frisbee gets to thread the projector tonight. It will be more than twenty-four hours before he sees the rack."

The morning came with reveille sounding at 0500. This allowed just enough time for the crew to get out of the rack, skip the shower, light a cigarette, grab a cup of coffee, and be at their General Quarters stations by 0600.

The bosun's pipe sounded at exactly 0600. "General Quarters, General Quarters, all hands man your battle stations. Close all watertight doors and hatches. Now hear this, General Quarters, General Quarters. The smoking lamp is out throughout the ship."

The call to battle was immediately followed by a rapid beating of the ship's bell followed by the boson's shrill whistle.

John stood on the bridge watching the coast of North

Vietnam growing closer. The crew knew that as soon as they crossed the magical 25,000-yard mark, they would immediately turn parallel to the enemy just as the dreadnoughts did at the Battle of Jutland in the First World War.

Over the 1MC came the command: "Batteries released, fire for effect." Immediately Mount 51 opened fire followed by Mount 52. Their twin batteries sent a profound shockwave throughout the ship. Both mount captains were free to fire as quickly as they could reload. Round after round was fired with the large brass shell casings filling the decks around them.

With each firing, John felt the sting of gunpowder on his cheeks. The strong smell of gun smoke filled the arms of the bridge and the wheelhouse of the ship. A percussion echo rang in John's ears.

"Hey Tom, why doesn't the Old Man issue us ear protection?" shouted John.

"He wants you to hear his bark, that's why," said Tom in between firings. When firing abaft the beam, the ends of the 5-inch guns were only a few feet from John's ears. John noticed that Tom had stuffed his own ears with abundant cotton.

Suddenly a shrill sound pierced the air. A short distance off the starboard bow, a large splash rose from the blue sea into the air. It was not a splash of clear water but one infused with a black-brown tint.

"Shit, they're firing at us!" Boats shouted from the edge of the wheelhouse.

John grabbed the unsecured bridge phone and shouted, "Counter battery, counter battery, we're receiving counter battery."

No one responded immediately. Then through static: "Snoopy, this is Cactus, we understand counter battery."

The Captain shouted, "This is the Captain, I have the con. Right full rudder! All ahead flank!"

The helmsman and lee helmsman echoed the commands.

What the hell? thought John as he braced himself against the plotting board desk while holding on to the radar repeater with the other hand. *He's steering us right into the barrels of the North Vietnamese guns.* The ship listed heavily to port as she turned at high speed. The Captain had outguessed the enemy gunners since the next rounds fired at the *Hyman* hit the water close aboard on the port side. Airburst soon followed with their dark gray plumbs of smoke.

As the *Hyman* sped seaward to escape the firepower of the shorebased gun batteries, she continued to fire with Mount 52 until the range was too great for the fire to be effective. The Captain then ordered a parallel course with the beach at a safe distance. John looked at the chronometer, it was 1430. The sun sparkled on the calm sea. Sea snakes swam past her hull.

It was not long until the roar of Navy and Marine Corps jets from off the *Ranger* passed overhead. In a matter of seconds, the palm tree-lined beach of Vinh became a series of fireballs after being repeatedly hit by napalm.

"Jeez, Tom, nothing can survive that pounding. They'll be out of commission tomorrow."

"Not from the scuttlebutt that I hear. They're like the phoenix, they're reborn instantly from the ash," said Tom in a confidential manner. "They'll be here waiting for us just like today."

"You've got to be kidding. Nothing can survive what I just saw."

Evening fell quickly upon the Gulf of Tonkin. The sky was saturated with stars. The moon was just rising over the sea when John and Tom appeared once more on the bridge for the midwatch, intoxicated with caffeine and fatigue. They had earlier been on the bridge for the transfer of black oil and mail.

They arrived early for the watch since every evolution on a tin can required the participation of all hands. Soon the air was filled with the sounds of two ships exchanging highlines at a distance of not more than 150 yards. No one laughed; there were no jokes for coming alongside a ship. The passing of ammunition was a serious and tense occasion. It was well known that in the past, ammunition ships have exploded for a variety of reasons, including poor ship handling. The large shells in wooded crates were swiftly sent aboard. *Hyman* and *Mauna Kea* then parted into the black void of the tropical night.

As the ships departed, John felt a great deal of relief for they were to steam a straight course along the coast of North Vietnam. A few bogies appeared on the radar screen but they were quickly identified by the ship's Combat Information Center as friendly.

Then John sensed something different. He peered off the starboard side of the bridge. Before him the horizon was lit by searchlights that stretched from the jungle canopy to the night sky.

It looked as if the dark mountains of North Vietnam contained large airport beacons. Then the sound of B52 bombers dropping tons of ammunition down the Ho Chi Minh trail was heard.

"Damn, it looks like the fourth of July!" said Boats with pride. Huge fireballs illuminated the coastline. The clouds above the mountains reflected the glare of searchlights as guns and missiles were fired at the B52s.

"What are the searchlights for?" asked John, staring through his binoculars at the light show.

"Just in case we send in helicopters or low-flying spotter planes. I think it's also a morale booster. To the civilians in Vinh, it looks like their North Vietnamese regulars are putting up a damn good fight."

"Maybe they are," replied John. "I took a few geography courses before my commission. You cannot win a jungle war by dropping bombs from 30,000 feet. Besides, the head honchos in South Vietnam are corrupt and everyone knows it. This war can't be won. Ho and the boys are not fighting in a conventional manner—discarded tire rubber for shoes, bicycles for transportation, rice and fish for food. Hell, their uniforms are nothing more than pajamas. I bet they have never seen a television set or a USO show.

Boats overheard the conversation. "No uniforms, no air force. Shit, they don't even have a Navy. No Anne Margaret for them. How do you whip a ghost's ass?"

Tom replied, "You're being a little dramatic. I suppose you're saying they're not a conventional target. In other words, they're not playing fair. Besides, if we don't stop 'em here, we'll have to fight 'em back home. Didn't you listen to Kissinger and his domino theory?"

"Damn right, that's what I'm saying," answered Boats.

"You really believe that political shit?" John asked. "Do you think they're going to swim to Los Angeles? They couldn't care less about attacking Hollywood."

The watch passed with idle chatter about a war they had no control over. They were simply doing what was ordered by those unseen to them. In war, a sailor knows it is best to never question the politicians, the intent of God, or himself.

The next day, reveille went at 0500 and General Quarters sounded promptly at 0600. At 1400 *Hyman* closed the beach to within 25,000 yards and opened fire. Once more the radar-controlled shore batteries opened fire on them, which was to become the pattern for the next nine days. Each afternoon *Hyman* approached the beach at 1400 and each evening Navy and Marine Corps Air dropped tons of napalm followed by the B52 strikes at night along the Ho Chi Minh trail.

"Tom, why the hell aren't the North Vietnamese using their missiles against the *Hyman*? Man, we're sitting ducks for such an attack. It would take less than a second for a missile to hit us at this range!"

"Yorktown, they know we have aluminum foil in the dash hanger. First we roll our cannon out of the hanger and ramrod the aluminum foil into it, just like in the pirate movies. Then we open fire. No missile can penetrate Reynolds Wrap."

"Are you shitting me? That's our defense? I thought the dash cannon was for starting a yacht race."

"Are you questioning our Mark 5 aluminum-foil spitting cannon?" Tom said, laughing. Sadly enough, he was correct about the missile defense system aboard the ship. The small cannon on wheels was all the ship possessed for defense against a missile attack. A rocket fired from 25,000 yards would strike *Hyman* in a matter of seconds. The ship's cannon, like the North Vietnamese night beacons, was intended as a morale booster for the crew.

"Tom, you didn't answer my question," said John, concern in his voice.

Tom drew closer. "Oh, they know that if they knock our ass totally out of the water, it will be a no-holds-barred war. Right now we're just hitting a ping-pong ball back and forth. If they put too much english on the ball, all hell will break loose and they know it," Tom said as he sipped his now cool coffee.

The Captain guided the ship day after day through both the surface and airburst that fell about them. Not counting the airburst, the sonar recorded over 500 surface bursts fired at *Hyman* during the ten-day ordeal. Just as quickly as they had been assigned to Sea Dragon operations, they were ordered to depart.

"Damn, I guess I'm now a warrior," John muttered to himself as the ship sailed upon placid seas as she departed the Gulf of Tonkin on her way to Hong Kong. The crew hoped they would not have to man their General Quarters stations for at least a few days. The routine of shipboard life was quickly reestablished with the monotony and repetition of each day.

CHAPTER SIX

Battle of the Movie Projector

NEW YEAR'S EVE, 1965
—*Detroit Free Press*, December 31, 1965

The day turned into early evening, and John was required to show the Captain's movie. Before arriving in the wardroom, he looked towards the sea that had changed in appearance as the moon hid behind clouds that hovered above the low swells.

John approached Paul just aft of Mount 52. "Goodnight Paul."

He did not answer but only looked seaward towards the ever-changing colors of the now visible moon, which had shed its clothing of clouds.

As John rounded the superstructure on his way to the

wardroom, he heard a commotion above him.

"God damn it, chief! What the fuck are you doing down there? I've been on this radar platform while you've been playing with your ass for the last twelve hours." The radar had once more faltered due to the constant shaking of the ship due to the heavy gunfire required by Sea Dragon.

"Sorry, sir, we have just about gotten her fixed." The chief smiled at John as he spoke.

Frisbee shouted to the chief, "If you plan on getting your butt ashore in Hong Kong, you'll get me down from here quick. If you had been doing your job, this would not have occurred in the first place."

Frisbee spotted John below. "Hey Yorktown, what's goin' on down there?"

"Hello Frisbee, it looks like you just can't get enough sea air these days. I bet the view is great up there, ocean and more ocean. Bernie thinks you're up there writing love poems to that hooker back in Taiwan."

"Eat shit, Yorktown!" Frisebee shouted down from his perch.

"What an attitude. You, an officer and a gentlemen. You're an example to your men even if you look like a chicken perched on a roost," John said, laughing.

John retired to his office in the communications shack before going to the wardroom to show the flick. Then he heard a knock on his door. Quickly he put his *Playboy* back into the safe and twirled the combination. He shouted loudly, "Enter!"

Phillips stepped in with his usual confused expression and Mississippi drawl. "Sir, I hate to bother you while you're decoding a message or whatever it is you're doing, but it's important, I think. It's Decker. I've seen him go to the starboard blower motor room off and on today."

"Well, what's wrong with that, Phillips? That's one of our spaces; at least I think it is."

"Sir, I figured there must be something special about that space. So I went up, and I'll be damned if there ain't a girl in there. I don't mean just any girl but a naked one; good-looking and built like a brick shithouse!"

"Phillips, this I've got to see. You probably saw some light reflecting in from the open hatch. Decker is not that dumb. At least I hope not."

John crawled up the ladder into the space after Phillips.

"See, sir, it's just like I said except she ain't a girl."

John squeezed himself into the small area. There before him was a beautiful, life-size inflatable sex doll. "I'll be damned. Get that balloon out of here!" John ordered.

"Wait, sir. I saw one of them for sale in Yoko. They have French mouths and vibrating hands. Damn, this one looks like the deluxe model." Phillips examined the inflatable girl with tremendous zeal. "Well, sir, here's her blower motor." He pointed to the D-cell battery compartment that was imbedded in her ear. "Sir, you gonna write him up?"

"No, on second thought, I'm going to deflate his love and

pitch it overboard," responded John.

John removed the plug in the love doll's ear and watched as her beauty diminished. It was very much like some type of horror flick. She turned from a beautiful young woman into a deflated balloon with wrinkles. John and Phillips lowered her from the blower motor compartment to the main deck and then gave her a shove overboard. As she vanished into the wake of the ship, Phillips and John both saluted.

"What a waste, sir," said Phillips in a serious tone. "She would have made a good life preserver."

Before a minute could pass, the 1MC blared: "Man overboard, port side! Man overboard, port side!"

"Oh no, shit! We're in for it now, sir," moaned Phillips.

After an at-sea recovery that consisted of the motor whaleboat being launched, which resulted in a rapid and successful maneuver, the Captain called all of the officers to the bridge.

"Gentlemen, I don't have to tell you that this type of sick behavior will not be tolerated on board my ship! I don't, however, care to know whose balloon this used to belong to." He held the limp object up. "I hope the pervert had a change of heart as was shown by his disposal of it.

"By the way, I want to commend the after lookout, Decker, who spotted the woman. I mean the thing. His alertness could have saved a real sailor. Mr. Yorktown, please convey my appreciation to him for being such a competent and alert seaman.

"I would like all of you to inspect your spaces very carefully from now on. I would hate to think we have any more functional lunatics on board."

John thought they would all receive a real ass chewing. Instead, the Old Man seemed to be restraining himself from laughing as were the rest of the junior officers on board. Only Pebbles possessed a worried expression, his tongue darting in and out in lizard fashion as though seeking sensory input.

The Captain always insisted on seeing a movie at night even though he slept through the last reel. The junior officer of the 0400-0800 dogwatch was required to show it. John had the milk-run watch coming up, and he wanted to get the flick over with as quickly as possible.

John entered the quiet wardroom early and moved over to the bulkhead seat and picked up the film can.

"You have got to the kiddin'," he relayed to Bernie, who was waiting to be entertained by the 16mm film. "Cary Grant, I can't believe it. You mean I've got to stay up and show this fucking 1950s love flick while the Captain sleeps through half of it?"

Tom overheard the conversation. "Yeah, boot. You ever wonder why he sleeps through the flicks, the cast ought to tell you. I'm certain, however, that this one has some good sex scenes in it. With a title like *The Art of Love*, this one may be a flick with promise."

The Captain read messages and talked about his home in Mississippi until 8:30. It was still 8:30 to John and not 2030 or whatever Zulu time it happened to be. Finally, John attempted to start the flick. The usually tricks were played on the boot ensign. The film was not rewound, and the lens had been taken out of the projector.

"Oh shit!" John whispered.

"Mr. Yorktown, I assume you know how to show a movie?" the Captain said, a worried expression overpowering his face. John knew that if he could not master a 16mm movie projector, how could he be expected to learn the steam cycle of a Gearing-class destroyer?

John replied smartly, "Yes sir, I do. I learned in high school when I was president of the AV club. I think I still remember." John noticed Bernie and Tom exchanging smiles. His face reddened with frustration.

"Mr. Yorktown, in this man's Navy there is either I can't or I can. There is no maybe. Mr. Yorktown, I repeat my question, do you or do you not know how to show a movie?"

"If I can find the lens, sir, I can show this movie."

"Jesus Christ, what kind of officers do I have on this ship?" the Captain scanned the wardroom for an answer as the junior officers tried not to laugh.

The lens was finally located by a steward and the flick began. John thought that maybe a cup of coffee would keep him awake through the flick or at least until the hoped-for sex scene. When John got up, he had to walk through the projection beam, which made the Captain shout, "Damn it, man!" As usual, he could not find the sugar and had to ask a steward, which earned him a "Damn it, Mr. Yorktown. Can't you keep still?"

After reseating himself and getting a first slurp of the strong burnt coffee, he realized the coffee must have been cooking in the pot for two or three days. His tongue burned not from it being too hot but from the acidic nature of the brew. As the ship rocked, he watched his partially full coffee cup sliding back and forth on the wardroom table.

The projector then began to hiss, and the picture became epileptic. Fear ran through his mind as he pushed every available button and protrusion on the Bell and Howell 16mm projector. The Captain spoke again demonstrating a great deal of frustration.

"Would someone get me a qualified operator?"

John, however, quickly found the loop reset button but now the audio was way behind the movement of Cary Grant's lips.

Before long no one was watching the action. Instead everyone, including the Captain, had to focus on Cary's lips in order to catch up with the audio. At 2330, the movie ended. The Captain had gone to sleep around 2245, snoring through the end of *The Art of Love*. What John had anticipated did not occur. There were no adult scenes in the film. Even the showing of a thigh would have been appreciated by the horny crew assembled that night in the small wardroom off the coast of China.

They were nearing Hong Kong. John could sense it among the crew and in the movement of the ship. Even Cary Grant couldn't erase the fact that each mile of sea drew the sex-starved crew closer to liberty call. For Abato and Boats, Hong Kong would be a place to get drunk and screw, but for Paul it would be the end.

CHAPTER SEVEN

Doubt Is a Visitor

25,000 IN CAPITAL MARCH FOR PEACE
—*Detroit Free Press*, November 28, 1965

A knock sounded on John's com shack door. "Enter!" he said loudly.

"Sir, this just came in. I imagine the Old Man will want to see this ASAP," said P01 Pierce who appeared to be nervous while standing in the hatchway.

John took the secret message and read it out loud, "*Hyman* to proceed to Tran Loc. Ship to provide gunfire support."

John only scanned the remainder of the message that provided further details related to the mission. He walked briskly to the bridge. It took a moment for his eyes to adjust to the bright sunlight.

Without acknowledging John's presence, the CO scanned

the message, then ordered loudly, "Get me the XO and OPS boss ASAP!"

In the background, John could hear Boats mumble, "Oh, we are fucked again!"

Tran Loc was not a great distance from their present location. They had passed close to it while on several missions along the coast. It was one of the prettiest villages that John had seen, almost serene in its quiet pastoral beauty.

After conferring with Lt. Smithy, the OPS boss The Captain ordered a course change and increased the speed of the ship. The ship vibrated from the rapid spinning of the turbines.

Within six hours, *Hyman* was once more at General Quarters.

"Mr. Yorktown, I don't want cotton in your ears or your finger up your ass!" shouted the Captain. "We need to keep the ship as stationary as possible. The Marines need accurate fire. Do you hear me?"

"Yes, sir," John said, removing the wad of sound-absorbing cotton from his ears.

Tran Loc was a small fishing village situated in a beautiful bay of azure blue water. Jungle-covered hills provided the backdrop to the small village. The houses had red tile roofs and were painted a bright reflective white. At a distance, it appeared like a Camille Pissarro painting of a French village.

As *Hyman* approached, children were playing on the beach while men fished in small colorful skiffs with their painted eyes drifting just off shore. It was a peaceful setting in a time of conflict.

"Mr. Yorktown," said the Captain," I'm going to throw this piece of wood over the side. I want you to keep the ship alongside it. Do you understand? Abreast of it!"

As the Captain turned away, John looked towards Tom and mouthed, "Why keep it next to a piece of wood?"

"Boot, you see the piece of wood is not affected by the wind like the ship is. It remains relatively stationary just like the ship has to be for accurate fire," replied Tom.

The Captain approached the squawk box. "Batteries released, fire for effect!"

The shells began to fall on the small village. One by one they struck one house after another like a neighbor calling. Like with the ancient Egyptians, there was no sacrificial blood on the doorposts. Everyone on the beach suddenly began to run. A few ran towards the water, others fled parallel to the oceanfront while many sought safety in the nearby jungle.

As ammunition ran low, the ship switched from VT frag to high-cap shells that were intended to explode as airburst when in close proximity to a target. With the change in ammunition, shells began exploding over the small fishing vessels. One by one, the boats with their painted eyes, vanished into the upwelling spray.

John continued to keep the ship alongside the small block of wood. When time permitted, he would look at the burning structures with his binoculars. The confusion of the villagers seemed to subside as the village with its lanes and sandy beach were vacated. The few remaining fishing vessels that attempted to reach the shoreline soon vanished in the flash of an overhead burst.

The squawk box buzzed loudly amid the roar of the two double barrel 5-inch guns that continued to shake the ship's bridge. With each new volley, gunpowder stung John's face. He realized he could not clearly hear any commands since his ears were ringing.

He could hear, however, the Captain shouting into the nearby squawk box, "Damn it, we're now down to Willie Pete? Very well, use the goddamn shells."

With each new volley, the white phosphorous fire rained down upon the houses of the village, burning through the wooden, flimsy materials. It covered the roofs, walls, and every person and animal it touched, releasing a jelly that water could not affect. To be extinguished, it had to burn itself out. International conventions allowed it to be deployed only as a spotting shell since its use was extremely inhumane. Soon only smoldering ash remained of Tran Loc and the jungle behind it.

"Mr. Fuller has the deck," shouted the Captain as he departed from the bridge.

After reaching the desired course and speed, John looked at Tom. "How the hell did they know Tran Loc was VC? It looked like a fishing village to me. It was the same yesterday as it was today until we took it out. Besides, what did that fishing village have to do with the Marines? There were no damn Marines there."

"How the hell should I know? My guess is someone didn't grease the palm of some bureaucrat in Saigon," Tom replied.

John looked at the smoldering village as it grew smaller on the horizon. The palms, with their fronds burned away, resembled small flues emitting brown, whitish smoke. He felt his idealist vision of war vanish. The world was no longer black and white but infinite shades of gray.

CHAPTER EIGHT

To Dream

The 0400-0800 watch was slow. There were only a few skunks on the radar screen, but *Hyman* passed well clear of them.

Tom quietly mentioned, "Yorktown, look at that barometer fall. There must be a low building up over China. It has fallen one point in the last twenty-five minutes." A frown swept Tom's face as he turned towards Abato. "Goddamn it, quartermaster. Why do I have to be the one on the bridge to tell everyone the weather is getting worse?"

"I'm sorry, sir. I didn't think it was necessary to check the barometer more than once on a watch. We just had a reading about an hour ago, and she was steady," replied the patriotic Abato.

"Can't you feel this old bitch rock?" Tom frowned. "You don't need any goddamn training to know when a storm is building up." Much of Tom's anger was an expression of his boredom and his dislike for the quartermaster. It was a straight steaming watch with very little to look at on the radar.

"Absolutely no bogies on the scope, thank God," Tom said louder than he intended to.

"Yes, sir!" repeated Abato as though given an order to change course.

"Get me a cup of Navy coffee," Tom commanded. "Make it strong!" He looked at John. "Yorktown, you want a cup?"

"Yeah, make mine with two sugars and lots of cream. That way it might not taste like it was made by a non-coffee drinking son-of-a-bitch," replied John.

"I'll take mine straight," Tom added, "like my sexual orientation." He then stared silently at Abato.

Abato's body language indicated his dislike of the request, an intense inward feeling of resentment magnified by streaks of lightning that appeared to hit the ocean in the southwest.

When Abato returned, John noticed stains on the sides of the cups. The coffee had a strange bitter taste to it, but it made the last minutes of the watch durable.

"Tom, we are to be relieved on time. I hear Frisbee stumbling up the ladder," said John. He was glad Frisbee was relieving since he knew he would not ask any of the required questions that John could not answer. He had written the course and speed on the radarscope with a greasy pencil in case the Captain appeared on the bridge. The grease smudges on the radarscope looked like small islands.

Luckily for both officers, the chief had fixed the radar, at least temporarily, before midnight. Frisbee was a creature of habit. He would appear on the bridge and look out the bridge window to let his seasickness pass. His staring at the ocean was always followed by an order for a cup of coffee: "Make it black." He would then come over to where John stood. Usually he would look through the field glasses to see if any ships were nearby. A task now impossible because of the low clouds that streaked lightning from their turbulent bottoms.

Both officers held tightly to the heavy line secured above their heads. With each roll of the ship, a different arm was stretched.

Today's early morning was no exception to Frisbee's pattern. "Anything happening?" he muttered through slurps of burning hot coffee.

"Not that I am aware of," responded John. "The course and speed are written on the scope, and that is about all you need to know except for the barometer falling."

"Do you expect us to hit anything in the next four hours?" inquired Frisbee, his words slurred by lack of sleep.

"No. Not unless we made a right when we should have made a left about an hour ago. We changed course a few degrees to give us more sea room from the reef. You know a fucking reef put the *Knocks* on the rocks not that long ago. There appears to be a storm building up over China. You can see the lightning over on the starboard bow."

"I get the watch just in time for a jackass hurricane." Frisbee frowned. "I mean a 'typhoon.' Shit, I forget what ocean we're on.

They all look alike. I haven't been doing too well since we left Taiwan. Haven't felt good since I sat on that damn radar platform. I'm probably sterile now. If that fart of a chief had done his job, I could have racked it after we left port. No, instead I had to sit like some dumbass on top of a pogo stick."

"Come on, creep, relieve me." John was too tired to hear Frisbee complain about getting a raw but well-deserved deal.

"Okay, nothing out in front. I relieve you," said Frisbee, his eyes partially closed from the newly arrived bright sunlight that lit fire upon the aqua-blue water on the leeward side of the ship. The color was intensified by the contrast between the clear sky to port and the turbulent black clouds off the starboard side. Frisbee put on his sunglasses as he stared silently at the sea. The Navy-issued sunglasses were designed to make a sailor look like a blind man. Instead of protecting his eyes, they actually opened the cornea so it let in more UV radiation than would have occurred by simply squinting.

What an opportune time, thought John. For as soon as Frisbee had arrived on the bridge, a ship started pinging at 20,000 yards off the port bow. Frisbee missed the contact during his brief viewing of the radarscope. It was customary for the watch to plot the course and speed of all new contacts that would close to within 25,000 yards.

"The old pogo-stick sitter will have to do his own plotting on this one," John said quietly to Tom. Raising his voice, he announced, "This is Mr. Yorktown, Mr. Frisbee has the conn."

"Steering course one eight five. Checking course one eight three, sir," the helmsman reported to the bridge.

It was immediately followed by the lee helmsman's: "All engines ahead standard for 17 knots, sir."

"Jeez! When are those two clowns ever going to learn the proper words to say when the conn changes hands?" Tom shouted, referring to the men on the helm and the engine order telegraph.

"Tom, I guess they have you as an example to follow," John said quietly since the Old Man could arrive on the bridge at any moment.

"Okay, boot. Let's haul ass from the bridge," Tom said. As was customary, they skipped the last few rungs of the bridge ladder by sliding their hands down the well-worn, skin-polished bannister rails.

John was very tired when he got to his stateroom. He had not slept after the movie and was completely exhausted. Even though he was expected to report to the com shack, he fell asleep instead. Sleep felt fluid to him as he was submerged into unconsciousness even though he realized that he would soon be missed from duty.

"Man overboard! Man overboard! Port side," screamed the 1MC. "All hands expedite mustering. Muster reports will be taken on the bridge."

John could not believe it. *Perhaps Decker lost another inflatable,* he thought as he quickly rose from his rack. *My first chance to catch some shuteye and some fart has to fall overboard with a storm coming up. Coming up? We're already in it!* His body was thrown against the frame of his rack when he stood up while his shoes slid into hiding. His clothing drawer, located above the fold-down desk, opened when the ship went into a heavy roll. As a result, his favorite coffee mug fell on the tile deck, chipping the rim.

Finally, he reported to the bridge after taking the muster of his own division on the ASROC deck. The truth was, the chief had taken the muster report while John leaned against the bulkhead and held back the rancid coffee that was attempting to flee from his esophagus. *Maybe that fart Abato leaped overboard or perhaps Decker did. Either way, it would not be a real loss. Hell, this may be a good day after all*, he thought.

A panting messenger stumbled up the ASROC ladder and reported to the Captain, "Supply Department reports that Mr. Passmore hasn't arrived to take muster."

The Captain walked rapidly over to the 1MC. "Mr. Passmore, lay to the bridge!" The Captain again had the word passed for Paul. The Old Man would occasionally say, "Damn it!" in between attempts to light his pipe. When Paul did not appear, the messenger of the watch was ordered to search for him.

The same thought was passing rapidly through all of the personnel on the bridge watch. The OOD had put the ship into a Williamson 180-degree turn the moment the lookout had reported a man missing from muster. Since the inflatable doll incident, the Captain had ordered the port sling to be used to pick up anyone who fell overboard. He now realized that it took too much time to lower a boat.

Sensing it may be a suicide attempt, he ordered, "Prepare the ship's boat. Launch the rescue party." The words were like adrenalin to the sailors as they raced to prepare the boat. John could sense their willingness to give their own lives for a shipmate.

"All hands man the rail," said the quartermaster. The command was unnecessary since each crewmember not on watch was already straining to see into the clear blue swells of the Western Pacific in the hopes of finding a man struggling for his life or any direction to follow for a successful pickup.

It was apparent that even with a life jacket on a sailor would have a hard time trying to catch his breath in the towering seas. The water was cold even though the air temperature was moderate. Under ideal conditions, a man could only last forty-five minutes in the tepid waters, and these were less than ideal.

"Forty-five minutes survival time. Forty-five minutes survival time," Boats repeated over the 1MC.

The ship rocked violently since the sea was now on her beam. For safety, the Captain ordered that no hands were to be admitted onto the lower weather decks to aid the search. From the bridge, he could see the heavy, now slate blue waves attempting to crush even the safety netting and the metal stanchions that supported them.

It was soon confirmed that Paul was the missing crewmember. The waves continued to give no mercy for it seemed as though the sea had heard his pleas.

The forty-five minutes passed unbelievably fast while sailors searched the sea for the missing crewmember. The Captain made the decision to search throughout the day even though Paul's body would, in all probability, be miles away from the ship's current location, provided the sharks had not already devoured it—strong silent swimmers that followed Navy ships, waiting for the discharge of their waste. The search was required and everyone knew it.

"Damn it, Mr. Yorktown," Boats whispered. "This storm has already slowed us down. Now this searching is gonna cost us another day. I'm so thirsty I can't take it anymore."

The Captain finally allowed the tired and seasick crew to return to their duties. The coordinates of the reported man overboard were carefully noted in the quartermaster's log.

John walked passed Paul's dark stateroom. A feeling of deep regret entered him. If he had stolen a wallet or hit another man while drunk, he would have gotten off fairly easy. *Shit, what am I thinking of?* said John to himself. *It's done and there is little good in thinking about it. I'll pray for him; someone should at least.*

In his stateroom, John knelt down on the steel deck. "Dear God, have mercy I pray upon Paul's soul. May his spirit rest in the bosom of your creation." Just then a huge wave hit the ship solidly on her beam and sent him sailing into the lower bulkhead. "Damn it!" he shouted to the empty cabin.

John then hit the rack and stared at the dimly lit overhead while holding his bruised head. He had hoped to get some rack time but sleep did not come. After several minutes of restless turning, he walked out onto the ASROC deck with his head still throbbing from the blow. Spray assaulted the metal stanchions that held the safety nets in place. The sky was lighter than before and the rain had suddenly ceased.

When he rounded the ASROC launcher, he noticed Marty leaning on the leeward railing while staring at the distant gray horizon. Marty was shorter and older than the rest of the junior officers. He had taught in an elementary school in New Mexico before going to OCS. His face was pockmarked and his appearance was that of a constantly serious person.

"Marty," John said softly, "even though I've been on board just a few days, I feel that my entire life has been spent at sea. The ocean is still beautiful to me. I guess I have always loved the sea even when my waves were the rolling limestone hills of Texas."

"John, I find that I can always think more clearly when I look at the ocean. You know, this is where life started." Marty spoke softly in the presence of his watery god of indifference.

"I don't believe it is our creator. How can you face death when your god is an inert force?" John questioned.

"The god you worship, John, is a god of paradox. A divine creator whose compassion is matched by his hate. The creator of heaven and hell. The god who led the stone to Goliath's head and yet did nothing to ease the agony of his innocent son. Your god punishes Paul in hell. My god gives him sleep; returning him to what he was in the beginning." Marty stopped speaking as the spray of a herd of gray whales appeared on the distant horizon.

"Marty, you didn't answer my question about death. What hope do you have? How does any of this make sense to you—our being here, I mean?"

"John, our entire culture is built on the knowledge of our eventual demise. It is death that gives us emotion. All of our literature revolves around and exists because of our mortality. We would not love if we knew we were immortal. It is the knowledge of our termination that is our beginning. Death is our resurrection."

John left the rail without feeling comforted and felt even more alone. Marty's eyes did not leave the horizon and the distant spray of the whales.

The morning passed quickly. The ocean was now covered with seaweed, which the dorsal fin of a large lemon shark cut through every now and then as it fed on the surface.

"Look at that shark feed. They devour everything they see," Tom said between gulps of black coffee. "They sometimes follow a ship for days, waiting on the garbage or for someone to fall overboard."

John thought how they must wait in the silent world of the ocean where they feed and grow strong.

The morning soon drifted into the noon. "Man, this rack feels good," John said to his bunkmate as he settled into the almost nonexistent, sweat-scented pillow and hard mattress. "There's nothing like a nooner. With Hong Kong coming up, it's great to have a chance to think about all that good liberty. Right, William?"

William Butler, a tall JG who usually said very little, shared his stateroom. Boot ensigns were not allow to call him Bill. In port, Boats claimed he would stay aboard and study the ship's diagrams, and even refused the invitation to go to Mother Wong's. He was acting so conscientious that Tom said he was the reincarnation of a senior officer.

"Uh?" responded William.

"Never mind, William, I was just thinking about Hong Kong." John paused. "I guess the Captain and XO won't have to write so many memos after all. Suicide and accident reports are not as complicated to fill out. For all we know, he may have accidentally fallen overboard. I hear it does happen. Some deck ape with the IQ of Decker may have forgotten to secure the railing properly."

"Accident? My ass!" responded William.

"Okay, suicide report."

At that moment, a loud rap on the stateroom door filled the small compartment with a thunderous echo as though they were being summoned by an ancient Greek god.

William shouted, "Come in! Come in! The way it sounds, it must be an angel sent to catch my soul or Boats collecting on his sludge fund."

One of the men in John's radio division opened the door, then hesitated as though reconsidering whether he should enter or not. "Mr. Yorktown, you in there?" he said, his eyes not yet adjusted to the dimness of the room.

"Yeah, Jones. I'm in here. Don't worry, Mr. Butler, your soul is safe for a while. Jones isn't the kind a god would send to collect souls."

"What's that, Mr. Yorktown?" Jones asked, trying to interpret John's remarks.

"Okay, Jones, now what's the problem that can't wait until my nooner is finished?"

"It's Decker, Mr. Yorktown. He said to give you this note. He acted very strange. Kind of like he was doing something important."

John opened the folded epistle:

Dear Mr. Yorktown:
I've decided to end my life. There is nothing for me to live for.
Give all my belongings to my girl, Stella, in Diego. Tell her I

love her and understand about the Buick.
Very respectfully,
Decker, SN, USN

"I'll be damned! Something like this happens every time I try to get some sleep on this ship!" John shouted.

"What's up?" William laughed.

"I guess Paul started a new fad on *Hyman*. It's that fucking Decker. He's decided to take his own life. I'm to give everything to that girlfriend of his. It has something to do with a Buick."

"Man, you should see that girlfriend." William's face wore a large smile as he spoke. "A Hormel hog if I ever saw one. Even Boats got to her back in Diego. He said one night he couldn't get anything else. Seems like she worked some of the bars around National City. You know? National City near TJ. Hell, Decker has been sending her money every month so they can get married. Well, according to Boats, that honey took their savings, or rather his savings, and bought a yellow Buick convertible with it. Even put the car in her name and was later seen riding around Diego with a jarhead in the front seat with her. Let Decker go ahead and take his own life before he buys another slut a new car. That's my advice."

"He might be serious about this. He's nuts enough to be." John leaped from his rack and ran for the bridge.

He found the Captain, seated in his bridge chair, in one of his pensive moods. He was staring out the bridge window towards the dark blue Pacific Ocean while smoking an extra-long cigar and being careful where his ash fell. Paul's death had obviously upset him. Suicides on ships are frequently attributed to bad morale, which is ultimately blamed on the captain.

"Captain," John said respectfully, "it's Decker. He gave Jones this note to give to me."

The Captain read the note twice intently and then returned it to John without saying a word. He looked back out to sea and took a long puff on his cigar.

"Thank you, sir," said John.

At that moment, SN Arnold ran onto the bridge. "Mr. Yorktown, it's Decker. He's in his rack, and he looks really sick."

John ran to the crew quarters where he found Decker groaning in his rack. "Decker, this is Mr. Yorktown. Can you hear me?"

"Barely, sir," came the weak reply.

"What's wrong?" John asked.

"Sir, I swallowed a can of... of..." mumbled Decker, accompanied by loud moaning.

"You did what?"

"Sir, I swallowed a can of Brasso. You know, metal polisher."

"Oh my God, where's the can?" John shouted.

"Here, sir, right here," Decker responded, his hand shaking as it held the empty container. Sweat rolled down his face onto his bedroll.

John scanned the empty can for instructions on what to do in case a man swallows Brasso. The inscription read in small type:

DANGEROUS OR FATAL IF SWALLOWED.
CONSULT A PHYSICIAN IMMEDIATELY.
DO NOT INDUCE VOMITING.

After reading the label twice, John raced towards the sickbay where he found the ship's corpsman, nicknamed "Regrets." Everything he did was painful, and the few that made sick call regretted it. Regrets was an overweight, balding corpsman with what appeared to be a very limited medical I.Q.

"Doc, Decker has drunk a can of Brasso! The inscription just says to call a physician, and you're as close to a simulation of a doctor that we have," said John, gasping for breath.

"Calm down, Mr. Yorktown. I'll look up the antidote." Regrets fumbled through a collection of mismatched manuals and finally produced a general medical volume with a cracked plastic cover.

After walking down the passageway with Regrets carrying his gospel, they arrived at Decker's bunk. Upon examining the empty Brasso can and cross-referencing his journal, Regrets said loudly, "My book don't say nothin' about what to do. Only thing I know to do with poison is to make 'em vomit."

Decker only groaned in response.

Upon returning to sickbay, Regrets continued, "This can says not to make 'em vomit. Hell, Decker ain't worth nothin' no how. Did you hear about that hog he bought a car for?"

"Yeah, I heard about that." John left the sickbay with apprehension. *What if I had accidentally swallowed a can of Brasso? It could me dying and not Decker,* John thought.

John went to the OPS boss's stateroom and found Smitty lying there. Smitty was tall and above average in looks. He had recently been passed over for LCDR. His large-framed body completely covered his rack.

John said loudly, "Smitty, Decker has swallowed a can of Brasso! No one on the ship knows the antidote. I flat don't know what to do. He's my man and I'll have to write up the report if he dies. Shit, I have the mid-watch tonight and this has to happen."

"Yorktown, I'll tell you what to do. Give him another can of Brasso." With that remark, Smitty started laughing. His laughter followed John as he walked slowly to the crew quarters where he met Jones.

"Mr. Yorktown, Decker's gone."

"'Gone' like in dead?" shouted John

"No, sir," replied Jones. "He's gone like in *gone*."

"Oh my God!" John raced to the fantail. Decker was the type to jump off the ship, especially if the weather was clear and the ocean was pleasant enough for swimming. As John expected, Decker was leaning on the ropes. "What the hell are you doing?" John thundered. "I thought you swallowed a can of brass polish."

"I started to, sir. I wrote the note and took a swig. Taste like shit and made me sick as hell just to smell it. Spat it all out." Decker paused. "I just couldn't take it any longer. It's my girl. I figure now that I've tried to kill myself, they'll say I'm nuts or some shit like that. They'll fly my ass to the States for discharge. Those two will be lucky if I don't kill them both."

"First of all," said John, "did you take anything else besides a sip of Brasso?"

"No sir, I wouldn't really kill myself with brass polisher. I would do it right just like Mr. Passmore did."

"Well, Decker, I admire a man of your integrity for wanting to do things right. I doubt, however, if they'll let you off in Hong

Kong since you didn't accomplish your objective. Sounds to me like you never intended to kill yourself. Perhaps if you try again."

"Maybe if I jump overboard then I can get off." Decker then paused. "The first thing I'm gonna do when I get to Diego is bust her lip. Did you hear about that car she bought with my money—a used Buick? I love her and all that shit, but I'm gonna bust her lip."

John felt depressed as he walked along the main deck towards his stateroom. He realized his nooner was gone and he had to write up a report. *Someday,* he thought, *I'll get back home to Texas, marry, and live again. Yes, someday I will go home.*

The sea, a copy of itself from the previous day, passed by as John stared at the undulating surface of the Gulf of Tonkin. Porpoises played near the slow-moving ship. The ocean was both comforting and peaceful. Seaweed floated like stormy clouds upon a blue sky.

After pausing to watch a sea snake dive, John went to his stateroom and lay down. He didn't care if Smitty got mad that it was still working hours. Rest, however, did not come to him. He began to remember what had happened in Yokohama just a few months before. Up until that moment, he had been able to shut Yokohama out of his mind, but now it came back clearly.

The trip from the States had been without any excitement. The plane touched down in Alaska for fuel, then took off for Japan. In a few hours, John and the other military personnel aboard were near the coast of Hokkaido. Light streaked through the windows and lit the compartment with a dying ember glow. Clouds began to thicken below them. Soon the sun entered into the bed of clouds and darkness engulfed the twilight.

John leaned towards his seat companion and said softly, "It may be bumpy going down. That's an amazingly thick cloud cover. Did you happen to hear anything about the weather while we were in Alaska?" Somehow he had hoped that the chief would reassure him about the climatic conditions occurring above Japan.

Chief Phillips said loudly, "Yeah, I heard something over the radio about some typhoon moving up from off Taiwan. It's supposed to hit some of the southern offshore islands this evening. I expect these clouds are the screen of that storm."

"Great!" John muttered. *Just what I need on a transpacific flight. A typhoon.*

John noticed that his companion merely glanced towards the window before settling into a pillow provided him by the stewardess. John continued, "Don't you feel any apprehension about storms?"

"Well," the chief confided, "what good would it do to be afraid? I figure we'll go when our time comes. Not much I can do about that, is there?"

John did not answer. In his mind, he felt he could do something. At least he could resent the storm, perhaps even hate it. *There's no reason,* he thought, *that I should feel neutral about anything that endangers my life whether it be war or a typhoon. However, the chief is right about not being afraid. You can't afford to be.*

On a military flight, a passenger would occasionally luck out and be able to go to the cockpit and talk with the pilot. It was also not unusual for one of the passengers, who had flown helos or bird dogs, to be given an opportunity to try his hand at the wheel.

While talking to the pilot just after the flight had left

CONUS, John noticed a bright light in the morning twilight just to the southwest. "Hey Jack, what's that?"

"Oh, that's the morning star. I guess you never had to get up early. It's probably Venus or Mars."

John watched the morning star as it grew brighter. Soon Venus passed beneath the plane at a few thousand feet. His flight had just missed an encounter with a 727 returning from Saigon with a group of 'volunteers.' John did not feel completely at ease with the pilot for the remainder of the flight.

Soon Navy Air began the descent. The plane hit the first updraft of a towering storm cloud, sending loose baggage into the ceiling of the compartment. John quickly forgot the chief's earlier advice.

"Oh my God!" He was now really afraid. The bumping intensified as they descended. *How the hell is he going to find Yokohama in this downpour?*

"You haven't flown much have you?" The chief smiled. "They got radar and homing devices. Just calm down and think about that good liberty. There's a Chinatown in Yokohama that's something else. Prices are higher there since it's a merchantman's port. Sailors have a hard time out buying civvy sailors but you should see the broads. There's one lady there with the biggest boobs in the Orient. Just ask any China sailor."

The aircraft dove under the clouds. Beneath them, city lights appeared eerily close. "Hey, we just ran a red light," shouted an E3 from the rear of the plane.

Abruptly, the jet headed back into the clouds.

"That damn fool driving this thing doesn't know where we

are," said John frantically to the chief. John's hands were wet as he clutched the seat in front of him as though his life depended on his grip.

Suddenly the plane dove back down and jerked hard as the wheels made screeching contact with the runway. Some of the passengers started clapping as John wiped a small bead of sweat off his chin.

The chief laughed. "Mr. Yorktown, you can release the seat now unless you plan on taking it with you."

The tired passengers walked to the airport terminal where everything was secured. They smelled the coffee floating from a small coffee shop. *That's what I need,* thought John. *Coffee—gallons of it. Everything seems better after a cup of Java.*

Inside they sat down and tasted the hot fuel. "Man, this is really bad," said John to the chief, who had accompanied him. "What did they make this out of? I'm afraid to swallow it."

"Hell, Mr. Yorktown," replied the chief, "you mustn't have drunk much Navy coffee. I bet you're a boot ensign. Right?"

"Yeah, you mean this is what real Navy coffee tastes like?" John muttered with disdain.

"You bet, sir. The secret is not washing the pot. Let me taste it." He put the steam to his lips. "Why this is the best cup of coffee I've had in years. It's a cup that brings back memories. Look, it ain't even corroded the sides yet."

While they drank their coffee, John noticed a lieutenant with salt-and-pepper hair staring at him intensely, obviously a mustang. *Maybe he wants to talk or maybe he's queer,* John thought. *No, impossible. He wouldn't have lasted in the Navy for so many years. It might be that since I'm the only other officer present, he thinks I should be sitting with him instead of the chief.*

John leaned over his coffee as he spoke. "Chief, that lieutenant seems to recognize either you or me. Have you noticed how he's been staring?"

"No, don't let it bug you. We all look alike. I bet he thinks he knows you from some ship he's been on. I done it myself a thousand times. Even bought a few bastards drinks thinking I knew them."

A small Japanese man appeared and said in English, "Everyone going to Yokosuka, please follow me."

"I bet that's all the English that Jap knows," Chief Phillips said loudly as if to test his theory. The guide did not respond to his comment as he led the procession from the building.

Everyone appeared tired as they slowly boarded the bus. Transpacific flights were long, boring, and John had been very tense during the flight.

After the bus left the airbase, the lieutenant stood up and began to stagger up and down the aisle. Chief Phillips leaned towards John and said with a pungent coffee breath, "Hell, that fart's drunk."

"Looks that way," replied John.

The lieutenant bent over the driver as though to whisper to him. Instead he sank to the floor of the swerving bus. The driver immediately applied the brakes, sending most of the sleeping sailors crashing into the back of the seats in front of them.

"What the fuck!" the chief shouted. "It doesn't make sense he's gotten drunk that fast. Back at the airport he was enjoying a cup of coffee just like us, and now he's passed out."

Two E5s approached the lieutenant and dragged him back to his seat. As soon as he was placed upright, he slumped against the shoulder of the sailor next to him. The sailor cried, "This man's sick. He mumbled something about his heart!"

John rushed towards the lieutenant who had regained consciousness. The mustang strained to have enough oxygen to speak. "Heart, it's my heart. Get a doctor. I'm scared. Don't want to die! Pain is terrible!"

John's hands trembled, and he felt the man go limp. He went quickly to the bus driver and tried to explain.

"He drunk! He drunk! Don't speak English," the driver protested loudly.

John kept pointing towards the lieutenant and towards his own heart. He then pretended to hold a small ruler in his hands. Then he broke the imaginary ruler into two. Finally it dawned on the driver what the problem was, and he gave the bus a surge of power.

The bus streaked down the narrow darkened streets and finally arrived in front of a small wooden hospital where several of the sailors and John carried the lieutenant to the door. John tried to open the door, but it was locked. As he pounded on the glass, he saw several hospital staff members running towards him. With great reluctance, the door was finally opened. The staff stood motionless before the uniformed intruders. The nurses and doctor looked frightened as though they had no authority to do anything.

"My God, he's turning blue!" one of the seaman shouted. John undid the lieutenant's collar and started mouth-to-mouth resuscitation. The lieutenant's lips were cold and dry. John was reluctant, but he had to do it. With his right hand, he pushed into the lieutenant's chest and at the same time blew into his mouth.

"Jeez, sir, you're killing him!" shouted a young seaman deuce who had just finished basic training at Great Lakes.

At those words, the lieutenant's bladder let go. He stared at the wooden ceiling as a Japanese nurse gave him a shot.

John went limp and had to lean against the bulkhead of the entryway hall. He had never seen a man die before.

"Is it possible I killed him?" John asked the chief who had been reluctant to participate in the whole ordeal.

"No sir, he was dead when we brought him through the door. Nothin' you could have done. However, I would, if I was you, practice giving CPR."

John walked out to the porch of the hospital and entered the deserted street. It was dark and rain was falling. The reality of death began to infiltrate his psyche for the first time. Death appeared so simple and complete, but what worried him most was that he felt so little. It was as though he had watched Armageddon in a dream.

He realized how lonely he really was when he reentered the bus. Already the talk had shifted from the lieutenant to Thieves Alley in Yokosuka.

John looked towards the chief. "I wonder what his name was?"

The chief leaned towards John. "Who?"

The memory of Yokohama faded as sleep dulled his senses.

CHAPTER NINE

Bridge Watch

THE TEXAS SNIPER
—*Life*, August 12, 1966

"Mr. Yorktown. Mr. Yorktown," a messenger whispered. In his sleep, he felt someone nudge on his shoulder. John barely heard his name being called for he was still submerged in a mixture of sleep and awakening sluggishness. The red light in his face had failed to rouse him.

"Uh, what? Oh, the watch. Yeah. What time is it?" he whispered, trying not to awaken his shipmate who was sleeping soundly nearby.

He did some mental calculation. "Let's see. Twenty-three thirty minus twelve. Yeah, it's time." *Shit,* he thought, *I slept through chow and didn't write up Decker. I'll do it in the morning.*

"Sir, please sign the Frisbee log." On *Hyman*, it was customary for those being awakened to sign a log sheet stating that a messenger had come down to wake up the sleeping watch. The tradition started when a messenger was ordered to awaken Mr. Frisbee one evening. The JOOD, whom Duane was to relieve, waited thirty minutes for him. As time continued to pass, both the JOOD and the OOD questioned the messenger about having awakened Duane. The messenger defended himself saying he left Mr. Frisbee sitting up in his rack. When the messenger completed his defense, the JOOD ran down the ladder to get Duane in person. The cursing could be heard all the way from the forward officer's country to the bridge. Duane, even to that day, claimed that the messenger never woke him. Regardless of his innocence, from now on each relieving watch had to sign the Frisbee log.

John stumbled towards the wardroom where the stewards were instructed to leave mid-rats out for the mid-watch. It was difficult walking since the tin can was taking heavy rolls in a beam sea. After entering the wardroom, John's first sensory impression was that of burnt coffee. Coffee that had obviously been prepared many hours before and left to evaporate on the burner. The only food in sight were a few green oranges and bananas with fruit flies living aboard them. The reefer contained unopened boxes and a small metal pitcher of milk. In the wardroom was another ingredient to the mix—stale cigar butts that assaulted his noise.

John heard the handle of the wardroom door being turned. It was Fuller.

"Hello Tom, another chance for us to watch the stars together."

"Up your intake," Tom answered, not smiling.

"Why don't you just relax and get into a better mood. Here, have a green banana and a fresh cup of Navy coffee," John said half-seriously.

Tom just stared at the fruit flies that were beginning to be annoyed. "Those no-good stewards, I'll write both of their asses up. They're supposed to have sandwiches ready for us."

"They may have fixed the sandwiches," John added. "With the roaches I've seen in the pantry, it would take two sandwiches to just fill one of 'em. I heard about a ship on the East Coast that was sprayed from stem to stern and still they couldn't get rid of them. It seems like they always stayed one bulkhead ahead of the spraying party. It was referred to affectionately as the 'USS *Roach Barge*.'"

"Those two stewards belonged to Passmore," Tom added with a frown. "The problem is, he's no longer around to write them up. The stewards now report to Pebbles, and he doesn't want to take the time to write another report."

"Tom, I'm still worried about Decker."

"Come on, you've got to be kidding me. The only reason I wouldn't want him to jump overboard is that we would have to search for him."

"Really, Tom, I'm not convinced that the fool will not try something."

"Yah, he probably will since he got so much attention last time."

"I'm telling you, John, Decker is a real loser. Damn it, why didn't he just drink the whole can of Brasso?"

John and Tom left the wardroom nauseous from hunger and fatigue. They would have stayed longer and relieved the watch five minutes late, except the only thing to read was a copy of *Duttons*.

"My God, Tom," John said as they emerged onto the bridge, "look at those bright and happy faces. It's a real pleasure relieving patriots."

"Oh God, it's that boot ensign!" Brandon the JOOD, said with mock disgust.

Allen, who was the OOD, called Tom and John over for an intimate conference on one side of the bridge so the enlisted would not hear them. "Have you heard about Frisbee? No, of course you couldn't have heard about him. Well, that fart had the watch in CIC. You know the 2000 to 2400 watch. At about 2200, he takes two of the folding chairs from the wardroom locker and places them behind the air plotting board and makes a bed. Yeah! A bed. He figured the Old Man had gone to sleep so what the hell. Well, at 2300, the Old Man walked in and noticed there was no officer sitting on the stool in CIC. He asked that smartass McFadden where Mr. Frisbee was. Well, you know McFadden, he just smiled and pointed towards the air plot. You realize how far it is from the bridge to CIC? You could hear the cursing coming all the way across. I never heard such shouting and I'm a Baptist. Well, to sum it up, we aren't going to see Frisbee for a few days if I know the Old Man. Probably put him back on to the mast again; this time with the power cut on."

"Frisbee doesn't have any sense anyway," Tom added with authority. "Anybody who takes an overnighter in Keelung has got to be a psycho." John grimaced at the thought.

They finally relieved Allen and Brandon. There was always a feeling of depression when a sailor begins a watch. The first wrong thing John did was look at the bulkhead-mounted chronometer.

"Tom, we have four fuckin' hours to stand up here," John muttered. "I bet there isn't a decent cup of coffee on the ship at this hour of the night."

"Yeah, it's going to be long and boring. Not even a contact on the scope." A long silence followed while Tom walked out onto the wing of the bridge and stood looking at the dark sea. There was only a witch's moon, but the abundant stars also unwittingly gave their light. The watch could see cigarettes glowing on the forecastle, being smoked by a few of the sailors who couldn't sleep in the hot, confined compartments.

"Tom, should you report their asses? The smoking lamp is out," John said out of boredom.

"Hell no! Do you think the Vietcong are going to see their cigarettes?"

John moved closer to Tom as they both stared at the sea. "Do you think you'll marry Big Bev?"

"I don't know, John. I guess I'm kind of afraid. We've had some good times, but that doesn't mean we'd be happy together for the rest of our lives."

John looked at the dim horizon of the sea. "You're lucky to have someone. Ever since Paula dumped me, I've been writing to several girls but they don't write back. It's strange how all the girls back home want to get married when you're in the States, but when your ass is overseas, none of them will write you. I'm so lonely and horny I'd marry just about any girl, excluding Cosby Ann of course, just to have somebody to write me. Do you realize it has been two weeks since I've received even a bill from the States?"

"What's wrong with Cosby Ann?" Tom asked, half expecting not to receive an answer.

"She was like that Pontiac I nearly bought—good to look at but wouldn't start." John laughed.

"Yorktown, you must be one great lover. I bet you're really romantic with a broad. You know, quoting poetry to her ass."

"Okay, Fuller, what about Big Bev? Are you going to marry her or not?" asked John after slurping more coffee.

"Well, we did have some good times back in Frisco. We stayed in one of the finest hotels there. I figured I would get killed over here, so I spent every cent I had. Boy, I'll never forget our last night in port." A long silence followed while Tom smiled and looked out to the white caps whose phosphorescent glow accentuated the steepness of the blackened waves.

"Okay, you got your point across," John said. "Now tell me what happened."

"The only reason I'm telling you this," Tom said confidentially, "is because I need someone else's opinion. When you think you love someone, you can't see things in perspective. Not that I think you're capable of giving good advice, but then it does help to talk."

"What a slap," John protested. "Here I am ready to hear your confession and you tell me that I'm not qualified."

"Now in bed she's something else. She was a virgin when I met her," Tom said with pride.

"Yeah, I bet!" replied John.

"Are you going to listen or be a smartass? I swear she was."

"You bet," replied John. Clearly this was a sore spot with Tom. This was surprising to John since he had never heard of a sailor who considered virginity a virtue.

"Well, anyway after I first met Bev, I couldn't stop thinking about her. You know, she is pretty tough."

"Now on that you're telling the truth. I thought about writing her myself after seeing the colored Polaroid."

"A boot like you couldn't score with her. At first there wasn't much action. We just sat around on the beach at Belmont Shores and shot the shit. I'll probably get skin cancer from some of our talks." He paused. "She's a great talker; reads a hell of a lot."

"With that body?" John noted. "I'm sure you wanted to review the *Great Books of the Western World* in bed with her. Come on, Fuller, cut out the bullshit, she doesn't look like a scholar."

"Yorktown, it was great just talking to her." Tom paused. "Anyway, I was sweating out some broad I had met down on the Pike. A real loser you know, what they call a 'WestPac widow'—some of these broads just can't help but sleep around when their husbands are away."

"Did you get her pregnant?" asked John. He noticed Abato moving closer in order to overhear the conversation. "Say Abato, give us a new position."

"Hell no, I was afraid of the clap."

"What got you afraid?" asked John.

"It was Boats. After I got back on board one night, I mentioned her name to him. You know, the local Pike expert. Well, he told me she's a walking clap trap. She even gave it to the chief steward, who used to be on board. What makes it so bad was that the chief was the ship's doc. If any man knew about prevention, it was him. To think that he gave VD lectures. Knew all about diseases that make your Luther fall off."

Tom showed some irritation in his voice. "Wouldn't you know it, a damn contact out in the middle of nowhere. With the thousands of square miles of open ocean, contacts end up passing about 200 yards off your stern. Jeez! That means I might have to wake the Captain. God! I don't know if I can stand his pipe smoke out here on the bridge tonight. It seems like he smokes cigars during the day and a pipe at night. The last time I woke him up for a contact, he spent the watch with me. Just sat in that chair and stoked his furnace for four hours. The first thing he'll want besides some matches for that cesspool of a pipe is good coffee. Now where the hell am I going to get some coffee that's worth a damn? Some of the other guys told me that your FITREP depends upon whether the coffee is sat on your watch or not."

"Fuller, will you calm down and get back to the story? What happened in San Francisco? I need to think about the States. The ocean and this old rusting motherfucker are getting to me."

"I didn't get a chance to score in L.A. So I figured that if I suggested she meet the ship in Frisco, I might have another try. We were going to Frisco to pick up a carrier to screen out of Alameda. So on my last night in Long Beach, I took her to see an old John Wayne movie. A real tearjerker. He plays a naval aviator who gets shot down. The show ends with him appearing in the clouds in uniform while a choir sings the Navy Hymn."

"Fuller, if she had any sense, she probably laughed through

the movie and you did all the crying."

"Boot, you're missing the point. I figured that if she thought I might die over here, she would put out. Walter Cronkite keeps telling the television audience that everyone is KIA over here. You know, nightly body counts to improve his ratings."

"The only thing that might kill you in the Orient," John added, "is some sort of venereal disease. I hear there's one strain in Bangkok that is incurable."

"Let me get back to the story, okay? I hope you're watching the only contact we have on the watch. After the movie we went down to George's Roundup to dance. It was there that I mentioned going up to Frisco to meet the *Hyman*. I emphasized the fact that this pig iron mother was going to be in port overnight."

John said softly, "That's pretty romantic—George's Roundup. I see why she was still a virgin."

"Jeez, I don't know why I even talk to you. Well, she flew up to Frisco and was standing on the pier while we pulled in. The minute I saw her, I got excited. I left my position on the sea and anchor detail somewhat prematurely and went below to dress. All of a sudden, I hear 'Mr. Fuller, lay to the bridge.' God! It seemed like Boats had suddenly forgotten how to secure the port anchor. We had it ready in case we needed to drop the hook in some fog around the Gate. That bastard knew that the Captain would ask to speak to me. Well anyway, when I heard my name over the 1MC, I ran half-dressed up to the bridge. The Captain didn't say a word at first. Just kind of stared at me, lit his damn cigar, and then laid in. What I heard, I can't repeat. Our Captain can out-cuss even Boats.

"I was two hours late getting out on the pier, but Big Bev

was still waiting. You should have seen the dress she had on. Man, it was short—and I mean *short*. Those new styles are something else. Strange that at the time we were homeported in the States, the dresses covered the knees and, now that we're overseas, they barely cover the ass. They had just started to haul 'em up when we left CONUS."

Yorktown and Fuller looked seaward, dreaming of short dresses. At times like these, however, John missed something more than fashion or sex. He deeply longed for home: warm August days when the locust would sing and thunderheads build in the east. Skinny-dipping in hot summer pools.

The dream was short, interrupted by Tom's continuation. "We hailed a cab and I asked her where she planned on staying. She said the Fairmont. My mouth fell open. How in the world was I going to afford a hotel like that? Her father's a doctor and sends her money; my father works on a metal press and sends me the bills I ran up in college.

"Well, anyway getting back to the story, I moved closer to her in the cab and whispered that I couldn't afford two rooms at the Fairmont. She just smiled at me, grabbed Luther, and said, 'I know.' Jeez, man, if I live to be a hundred, I'll never be that excited again. Of course I wasn't sure what she meant. Knowing Bev, I thought she probably brought along some of her roommates from Belmont Shores and I had to sleep on some damn couch.

"We pulled up in front of the Fairmont and the doorman opened the door for Bev. You should have seen his expression. He looked like Henry VIII eyeing a leg of lamb. We didn't even stop at the front desk. She already had a room signed in her father's name since she was using his credit card. I just smiled at the clerk as we went by. The elevator seemed to take forever to reach the floor. Finally we entered the room. It was beautiful with shag carpet and all. Man, the view was magnificent. You could look out over the other buildings and across miles of city and even to the distant mountains that frame the Bay."

"Fuller, you mean you went directly from the ship to the Fairmont? I figured you two would have at least hit Broadway and seen some of those silicon tits. While I was waiting on a flight at Travis, I went over to Broadway. They have a gal there that must have had forty-eights. She came down out of the ceiling onto the top of a piano, gyrated for a while, then went back up into the ceiling. I think her name was Carol Doe Doe or some shit like that. It's a hustle joint, but she's something to see. I swear they get you to drink two drinks in less than seven minutes. When you finish, you're escorted out of there in order to make room for the next sucker."

"Well Yorktown, if that's your idea of an evening on the town, be my guest. A few of us more experienced guys would just as soon go to the Fairmont than watch some gal saddle up on a piano. Let me finish my story before the Old Man decides to visit us on the bridge. Back at the room, I walked over to her and held her close to me. She starts breathing harder, and I figure that's a point in my favor. Then we kind of shuffle across the shag carpet to the bed and fall down on top of it. Before long I had my hand up her dress, and this really turns Bev on. Her breathing became gasps. Then she whispered in my ear, 'Have you got anything?' Talk about Luther wilting. Can you imagine being the most excited you have ever been in your life, then your girl asks you, 'Have you got anything?' Jeez, of course I didn't have anything. I thought everybody was on the pill or had some mechanical device shoved up their ass. After all, this is the 60s.

"I told her I didn't have anything, but that I would be careful. She then tells me it's her time of the month and she can't take any chances. What an opportunity, and now there was a possibility that I might lose it. So I told her I'd be right back. I took the elevator and went down to the curio shop in the main lobby. What an experience. The clerks always want to know what you are looking for and of course they're always women. I'm not shy except when it comes to buying rubbers. So finally, after the young salesgirl kept bugging me about what I was looking for, I told her, 'Gum.' 'Gum!' she said. 'You mean you've been looking for gum? Why it's right on top of the counter in front of you.' A real smartass she was.

"I got to thinking I will never be back there again, so I just came out with it: 'No, it's not gum that I want, but ... but rubbers.'

"'Oh, I see. Yes sir. What kind do you prefer?' I didn't expect a hotel to have a selection. I told her I preferred Sheik. That was the only brand name I could think of. They're the kind they put in the large bowl on the wardroom table at liberty call. Then she asked me, 'Do you prefer the reservoir end or plain and with or without sensi-creme?' I told her I didn't know a damn thing about rubbers since I was a devote Catholic and didn't believe in birth control. You should have heard her laugh.

"Then she asked me how many I needed for the evening. I told her three. In reality the way the night was going, I figured I wouldn't even need one. Bev would probably be out of the mood by the time I got back to the room.

"When I finally returned to the room, I found her sitting on the edge of the bed. She stood up, smiled, and walked towards me. I held her, and she felt warm and so good. I knew I had won. It was as though what we were about to do should be done. She took the rubbers from my hand, put one in her mouth as though to tear it with her teeth, then threw all three of them on the floor. By the way, what's happened to that contact on the screen?"

"I haven't looked in a while," John said hesitantly. "Just a minute." John walked back into the darkened bridge and looked at the radarscope. "She's going to pass close to port. Damn it, just when the story was getting to be good! Tom, I hate to say it but the contact is closing fast. She's at eight thousand yards."

At that moment, John picked up the CIC phone and asked for the status of the contact. "CIC expects a CPA of 1200 hundred yards astern. Do you want me to wake the Old Man?"

"Hell no!" Tom whispered. "You read the night order. It says to wake his ass when a contact is at twelve thousand yards. It's already eight thousand yards. We're both going to catch it. Twelve hundred yards astern will do just fine. However, let's walk over to the other wing of the bridge and keep an eye on her. There's no point in ruining my perfect record of near misses."

They both walked through the bridge to the other wing. The sky presented a new arrangement of stars. It was a tropical night filled with strong island and sea smells. The bow of the ship pointed towards the Southern Cross.

Tom continued, "I started undressing her. I really fouled up that part. I caught her blouse zipper on some material and ended up having to pull it over the top of her head and it just about choked her. In the movies you see the man completely undressing the woman and she just flows out of her garments. Well, it's never worked that way for me. Something always gets snagged. Besides, most girls don't even bother to play the role. Finally I get her undressed and she reminds me she's a virgin, so I have to take it nice and easy.

"Despite her protest, I picked up a rubber off the deck. Man, I didn't need a pregnant girlfriend. My problem really started when I undid the package. I thought you were supposed to unfold the damn thing first. Hell, I couldn't admit to her I had never used one. It's against my religion, and she's Catholic too and couldn't give me any advice. Boy, what a mess. The damn thing wouldn't fit on anything except a pencil after I unfolded it. Hell, I couldn't wait anymore, and I figured she wouldn't know the difference. She's not the brightest girl on the beach even if she does read a lot."

Tom looked very serious. "It was over in less than a minute. She didn't even groan with ecstasy. Yorktown, you ought to try one of those Yokohama broads. They holler, claw, and beg for more—real actresses. Anyway, as I lay there exhausted, I began to think about what all the evening had cost me. I had gotten into trouble with the Old Man. I had spent seven dollars on a taxi and ninety-five for the room since I insisted on reimbursing her. And with my luck, I was going to end up paying for a honeymoon with a pregnant bride."

"Tom, that's just about the most romantic thing I've ever heard," John said, laughing. "Is she pregnant?"

Tom cut him short. "What about the contact?"

John raised his binoculars. "Hey, look through the glasses!

It's a luxury liner. May even be a Cunard." He could tell that Tom wanted to drop the subject. Her being pregnant didn't seem like such a bad idea to John. At least she would write to him. What he would have given for some mail.

Both strained their eyes looking at the liner. She was pure white under the witch's moon and starlight. The liner was ablaze with a myriad of lights: port holes, veranda windows, even to the masthead. She cut the smooth sea with her bow. As she approached *Hyman*, the moon appeared on the opposite side of the liner, framing her in soft moon glow.

"Fuller, we better change course," John said hurriedly. "This bearing is closing constant now. We might end up eating some of their mid-rats if we don't do something quick."

"Come right five degrees," Tom ordered the helmsman. After a few seconds delay, he added, "Come right to course one three zero."

"Aye aye, sir," the helmsman replied. "Steering course one three zero."

John thought, *We're lucky we turned when we did since the liner passed only one thousand yards off the stern. Damn lucky.* Through their glasses they could see passengers dancing and hear the muffled music of the ship's band.

"What a contrast, Tom. Here we are defending what they're enjoying. They don't even know a fucking war is going on. All they have to do tonight is eat, drink, and fuck. We have to wait another hour to get relieved. Not even a cup of coffee on this mother that's worth a damn. Would you look at that broad up on the third deck pointing and waving at us? What I wouldn't give to get in her pants.

Hell, I don't even care what she looks like up close or even how old she is."

"Man, we were lucky. If there had been anyone on the bridge besides Iron Mike, they would have sounded the whistle. That would have awakened the Old Man alright!" said Tom.

"Thank goodness Iron Mike can't see. The liner's captain is probably in bed with a passenger." John laughed.

"Yeah, Yorktown, it doesn't seem fair. I guess our time is coming—that's what makes it okay. At least I think it does."

CHAPTER TEN

Sign of the Crab

The day had started off hot and evidently planned on getting even hotter. Everything seemed to be going wrong. John had overslept and missed breakfast that included his three mandatory cups of coffee. The lack of caffeine always gave him a coffee headache. The ass chewing he received for being late to the officer roll call was prompt and lengthy in detail.

The worse thing so far that morning was the Pepsi machine being broken again. The machine seemed to run on a port and starboard timetable. One day it gave pure carbonated water with no syrup, the next day it gave pure syrup with no carbonated water. Today it didn't give shit.

After groping the machine, which resulted in hurting his hand, John sensed a new problem in the form of his approaching chief.

"Sir, I hate to bother you, and I realize the XO's pissed at you for missing roll call, but it's that fucking Decker again. I can't find the bastard anywhere. The only thing that cheers me up is that Abato says he can't find his Brasso. Maybe you should check the sickbay," the chief said, smiling.

"Why don't you check on him yourself, chief?"

"Are you serious, sir? Go in the sickbay. You must be kidding. At least the XO is on to that fat-assed corpsman. Did you read the P.O.D?" When John shook his head, the chief continued, "Well, you ought to. That fat ass had been on me to lose weight. Here, read what the XO put in it." He handed over a coffee-stained Plan of the Day. John reluctantly scanned it:

```
HM1 Justice says all hands are reminded of
the new Navy weight limit. If you don't
meet the standards, you are required to go
on a diet. To emphasize the importance of
weight control, HM1 Justice did a pushup
and drank a tab forgoing his usual donut
and Mountain Dew.
```

"Sir, here comes Boats. He'll go to sickbay with you. He hates Decker enough to risk encountering that fat ass."

"Okay Boats, let's check it out," John said, his frustration showing. There was no way John could avoid searching for Decker.

The medical department was an area to avoid at all possible costs. It seemed that if a sailor ever entered the hatch to the stainless steel, rubbing alcohol-scented infirmary, then a shot awaited the swabbie. Regrets would suddenly remember that the sailor needed a TB patch test, a typhoid or maybe even a yellow fever shot that made the victim ache like hell. Regrets was not a small man if you measured his circumference and did not concern yourself with his height. His bottom button never could secure his shirt that stretched at its expansion joints while his belt supported a sea chest of a stomach. His fly perpetually remained at three-quarters hoist.

No matter who entered his serfdom of medieval care, they were always asked, "What's your weight?" If the sailor was not within Navy standards, Regrets would report him whether he was a seaman deuce or an officer. Of course, if the swabbie had been around a little and was at least a first class with two hash marks, the potential victim simply had to ask him what the requirements were for a 5'7" person—the doc's height. Regrets would then be immediately defused, becoming almost apologetic.

As they entered sickbay, Boats said, "Shit sir, Decker is the only fucker willing to get one of the corpsman's shots in order to miss work."

John frowned at the approaching corpsman. "Look, I don't want one of your shots, and I weigh 165. All I want to know is if Decker is behind that divider, recovering from a shot or whatever else you've done to him."

Regrets stared at John for a moment and let out a puff of Swisher Sweets cigar smoke. "Do you know the three signs that indicate an early heart attack? One of them is flab under the arm." Regrets demonstrated this by pinching his own arm. "The second is having two chins, and the third is a pig's belly."

Boats smiled at Regrets. "Well, I hate to hear that you won't be with us much longer. Mr. Yorktown, wasn't it nice of Doc to tell us he's being discharged over the side?"

John left sickbay as Regrets demonstrated to Boats that his arms were firm and that it was impossible to pinch his second chin. *Shit*, thought John, *who cares where Decker is anyway?*

John's problems were not over. He found Abato waiting for him outside sickbay.

"Mr. Yorktown, the Captain wants to see the message board, and I can't find Decker anywhere," Abato said quietly, fearing reproach for what was not his error.

"Oh hell, give me the board. Go find Decker and tell him I'm going to write his ass up."

"Yes sir, I'll tell him you're going to write his ass up."

What an IQ, John thought.

John found the Captain sitting on the bridge surrounded by a cloud of cigar smoke. As usual, he didn't speak or acknowledge John's presence but stuck out his hand to receive the crowded message board. "Great God alive! What the hell is that?" The Captain pointed towards a small insect that paraded down a "secret" message.

"Uh Captain, it looks like a small crab to me. Never seen anything like it before," said John with a tone of innocence and shock in his voice. Had the Captain looked closely, he would have noticed perspiration forming around the brim of John's piss gutter.

"I know what the hell it is. It's a crab, that's what it is. And I don't mean the kind you eat, but the kind that eats sailors. Bloodsucking sons of bitches!"

"Captain, it must be Decker. He's the kind that would get

the crabs. Yes sir, if there's anyone in my division that would be prone in that direction, it would be Decker," said John.

"Mr. Yorktown, I'm not going to risk it. Once these things get started on a ship, there's no stopping them. Before long a tin can gets a reputation as being a crab can. I want you to muster your division and send them all to Doc. Tell him that I want the one with crabs put on report for not reporting to sickbay on his own volition. Do you have that straight, Mr. Yorktown?"

"Yes sir, we will muster right away."

John had the word passed throughout the ship. Soon he was standing in front of his division trying to think of how to put it. "Today, the Captain found a crab on one of his secret messages. He has ordered that each of you proceed to the sickbay for a complete crab examination. I expect each of you to do your part to see that our mission is not hampered in Southeast Asia and to promptly report any sightings of crabs on this ship. I especially don't want any crabs foraging in my division." Only one man in his division caught the humor in his remarks and laughed. The rest were trying to grasp the import of the order and were fearful of being the one who had dispatched the solitary crab.

Slowly it dawned on John that ever since that mistake at Mother Wong's, he had been itching. Not a persistent itch but an off and on one. *Oh, no*, he thought. *It cannot be me.* He immediately walked to the nearest officers' head for a personal inspection. There in the toilet stall, he experienced his first intimate onboard anxiety. Nested in his body hair was a beach scene at low tide.

The next few days to Hong Kong can't pass fast enough, he thought. *Maybe I can keep them pastured in my boxers. I will have to remember when to scratch and when not to. Maybe in Hong Kong there will be a SupeRx drug store where I can get some serum or suave, yah, and someday that Pepsi machine will work and give me change for a quarter.*

CHAPTER ELEVEN

Sailor's Prayer

WALT DISNEY DIES
FAMED CAREER ENDS AT 65
—*Herald Examiner*, December 15, 1966

Each day seemed to duplicate the preceding one. However the hours did pass, and before he realized it, John was being awakened for his last watch prior to the ship's arrival in Hong Kong. The night had already been too short when a stream of red light splashed upon his face.

"Time for your watch, sir." The messenger's voice was muffled in an attempt not to awaken the other officer who shared his stateroom.

"You've got to be kidding me," John muttered. The stream of light vanished into its source and only the night lights filled the stateroom. After signing the Frisbee log, John asked himself out loud, "Where are my damn pants?" He was not in any mood for the watch.

Hyman was taking mild rolls off the coast of Hong Kong. Lulling, cradle-like rolls that made walking up to the bridge a mixture of wakefulness and sleep. "Good morning, Tom," John said quietly as he nested his cup of coffee. Tom did not return his greeting. Instead, he continued to peer out at the moon-covered sea whose waves were distorted by the salt-covered bridge windows. After a silence in which Tom appeared to awaken, he lowered his binoculars. "What's good about this morning, boot?"

"Hong Kong—that's what's good about it. No more sea. I'm gonna find a hotel without a view of the ocean. No damn room with a view. A hotel where there is only a panorama of dry land. I can already smell the soil."

"Yorktown, you aren't smelling land. What you're smelling is fucking pollution. A China sailor can tell what port he's entering by smelling the air miles before he can sight the harbor. Even I can tell the difference between the smells of Olongapo and Kaohsiung."

Their watch was the four-to-eight, a waking watch. A watch that morning in which the sea appeared to be changing into earth. Gradually they saw the out islands of the British colony appear, adorned in lights. Tom, who was beginning to take a more earthly form, pointed towards the island of Hong Kong. "You see those lights? Just think there are people there. Land people just beginning to awaken and have a cup of tea. Hell, I'm ready for a cup of coffee. Abato, get Mr. Yorktown and me a cup of Java. Don't spill any of the damn stuff on the deck. The Captain has been bitching about coffee getting on both the deck grate and his chair."

Tom turned towards John. "Abato's mind is in his ass if you want my opinion. That bastard destroyed Paul." It was apparent that Tom neither forgave nor forgot.

John looked at him. "I know Paul had it coming to him for what he did to Abato. Can't violate UCMJ. Oh hell, there's no solution and no point talking about it. However, I didn't care for that deck ape the first time I saw him."

After a short delay, Abato brought up the coffee.

"Thanks, Abato," uttered Tom quietly.

"Yes sir," Abato replied, casting a smiling face towards the helmsman. Abato, since John had known him, only smiled when he cursed a seaman deuce, especially if that seaman happened to have attended college.

Tom took a drink of his coffee and immediately spat it out on to the deck. "You son of a bitch." He stuck his finger into the coffee cup and pulled out a wad of curly short hair. "You son of a bitch," he repeated at least two more times. Tom was careful to speak softly, however, since the Captain slept right behind the bridge. "You put goddamn short hairs in my coffee! I'm gonna write your ass up for that!"

"Hey Tom, come over here," said John, laughing. "What are you going to write him up for? I just took a correspondence course in UCMJ, and it doesn't say anything about hair in an officer's cup. Besides, the Captain said not to order the quartermaster to get coffee for the watch. To me it looks like Abato got one over on you. You can't report him without catching hell yourself from the skipper."

"I'll write that son of a bitch up for something," Tom promised. For the rest of the watch, they observed Abato closely. They tried not to be obvious in their glances, but Abato sensed their vengeance and sought the solitude of the starboard wing of the bridge.

The hours flowed like ketchup from the dispenser at John's hometown city café. It was a feeling derived from anticipating a great event such as liberty in Hong Kong. John was looking at the distant lights when Tom tapped his shoulder.

"I've got him. I've finally got the bastard, but I need a witness. He's asleep on watch. Come on, Yorktown. Take a look."

They walked quietly to the starboard wing of the bridge where they found Abato leaning on the railing apparently asleep. "Tom, how do you know he's asleep? He's not lying down but leaning on the railing. Can a man be asleep while standing up?"

"Abato, Abato, this is Mr. Fuller," Tom whispered in a barely audible voice. "See, Yorktown? This dumb ass is sound asleep," he said with a smile. "Abato, I am reporting you for sleeping on the watch!" Tom said loudly so that everyone on the bridge would become immediate witnesses.

"Sir, I ain't asleep," Abato said as though reentering consciousness from a hangover.

"Abato, I called your name in the presence of Mr. Yorktown, and you failed to reply. If you can't hear what's going on during a watch, I must also assume you can't see what's going on, and that makes for one hell of a quartermaster. Just consider yourself on report."

Tom motioned for John to follow him to the port wing of

the bridge. "I knew I could beat that fucker at his own game. You want to know how I knew he was asleep? It was easy. If he isn't holding a coffee cup, he has got to be asleep. I have never seen a boatswain mate or a quartermaster of the watch on duty without a coffee cup stuck on their thumb."

"Wow, Fuller, that's overpowering evidence," said John, laughing. Tom had finally triumphed. College and NROTC had won a decisive victory. *What the hell,* thought John. *Abato deserves to be written up for something.*

As their watch ended, the ship began to slice through the morning fog of Hong Kong harbor. John could barely make out the city crowding the flank of Victoria Peak. The sea and anchor detail relieved them both on the bridge. Tom walked to the ladder and descended to the main deck where he attempted to perform the duties of the first lieutenant.

John's function was to remain on the bridge and contact the port by radio. He always tensed up when it came time to contact the harbormaster, and he was sure that today would be no exception.

The Captain leaned over the edge of his chair, tipping slightly his cup of coffee. "Have you got him yet?"

"No sir, I'll try again," John's voice displayed a mixed tone of fear and respect. "This is *Hyman,* radio check over." There was a prolonged silence followed by Chinese conversation.

"Goddamn it!" The Captain picked up his own phone and called the com shack. "Chief, fix that radio!" Some seaman in radio then flipped the squawk box switch twice to indicate "Aye aye." This sent the Old Man into a tirade about the lack of military courtesy in John's division.

Because of his now fully awakened fear, John had forgotten the large city looming before him. As his heart rate returned to near normal, he was amazed by the tiers of buildings solidifying through the fog. In front of him was a busy harbor filled with foreign warships, freighters, junks, sampans, ferries, and floating waste. From the appearance of many of the harbor's native vessels, the garbage stood a better chance of staying afloat.

The order to let go the anchor was given by the Captain. The sound of sliding chain filled the air. From the forecastle, laughter was followed by cursing. Boats was now in his haven with a coffee cup in hand and a gravity-defying cigarette perched on his lower lip. Orders, mixed with a continuous source of unrestrained profanity and humor, flowed from his mouth.

The crew worked steadily to secure the ship since the time for liberty call depended on their speed in completing the delegated tasks. Soon the most beautiful words that a sailor can hear filled the ship: "Liberty call, liberty call. Liberty expires on board at zero seven thirty for duty sections one and two. Now liberty call."

John stood on the bridge, attempting to secure some of his gear while watching the streams of sailors form pools of white on the quarterdeck as they waited for the liberty launch. The great desire to get on the beach left John as he watched the swabbies struggle to get aboard the already crowded bam-bam boat.

Due to getting up at 0300, exhaustion, and the growing fear that Hong Kong would be another Taiwan, he decided to spend his first day and night in port aboard ship. He would eat aboard and watch a flick in the wardroom. It would be great to spend just one night without someone waking him up for a watch. Besides, he could go on the beach tomorrow morning. He was sure that Boats and his friends would not exhaust Hong Kong's potential the first day in port. Even though *Hyman* was a "small boy"—that is, a ship smaller than a cruiser, they represented the U.S. Navy in Hong Kong that day. There were no other capital ships present to assume that task.

John went below and found Tom lying in his rack reading *Lord of the Rings*. "Going over, Yorktown?" he asked.

"Are you kidding?" John replied.

"Come on, let's go. Whoever heard of a sailor staying on board the first day in port? Hong Kong is no place for saving your cherry. Let's get some beer and everything else that's available."

"Hell Tom, I'd rather read Navy regs than blow my money on some gal and Tiger Beer."

Ten minutes later they were standing on the deck of the *Hyman*. They waited impatiently in the cool, pungent morning air. A strong sea breeze had removed the fog, revealing the city and its crowning mountain, Victoria Peak, while Hong Kong's nightlights were being submerged by the brilliant rays of a newly risen China sun.

Tom broke the silence. "Here comes the mother now." An old, slow bam-bam boat came around the *Hyman*'s stern, its two cylinders making a popping Johnny Tractor sound. John and Tom managed to get ahead of some of the enlisted men who had gathered with them. They could hear their expressions of discontent, but then Tom said, "We are officers."

Boats and the other enlisted responded through their

expressions, "No shit!"

The unreal became real as the boat struggled to reach Fenwick Pier, a concrete landing near the British China Fleet Club. Spray from the rough waters of the harbor dampened the sailors who huddled in the bow of the boat. Blurs became images formed by the fleeing fog. An Impressionist painting had become one of Realism.

Up until their arrival at the pier, they had heard only a mixture of harbor sounds: ship whistles, seagulls—or sea vultures as Boats referred to them—and metallic ship noises, but now their ears were filled with strange words, car horns, and sailors bragging.

They stepped ashore with unsteady legs. "Land!" Tom shouted. "Which way you want to go, boot?"

"I don't care," replied John. It did not matter to him for right then he wished he had stayed on the ship.

"Follow your nose," Tom commanded. He sniffed the air in several directions. "This way—I smell beer." Tom was right for as they rounded the corner from Fenwick Pier, they entered the main street of the Wan Chai District, a place of bars, brothels, and exhaust fumes.

Most of the shops and bars were closed for it was still too early in a city that depended on the masquerade of night to create its mask of perfection.

"We may have to play pool at the China Fleet Club until some of these spots open up. John, I don't know about you, but some of these odors are beginning to get to me."

As they neared one cabaret, loud music came at them like a

wave that washed them into the bar. Within the darkness of the lukewarm room, shadows moved towards the new arrivals.

"Hello sailor, what's your name?"

"Uh, my name is Tom, and the creep with me is Johnny Yorktown."

"Tom-son, Yorktown-son ... Navy, no?"

It occurred to John that he had heard the word "son" in Japan and wondered what it meant. He assumed it was universally translated as "sucker."

"Yeah, we are U.S. Navy," John replied. They were then led to a very dark booth. It was so dark that John didn't know who seated them. He assumed she was young or at least he hoped so.

"My name Mary and her name Jane."

"Oh God," John whispered to Tom, "this is a come-on to sell us weed. If we get caught with two pushers in Hong Kong, it means jail time under Chinese law. I think they are prone to throw the key away here."

"Isn't Hong Kong a British Crown colony?" Tom smiled.

"Guess who runs the jail?"

"Okay, okay," replied Tom. After thinking further, he said, "John, what the hell are you talking about? All they said were their names." Tom then reached over and pulled Mary towards him. Tom was apparently in ecstasy. Earlier he had explained that a sailor's love is different from a landlubber's. A sailor didn't have time to wait for tides or orders when ashore. This rule applied to both swabs and admirals.

In the selection process, John ended up with the Jane half of the duet. Their eyes were now used to the dim light that made it possible for him to see Jane for the first time. Her straight black hair hung below her shoulders. Her frame was small and her face was more slender than many of the Chinese girls he had seen in Taiwan. Her mouth appeared continually in a puckering position.

"You got cigarette, Yorktown?" Jane asked, lightly rubbing his leg.

"No, but if you keep on rubbing my leg, I will light up."

"You got cherry, Yorktown-son?"

"Damn right he's got his cherry." Tom laughed.

"Cherry boy-son." Jane laughed. "I got mine too. See?" She twisted her forearm so a stray ray of light landed on the lightly etched tattoo of a stemmed cherry on her skin.

A jukebox began an old scratched Patti Page number that John had first heard as a small child back in Corsicana Texas, "Mockin' Bird Hill." The jukebox had started reluctantly and was to continue in that fashion throughout the song, slurring the words.

"Buy me drink!" Mary commanded, looking at Tom. No doubt she was rubbing his leg too. She was heavier, shorter, and less attractive than Jane. But as Boats was apt to say, "The less attractive, the more willing to please."

"What for?" Tom asked with a smile of anticipation on his face. Mary leaned towards Tom and whispered something that John could not make out. He spoke quietly into her ear while she remained silent. Mary then stared into space as if giving an important business transaction ample consideration. Finally she nodded her head in a slow and very reluctant sign of approval. This indicated to John that Tom was getting a real bargain.

Ha, ha, John thought. He leaned towards Jane and whispered what he thought would be appropriate, "How much?"

Jane was silent. She starred into space and, after deliberate consideration, whispered, "Twenty-five American dollar."

"Twenty-five American dollars!" John shouted. Tom and Mary smiled at each other.

I bet that son of a bitch got a better deal that I did, thought John. *Probably got some extras thrown in.* Then he calmed down. *It's my first night in port. What the hell, might as well blow my money now, then I can't be suckered into anything later.*

"Okay, Jane, let's go," said John in a tone of resignation.

"No, can't go now unless you buy me out of the bar," Jane said with authority and experience. No one commands greater respect than a B-girl with attitude, especially when a sailor is horny.

"How much to buy you out?" John asked weakly.

"Ten American dollar," she answered.

"Ten American dollar!" he shouted. This time it was his turn to be silent, gazing at the ceiling for an answer. He stalled for time while he tried to remember how much money he had in his billfold. "Okay, ten American dollars and no more hidden fees."

Fool! John's conscience shouted at him,

Jane said, "I go ask Anne Sung when we can go." She vanished into the darkness like an inkblot. Ten long minutes passed before she returned. "Anne Sung say we must wait two hours. Some of my other boyfriends come at this time, and she say it make them mad if I not be here. Cause great trouble for cabaret."

"You've got to be kidding!" John couldn't hide the astonishment and irritation in his voice.

"Yorktown, buy me drink while we wait on my other

boyfriends." And so began a steady request for "lady cocktails." They were but colored water that cost two and a half American dollars a drink. With each new request, she rubbed John's leg with quick short strokes in a pump-priming fashion. When she wanted a double cocktail, she would let her hand rest on his fly. He began to wish her other boyfriends would arrive before he went truly broke.

After thirty minutes of "priming the pump," she asked John if he wanted to dance. He reasoned that this must be an attempt to let her bladder rest after three single and two double lady cocktails.

John told her he was willing to dance, but didn't dance very well. He hated to admit he had never danced a "fast dance" in his life, but he figured that something had to be done, or he wouldn't have enough money to pay the taxi fare to her place.

On the dance floor, she danced the monkey, twisting, turning, bumping, and grinding as she stared at other nearby sailors. In front of her, John shook spastically with the music.

From the darkness came the familiar voice of Boats, "Way to go, Mr. Yorktown!"

"Why he call you Mr. Yorktown?" asked Jane.

"That's Boats' way of treating other sailors. He believes the enlisted need respect, too." Jane's stare indicated she needed to think over his last comment for several minutes.

John had earlier reasoned that she might charge him more for her favors if she suspected he was an officer since he would be able to afford it. He was now afraid that Boats had ended the charade.

When the music ended, they seated themselves closer to the dance floor than before. John decided it was easier to buy her drinks than to dance to a rhythm he didn't feel.

Boats and his "date" continued dancing. He now appeared as a tank reed from the ankle up. He bent and twisted as though caught in a Texas whirlwind. As a result of his pride and the heat of the dance floor, Boats rolled up his sleeves to reveal his tattoos. Above the tattooed chains around his wrists, the heads of his finely done Yokohama dragons appeared. John had seen the menageries at different times while he supervised his sailors on the lower decks. A red cherry adorned one arm above a devil with the inscription: *Born to Raise Hell*. On the other arm were *Ruth, Eternally Yours* and *Mother, the Girl of my Life*. A fully rigged ship sailed across his chest. He was like a seagoing billboard carrying tattooed messages along the coast of China.

John's two-hour waiting period soon passed rapidly. At first, he attempted to kiss Jane, but the strong smells of lady cocktails, coffee, beer, and cigarettes worked like a bulletproof shield over her face. There was no great need to kiss her since he knew he would eventually find a girl in Hong Kong with better breath.

Unfortunately he was not in total control. She continued to rub his leg and occasionally his fly for a double cocktail, further whetting his expectation.

While sitting at the table, John tried in vain to keep time with the music by tapping his foot. He soon found it to be too heavy to lift after being required to drink Asahi, San Miguel, and Tiger Beer for two hours.

John had a straight flow system when it came to drinking beer. Due to his numerous trips to the head, he had diverse opportunities to read the thoughts left by his predecessors above the urinals. Many of the expressions were simply names, dates, and hometowns. Others dealt with their impressions of the Navy and, as typical of the heads around the Pacific, sailors wrote about the Marine Corps and the Marine Corps wrote about sailors. Both branches claimed the other one performed unnatural sex acts.

While he was washing his hands on his fifth trip to the head, a young lady walked in. Immediately he felt uneasy since he had not read any signs on the door that said MEN'S, GENTLEMEN, SEÑOR, BULLS, or COCKS. Instead of paying him any attention as he fumbled for the dropped soap in the basin, she raised her skirt and squatted over the hole in the floor where in America there would have been a toilet bowl. John assumed that the hole had been installed during the Japanese occupation.

"Excuse me, ma'am, but isn't this the men's room?"

"What you say?"

"I said isn't this the men's head?"

"You crazy American, no need two heads in Wan Chai when one will do. I no see you, and you no see me."

"I'm sorry for 'seeing' you. You go right ahead," John said, flushing the urinal, a trace of perspiration having formed on his brow.

After he returned from his trip to the restroom, Jane touched his arm and leaned towards him. "Let's go. Anne Sung say she like you. Do you favor. She let me go early." Her words were preceded by her breath. Anne Sung had done him a favor alright. Instead of buying her out of the bar directly, he had been allowed to buy her two-dollar-and-fifty-cent American dollar drinks for two hours plus ten dollars for letting her go early.

They fought the tidal inflow of the bar and finally emerged onto the crowded sidewalk. As alien as the bar was, it seemed friendlier and safer than the street. It was as though the street was paved with automobiles as tightly packed as the red bricks on the roads of his hometown in Texas. John began the traditional waving and shouting at the cars, hoping that one of them would be a taxi.

In the brilliant sun that required another period of eye adjustment, it dawned on him that Tom and Mary hadn't followed them out. Jane answered his unspoken question, "Don't worry. Mary knows where to take Tom-son."

"I bet she does," replied John.

A taxi stopped, and immediately they got in. Without a word from either one of them, the taxi driver applied full throttle and roared into the traffic honking at other cars and objects that he alone must have been able to see. Jane leaned over the seat and spoke loudly to the driver. He acknowledged her comments by sucking air between his teeth. The taxi was in almost continuous acceleration with every approaching corner or intersection being a target for more speed. John prayed out loud to a non-listening congregation, "Dear Lord, let me get out of this thing alive, and I'll start going to church. I mean it, I'll go!"

The taxi stopped abruptly, launching him against the back of the front seat. John glanced around and noted that they were not in the best of districts. It was also apparent that he was the only American in the area. Tall, soot-covered brick buildings hovered on both sides of the narrow street. The buildings looked like a Chinese version of the French quarter in New Orleans with iron grillwork on each balcony. The sounds and odors, however, were very different.

Obviously they did not serve Cajun food here.

Thankful for being alive, John handed the taxi driver five Hong Kong dollars and told him to keep the change. His meter didn't work, but John figured that five Hong Kong dollars would be enough. A vengeful look came over the taxi driver's face.

In response to John's attempted generosity, Jane said, "Stingy American! No-good first class bastard! Give him ten Hong Kong dollar!"

"Ten Hong Kong dollar?" John questioned since they had only driven nine blocks. This trick had been pulled on him before in Tokyo when the taxi driver claimed he had given him a tour of the city. Some tour that had been. The driver hadn't said one word. His meter wasn't working either, and it seemed that he too sucked wind between his widely spaced front teeth.

They had stopped in front of a small, paint-blistered brick hotel where Chinese kitchen odors, mixed with a portion of spilt Tiger Beer, awaited them as hostesses at the entrance.

Jane said firmly and proudly, "This way Yorktown-son," as she grabbed his arm. John was glad that she hurriedly entered the decaying structure. He assumed that the rest of the building was more substantial than the entrance. In Texas, some people did not repair the outside of their homes in order to avoid paying higher property taxes, but a few were plush inside.

Quickly his thoughts of the structure's vulnerability vanished. *At last, at last, hallelujah!* John thought. He was finally safe from the bars, the congested streets, and taxi drivers. The odors increased as they penetrated the semi-darkness of the hall. It smelt like someone was burning a pasture off with an occasional old tire thrown in.

Their procession ended when Jane opened the door to a large room. Smoke covered the upper two-thirds of the interior. There on the floor, holding on to a slopping bottle of Jameson Irish Whiskey, was Boats and his new girlfriend. The girlfriend was older than John deduced when he first saw her in the dimly lit bar. The room's lights were destructive in their revelation. Boats, however, was already past the state of critical awareness.

John looked at Jane to see if she too had been altered by the light. Her body was still thin with small pointed breasts and full hips. The side slits of her long light-green bar dress revealed beautiful legs.

Boats waved his spilling whiskey bottle with an exaggerated expression. "Come in, Mr. Yorktown. I want you to meet one of the finest ladies in Hong Kong. This here is Madam Po-Chun."

Madam Po-Chun was as drunk as Boats. It was obvious that some of the B-girls preferred real whiskey to colored ginger ale. The madam was losing her business sense since it became more difficult to pump a sailor dry when she was on the same sobriety level as her customer.

She raised her arm to shake hands with John but made contact with his knee instead. Madam Po-Chun made another attempt for John's hand but missed his knee on the second try. Since she was determined to make physical contact with John, he got down on the floor with her and placed his hand in hers.

Madam Po-Chun said in slurred English, "You good American bastard. I like you. You be my boyfriend when this son of a bitch go back to ship? He too drunk to be a good lover."

"Madam, I would love to, but Jane is with me, and I

promised to be hers for the evening." He thought, *Paid for but with no guarantee—that's the real truth.*

Strangely, Jane didn't interrupt their conversation. In Taiwan, John had witnessed one girl's attempt at taking a sailor away from another. The lady with the sailor had rapidly produced a rather large butterfly knife, waving it in front of his startled face.

The truth dawned on John. "Madam Po-Chun" was her professional title, much like Dr. Smith or Admiral Hays. Jane was obviously her employee. Therefore, her subordinate role afforded her only limited privileges such as saying, "Yes, madam."

With a loud burp, Boats collapsed on the floor and proceeded to moan loudly. As if Boats were the doorman announcing a royal arrival, Tom and Mary entered the room from a small side door. Mary walked over to Jane and the madam and began a rapid conversation in Chinese during which they would point at one of the three sailors and laugh.

"Tom, this looks just like Hilton," John said, gazing about the interior of the room.

"Boot, it's been so long since I've been in a real hotel that I have forgotten what they look like."

"I bet each toilet lid here has a sanitary wrapper on it, and there are miniature bars of Sweetheart soap on each laboratory basin," John said with a wink.

"Yorktown, we'll be lucky if this place even has one john with a bowl."

John glanced at Jane. "Which way is the room? I'm worn out from a day of hard work on the ship."

Tom caught his meaning. "Mary, let's get our room before

this hotel fills up. I bet this place is listed in all the better-known travel guides. Probably recommended by the local chamber."

They entered the hallway again and began their ascent up the stairs. On John's third step up the extremely narrow passageway, a door opened at the top of the stairs and the largest steward on the ship heaved out of the entrance. He was in his early forties and still a seaman apprentice. At one time in his twenty-two year career, he had managed to become a second class, but then he went UA for twenty-five days and got busted back down to seaman deuce. From then on, every advancement was followed by another career setback.

"You can have my room, Mr. Yorktown," the steward said, mixing his words with his bourbon breath. "I done learned my lesson. I'm getting back to that ship and saving my fucking money. I ain't spending another cent on no bar girl. She got everything I had, even my peacoat. Mr. Yorktown, I need a couple of Hong Kong dollars in order to get back to the ship. That is, if I don't get one of those Hong Kong tours I've heard so much about, then I'll need about five U.S."

John dug into the wallet that he had owned since attending Commerce High School. "Here you go, White," he said. "Just tell the cab driver to give you a two-dollar tour."

"Thanks, Mr. Yorktown. You sure have saved my feet."

"You mean she even got your peacoat?" questioned John. "That's Navy issue."

"Sir, I knows that. But what can they do to me but bust me back to seaman recruit? It won't be but a few beers difference in pay each month. If I work hard, I can make apprentice again."

"White, may the sea gods praise you for your motivation."

"Thank you, sir. I always felt that they was on my side." White then appeared to think deeply for a moment. "What you mean sea gods? I thought there was only one God, and he was a Mississippi Baptist."

"Yah White, now that I think about it, you are completely correct. Why don't you go get your two dollars' worth before the evening taxi rates go into effect?"

"Yes sir, I sure will. Thanks again." His heavy steps down the old wooden stair yielded loud thumping echoes.

Inside the room, White's girlfriend was making up the "just used" bed for them. Jane walked over to Smiley, and the two of them began a loud conversation in which they appeared to compare notes. From the expressions on Smiley's face, White had not been the greatest of lovers.

Smiley was unusually short and fat, her plumpness accented by the large peacoat she was now modeling.

As the two girls talked and giggled, John felt like a lamprey awaiting dissection in a University of Texas zoology lab. Jane would point to a particular sector of John's body. They would then discuss it for a period of time and eventually climax into laughter.

As the conversation continued, Jane began to undress. She fumbled with the buttons on her blouse, but they gave her no problems since the buttonholes were well-worn from taking the blouse off so many times during her workday. Next she undid her bra. Her breasts, which were pointing horizontally, suddenly pointed down vertically like a water-witch on an underground stream. The dress and slip offered no more problem than her blouse and bra. Next came the panties that had MONDAY written on them. This fact bothered John since it was now Saturday evening. Jane slid her pants down, lost her balance, and ended up falling onto the bed.

The well-worn bed could not take such a blow after having been rocked by White and Smiley unmercifully. With a loud crash it collapsed. Smiley started laughing and Jane began to curse. Neither one made any attempt to pick up the broken parts of the bed.

Standing naked before Smiley and John, Jane lit up an extra-long cigarette and took an exceedingly strong puff that she allowed to ooze out in a small continuous stream from her nostrils.

John felt very much ill at ease. Apparently they were expected to make love while she and Smiley continued their conversation. Not only did he feel mentally uncomfortable but physically stressed as well.

CINCPAC required all officers on a deployed Navy ship to wear a suit ashore. The old black suit he had on was appropriate for a cheap rural burial; his vest fitted like a turn-of-the-century corset. His outfit stemmed from poverty not only in high school, but in college as well. He had worn it for his high school and college graduations. Thus dressed, he felt like he was about to receive another diploma.

Smiley left the room as if she had forgotten an important appointment. Jane walked over to an old Philco radio and flipped it on to some loud American music that consisted of a beat without audible words. If a human was singing, he was drowned out by the guitars and drums. It was music composed and produced by randomly selected electronic components.

Jane then lay down and stared at John. Under her professional stare, whatever lust he felt dwindled to nothing. A slow fear began to creep over him: What if she had VD? According to rumors circulating on the ship, there was a incurable strain of VD in Bangkok.

He hesitantly undressed down to his skivvies. He then found an old coat hanger and tried to fold his shapeless pants upon it, but since the legs had no visible creases, he gave up and threw his pants over a small stool.

My Lord, I must talk her out of this, he thought. *A prostitute in Frisco is one thing, but a call girl in Wan Chai is another.* He was rapidly recalling the Executive Officer's lectures and films on VD frame by frame. *Let's see, first there's burning urine, next a drip. I have to get out of here!*

He lay down on the opposite side of the bed as far away from Jane as possible. As he tried to feign instant sleep, he could hear sounds coming from the other rooms. Nothing in the building's construction prevented the pantings, sighings, snickering, and occasional cursing from infiltrating their room. The walls and floors even shook with erotic rhythm.

"Yorktown-son, what wrong with you? You queer?"

"Hell no, why don't we just talk a little while and then go to sleep?"

"Uh?" she replied.

"Jane, why don't we just go to sleep?" John then whispered to himself, "Lord, if I get out of this one without the clap, I'm gonna repent and go to church. I mean it this time. Amen."

"What you say?"

"My bedtime prayer. Come on, Jane, I'm tired and my back aches. Let's just get some sleep."

"Me not pretty enough?" she said loudly

"Beautiful, just plain beautiful!" He would tell her anything to get out of this most elementary of financial transactions.

"No-good first class stingy lying bastard! You think me not good enough for you to screw."

John could tell he was going to lose the battle. Jane was determined to have sex with him, or she would lose face with the other girls. As her anger mounted, John began to fear clap less and her temper more. Besides, Bangkok was far away.

He pleaded, "Okay, but get me a rubber."

"You think me have VD?" Her voice trembled with anger.

"No, I know you're clean. It's me I'm worried about. Too much playing around in Japan." It was definitely a lie but then it might serve the purpose of saving her professional honor.

"Okay, I get." Jane hurriedly put on her panties and bra and left.

Some hotel, John thought. *All you need on is your underwear when asking for room service at the main desk. The window? Why not escape?*

He hurried to put his pants and shirt on. The zipper of his pants caught his shirttail and ripped the material. He then raced for the open window.

"Oh my God, this place is on a cliff!" The hotel was built overlooking an uncovered ditch of considerable depth through which raw sewage flowed at a tremendous velocity. "I'll just have to get the clap. I'm not diving into any sewer." He returned to what was left of the bed.

He jumped when Jane entered the room without knocking.

He was not expecting her to return so quickly.

"Why you dressed? You try to leave me?"

"Hell no, Jane. I thought I would try to buy some gum in the main lobby. My breath is not so good after all those drinks." This explanation seemed to satisfy her for she jumped onto the remainder of the bed that hadn't collapsed.

John remembered why she had left. He guessed that a woman clad only in underwear ordering rubbers in the main lobby was nothing unusual in the hotel. He expected her to hand him a rubber, but no Sheik appeared. "Where is it? Don't tell me they ran out during the rush hour today?"

"It's coming," she replied.

"Oh my God, what's coming?"

The door suddenly opened and an elderly Chinese lady entered with a tray strapped about her neck. On the edge of the tray the logo read SUNSET BAR AND GRILL.

"What you want—Japanese, American, or African?" she asked in broken English. She was apparently referring to size descriptions. John hated to admit it, but he felt that he should request Japanese. However, his pride said otherwise.

"I'll take three Africans." His voice displayed his uneasiness. She smiled and produced three of the largest rubbers that imagination could conceive. She then took his money and meandered out of the doorway. John had no doubt she would want a description from Jane of what happened later. The great issue would be whether he was really African or Japanese.

Jane once more removed her bra and panties with the inhibition of one undressing before a piece of furniture. John removed his suit again, but this time he didn't bother to look for a clothes hanger. His thoughts were still not on sex but VD. He was afraid she would give him a WestPac souvenir, a term borrowed from Boats. Another thought then entered his mind: *What if I can't get it up? Jane will want blood if that happens. I can't do a thing when I try consciously. Oh God, if I can only get out of this one ...*

Through Jane's skillful maneuvering, his last fear proved unnecessary. After what must have been one of the shortest love making sessions in Jane's memory, he came. Then a new fear gripped him as he mumbled, "Where's the rubber? It's not where I put it?"

Jane started laughing. "You Japanese boy-son, not African. You lousy lover. You too quick. Give me no time to enjoy. You just like a chicken. I should have charged you more."

"Come on, Jane, help me find the rubber," John said with increasing fear.

Jane's laughter grew in intensity as she pretended to look between the sheets. John, however, was not pretending in his desperate search. "It just can't disappear into thin air!" he shouted. He then repeated the concept. "Jane, a rubber that big just can't vanish." She did not appear the least bit concerned.

"Yorktown, let's take bath."

"A bath? I don't want to do anything except find my rubber."

Jane's laughter became increasingly louder.

"Okay, okay, let's bath! I'll do anything. Just stop laughing," John said in a serious tone. "People can hear you through the walls, and I probably have some friends staying here. Yah, like that fat-ass steward. Hell, for all I know Decker is here."

The hallway was lit by a yellowish globe that was covered in dust and supported by a partially insulated wire. As they made one sharp turn after another, the hallway became narrower.

"Are you sure this hallway leads to a bath?"

"What wrong with you? I know where bath is," Jane said harshly.

With her assurance, John felt as secure as Columbus' crew during their voyage to America. She opened a small door at the end of the hall where a gush of wet heat pushed against them. A splattering of fluent Chinese came from the bathroom.

Jane informed John of what was all too apparent, "Elderly gentleman still in tub." Through the hot vapor, John could see an old Chinaman buried in the fog. His head looked like a cypress knee above the fuming water.

As John turned to leave, Jane said, "We wait."

"Good grief, Jane, what if someone comes down the hall and sees us standing here naked? There are probably obscenity laws in Hong Kong that forbid this kind of action. I'm respected on the ship, and this could hurt my men's morale."

"You officer? You no enlisted man! No-good lying bastard. That much I know is true. Claim you African and really Japanese. Not seen such prick except on small boy."

"Where did you hear such a term?" John asked loudly.

"Chief tell me that. He fine lover; built like a man and not like a boy.

At that moment Boats entered the hallway with his date. "Good evening, Mr. Yorktown. A little bit cool in the hall, sir?" Boat's voice bubbled with joy.

John replied with an intense frown. Boats rocked on down the hall, moored to the bar girl with him like a small boat rafted against another.

There was no telling whom John would meet next. So he forced Jane into the steam-filled room to wait. The old Chinaman began to curse them for hurrying him out of the water. No doubt he had planned on sleeping in the hotel tub rather than paying for a room.

"Enter water fast; don't move when you in hot-sea-bath," Jane ordered, demonstrating the action.

As John stuck his toes into the water, he couldn't help but yell, "Damn it, my foot's cooked! This must be the entrance to either hell or the boiler room."

"You American fag, can't take hot bath."

At her remark, he dove into the cauldron which was a mistake. John struggled to keep his screams low and to keep his soul in its proper place.

"Jane, I bet you not only bathe in this water, but cook in it too. Just add vegetables and you'll have a stew." John couldn't take it any longer. He tried to get out of the tub as quickly as possible. He reached the rim and flipped his body onto the tile floor. From neck down, he was a sweet potato red. Jane laughed at his red body and continued to enjoy the comforts of the lobster-ready water.

Jane soon emerged from the inferno of steam. "John-son, I found the rubber. It's were you put it."

John wondered when it came off. If it came off at the end, he was alright, he guessed. If it came off at the beginning, then he was in real trouble: Clap.

After drying off, they returned to their room. It seemed strange how religiously quiet it was except for a child crying in the street and an occasional squeak from an old bed.

"Jane, I have to go."

"Why you go? Only four in the morning. Real man last until six."

"I've got a watch coming up, and I need some rest."

John was afraid to tell Jane the truth. He was really sick of the hotel and of her. His money had gone too quickly, and now he had a new worry—VD. He reached into his wallet. "Empty, oh my God!" Then it dawned on him that he had given everything he had to Jane and the ship's steward.

"Jane, give me some taxi money. I've spent every cent I have."

"You no-good fucking sailor. I don't have any money to give stingy butterfly. You take my money and go to some other girl."

"Come on, Jane, it's going on five in the morning. I don't know a soul in Hong Kong I can call, and it's at least three miles to Fenwick Pier or more."

"No give my money to stingy first class asshole."

It was useless and he knew it. He had injured her pride by not wanting to spend the few remaining moments of the night with her. It then occurred to him that she wanted to show off her conquest to the new shift that arrived at 0600.

"Okay, okay, just see if you get me or my friends for customers again!" It was senseless to use this threat since he was not dealing with Sears and Roebuck. John was dealing with a career girl whose sales did not depend upon a consumer report.

"Haul ass, sailor!" she shouted.

At her command, John zipped up his pants and entered the darkened hall that smelled strongly of cigarettes and bourbon. He pushed the hotel door open and stepped into the night air that possessed a strangely sweet breath. It felt great being free of Jane and the hotel's odors. As he began to walk, he cursed to himself, "How stupid can you get? Not even a Hong Kong dollar for a cab. Even a boot like me should know to carry money in his shoe. Yeah, a real dumb ass!"

Twilight began to give shape to unsure forms. Occasionally he would pass a sailor who had probably encountered another Jane. As they would walk past, neither of them acknowledged the other's presence. It was strange how, in the very early morning hours, no one wanted to be a friend. "This is what I deserve. Tomorrow I'll go to the museums and visit the church brethren here. You bet I will. No more of this crap for me," he said to himself. The echo of his footsteps followed him to Fenwick Pier where the night ended in a brilliant sunrise over Kowloon and the out islands of the Crown colony.

CHAPTER TWELVE

Among the Clouds

The day passed with the customary monotony and ass chewing. The conversations were more interesting than usual for each man related his victories ashore. Boats told of a lodge located on top of Tit Mountain that he had visited on a previous cruise.

John had noticed Tit Mountain from the sea. It appeared like a large breast looming above the ocean's belly. It was the first landmark that a sailor recognized—the promise of good liberty, freedom filled with the expectations of Tiger Beer and good sex. As Boats would say, "Used to be the best damn ass in the Orient was up there."

"Mr. Yorktown, there ain't a damn thing now to do on Tit Mountain. Nothin'! Hell, I doubt if they even still serve any beer up there. The only reason I bring the Tit up is that I had me one hell of a piece up there a few years back, you know during Korea. You could get a woman cheap back then. A man didn't feel like a fish every time he entered a bar. The girls were square shooters. I met this little hostess down in Wan Chai and she took me up there for the weekend. Screwed myself sick. Yah, that was the war to be in—Korea." John agreed with Boats with a small amount of doubt entwined in his words.

His great expectations of liberty had faded after his night with Jane. The thought of beer on a mountainside now seemed like a welcome relief from the city's noise and smells. A sailor sought mountains when the valleys became barren of dreams.

Even the slow passage of the bam-bam boat depressed John. *Maybe up there is a grove of green wet bamboo where the only sounds come from the wind. If there are no 'Janes' there, I can count myself blessed. As far as Tiger Beer goes, they can have it*, thought John.

After John's arrival on the pier, he spotted the damage control assistant on the ship. "Hey, Mark!"

Mark was slightly overweight. His hair longer than a crew cut while his clear-rimmed glasses rested upon the bridge of his large nose. Mark leaped across the street, barely missed by some oncoming traffic that showed little signs of yielding to his perilous position. He approached John panting. "Yorktown, what are you up to?"

"Mark, I have a great idea. Let's go up to Tit Mountain. Boats said there isn't much to do up there and that's what I'm looking for. There should be a good view and some fine food. I know how you like to take photographs."

"Might as well, John. I've seen all the curio shops that I can stand. Those shops haven't changed since my dad was over here just after World War II ended. The place was pretty messed up then, but still they managed to sell pillows with dragons on them. I remember he brought back one with the name "Sally" on it. The only problem was that Mom's name was Christine. He told her that names don't mean a damn thing in China and that every woman was called Sally. I'm not sure she believed him."

Catching a taxi required no great mental process but did demand courage. Waving at a Hong Kong taxi was pointless. It was necessary to step out into the oncoming traffic and confront an approaching cab. The driver either stopped for a sailor or he ended up hitting him. Few alternatives were as clear in life. Luckily a cab stopped, allowing them just enough time to get their feet in before the driver accelerated through a band of honking cars.

Mark was silent as the cab raced through the streets that flanked Tit Mountain. The clicking of the cab's meter made a metronome-like rhythm. People leaped from the pavement at the approach of their taxi's piercing horn. No one hesitated to give way to their driver.

"Good Lord, Mark, how did he miss that old fart back there?" shouted John. Mark did not reply. He just stared straight ahead while holding on to the backseat strap, hoping his head would not hit the overhead as the cab bounced along.

The city became smaller with their ascent. It now looked like a postcard view—clean, artistic, and dehumanized. It was strange how poverty could look so beautiful from a distance. The hues of poorly kept buildings and squatters' huts blended like paint on an artist's pallet. Cities to John were three-dimensional: sights, sounds, and smells. Since the real Hong Kong could not be captured in postcard views or from heights, it was no wonder that a god had to descend to earth.

The cab stopped abruptly near the mountain's top. The driver glanced at his meter and then transferred his attention to his passengers. "Thirty-six Hong Kong dollars."

"Huh?" Mark uttered politely, hoping to avoid any confrontation.

"Thirty-six Hong Kong dollar, now!" the driver shouted

"Good Lord, Mark, he sounds like an old Navy chief boatswain's mate. Here's the thirty-six Hong Kong dollars." John placed some deteriorated bills into the driver's palm, but he continued to hold out his hand.

"Here you go," Mark said. "I'm not only giving you the extra money as a tip, but also in appreciation for not killing anyone on the way up." The driver took the money from Mark and then gunned his engine while they struggled to open the bent doors of the taxi.

The eatery before them appeared to have aged with the gracefulness of the wealthy. It had, during an earlier dynasty, been painted a deep red. Smells of incense and Chinese cooking wafted from the entrance as they ascended a small flight of steps. A lean waiter greeted them at the door and guided them to a small room whose view encompassed Hong Kong harbor and the distant lands of Red China.

The waiter placed huge menus covered with dirty fingerprints in their hands, and then stood at attention. Unfortunately the menus were completely beyond their abilities to comprehend. Next to the Chinese logograms were translations in

Portuguese—a tribute to nearby Macao.

"Come on, Mark, how the hell are we going to order anything? Not only can we not read what to order but we have no idea about the prices. If I spend all of my money here, what will I do for tonight?"

"Yorktown, just point," said Mark. "The waiter will acknowledge a wise selection with a big smile of approval; if you blow it, he will indicate that with a scowl of disbelief."

John inclined the menu towards the waiter. "Uh, waiter, I will have this one." The waiter bent over the table and sucked air as he examined John's selection.

"Mark, I guess that wasn't the right thing to order, probably too cheap." Whatever John had ordered, the waiter busily wrote it down and then moved over to Mark.

"Waiter, make it this one," said Mark. This time the waiter not only sucked air, but shook his head in disbelief. Mark had ordered the same selection that John had. "Yorktown, even if we just ordered poison, at least the view is beautiful and the wind feels good. Man, fresh air and real wind are great, no blower motor attached here."

As they sat admiring the view of freighters and junks in the harbor, they could hear their waiter talking loudly in the kitchen. His conversation was producing restrained laughter from the cooks.

"You know, John, I sense a great contrast here. Just think that less than two weeks ago, we were helping to burn so-called communist villages, and now we are sitting comfortably in a Chinese restaurant overlooking the mountains of Red China."

"Shit, I know what you mean, Mark. It probably isn't

important whether it makes sense or not. Boats says that the only important things are screwing, drinking, and eating in that order. I figure he has examined the universe as closely as anyone considering that he has been drunk over much of the Earth's surface."

The waiter approached them with what they hoped would be their meal.

"Good grief, now I know why it's important to learn Chinese," said John. Before them was some type of chicken soup. Each bowl contained two whole chicken legs wading in a clear broth of salty water. A few small fuzzy feathers remained on both legs.

"My God, John, it looks like someone raided a chicken yard with a sickle. They could at least have trimmed the nails. I guess we're supposed to eat those with a pair of nail clippers, and look at the hairs running up those claws."

"Shit!" John uttered, forcing out a smile of approval for fear of making their waiter mad. He trusted that the man spoke not a word of English. It was the only word that he could think of that expressed how he felt. The waiter smiled back and nodded to acknowledge the compliment.

"Mark, I've got it figured out. Once you finish your meal, you pick your teeth with the claw."

"I just hope it is well done. Nothing upsets my stomach more than a medium-rare chicken claw. To be truthful, I'd like to shove it up his ass until he crows."

The waiter opened the sliding doors to their small room and ushered in two very attractive Chinese women.

"Mark, pinch me. I've got to be dreaming. Now I know why the prophets went to the mountains."

"Yorktown, how old do you think they are?"

"Hell, what does it matter? Boats told me that age 'don't matter none, it just makes 'em appreciate a real man more.'"

"John, I can't question your source. He told me to put a sail bag over their heads, and they would all look the same."

The two new arrivals in their small room did not look in their direction. John and Mark felt like Sears, Roebuck & Co. reprints hanging on a wall. The women were wearing American-style dresses that were very short with a long slit on each side. Being a good sailor, John noticed women's fashion. The taller one lit up a Marlboro. Before long, heavy smoke curled out of her mouth and was immediately sucked up her nose. After four tremendous puffs, her lips touched the filter. She reached for another cigarette and offered one to her partner.

"Mark, it's just like classical China," said John, staring at the women.

"Sure it is. You know, I might be wrong, but they look like our kind of women. Of course I could be in error, but I don't think that the ladies in Classical China wore ass-high skirts and smoked cigarettes. Man, just look at those legs," Mark said.

"Hell, Mark, I thought you were the spiritual kind. You know, void of any material hang-ups. Now you need to understand that it's not what's between the legs, but between the ears that's important," John said in a serious manner as he considered the potential risks involved.

"Sure, Yorktown. But hell, let's be reasonable and get things in a proper historical perspective. Even the prophets got horny," added Mark.

"Man, look at the legs on the one closest to the open window. Oh wow, how do we approach them? They might be a couple of schoolteachers for all we know," John said with a smile.

"Here's how: Go ask if you can buy 'em a drink. If they giggle or laugh out loud, they are schoolteachers. If they give you a go-to-hell look, then you'll know they're what we're looking for and we can get down to terms," said Mark.

"I don't understand," said John with an expression of curiosity.

"Well, boot, even hookers have to save face when they're away from the bar. It is through their looking mad that they acknowledge an understanding of what we want. When you go over there, if one of them shoots you a finger, motion for me to join you. We'll have us one hell of an evening."

"Wait a minute, Mark. First of all, I came up this mountain to get away from all of that. Secondly, why should I be the one to go over to their table?"

"Haul ass, boot. The reason you have to do the legwork is because I'm the brains in this duo. Besides, I outrank you based on longevity. I have the necessary experience that comes from being in this man's Navy for eight months. You haven't even been on active for four. Experience costs you something. Now get over there and act like a China sailor," Mark said, pointing towards the two young women.

Without any further protest, John walked slowly towards them. He spoke loudly and without any hesitation. "My friend and I would like to buy you two ladies a drink."

Both girls frowned and looked away as if contemplating his

murder in private. After a brief silence, they began to make rapid remarks in Chinese.

Mark glanced towards John with an all-knowing smile. He also felt for his wallet, not to see if it was there, but to check on the thickness of it. This might cost quite a bit.

Apparently Mark was correct and this gave John greater courage. "Why don't you two ladies join us at our table? We have a lovely view of the harbor and a couple of packs of American cigarettes." Not that these women appeared to be poor, but John had heard that after the war, any girl would be your servant for either a Hershey or a pack of cigarettes, and hell, maybe things had not changed much in twenty years. *I wonder if Hong Kong was ever occupied. Maybe I'm thinking of Japan,* John thought.

Mark's theory did not, however, have a hundred percent validity. The two women glanced sharply at John, and then shouted to the waiter who immediately appeared, looking ashamed and very reluctant to perform his next function. "You go, you go!" he said weakly, pointing towards the door.

"I didn't mean anything improper," John replied, a touch of pleading in his voice. But it was useless to discuss anything with a waiter whose only knowledge of English consisted of "You go!" John also knew that if they protested some more, he might call the shore patrol, and that would result in their being restricted to the ship. "Oh God, what a dark thought," he said loudly to himself.

"Come on, John, no point in arguing with the deacon. Let's get our asses out of here," said Mark.

John looked at Mark. "Some leader you are. Yeah, you had it all figured out. Hell, now I'll never know what chicken feet taste like. Something else we better do—let's leave some money on the table or that fart will turn us in for not paying the bill."

It felt good to be out of the building. A feeling of great relief. The wind was strong and determined, intensifying the feeling of natural freedom. "Look at those clouds coming in from the sea," Mark said, pointing towards the top of a higher mountain that appeared to pivot the fast-moving carousel of clouds about its weathered, rocky crown.

"Hey boot, here's a path to the Tit's summit. Let's go up and take a look," said Mark. "Who knows, there might be some broads up there just looking for a couple of horny sailors."

They followed the path, walking briskly. It eventually led to a small shrine that rested on the mountain's crown. As they approached, heavy rain began to fall, forcing them to take shelter inside the shrine. The earth soon became intensely dark and even the restaurant below disappeared into the rain. It was as though they were among the clouds.

The storm would occasionally pause long enough to allow John to see the harbor. Then thunder sounded and a fresh breeze blew followed by more rain. John looked a Mark. "Life seems different in the rain. It is peaceful now with the rest of the world hidden from view."

It reminded John of his childhood. Days when the earth was hot and expectant. Moments when great clouds would appear out of the Southwest. He remembered lying on his back in the early spring cotton fields, seeing all kinds of faces and forms in the clouds. Soon the fresh smell of lightning would come to him followed by his mother's call to come home, "It's lightnin'." Warm, secure, and safe, he would watch the storm from the farmhouse porch.

"John, I guess I shouldn't have had you approach those two girls back in the restaurant. I still believe they were a couple of hookers off work. It seems like everybody demands time off these days. Oh hell, let's get back to Wan Chai where you don't need an introduction. I don't want to stay on this mountain too long. Besides, the days are going by too quickly, moments that cannot be returned to us. Pretty soon the pig iron mother will be heading to sea again, and you and I will be back on her. The way things are going, I won't have a single memory to look back on that's worth a damn."

As they climbed down the steep path, John turned and looked once more towards the mountain's peak and the small shrine. A cloud quickly covered it from view. There was something about this mountain's summit that he couldn't grasp. He guessed it was the rain and the feeling of detachment. *Oh hell, why think more about it?*

CHAPTER THIRTEEN

Combinations

MARCHERS ARRIVE AT CAPITAL
—*Los Angeles Times*, March 25, 1965

Boats approached John with unnerving information. "Mr. Yorktown, I hate to bother you, sir, but the XO wants to see you. I just seen him. He wanted to put my ass in the noose for missing this morning's muster. I told him that I would tell him the truth about why I was late, and that once he understood, he wouldn't see any point in putting me on report. So I told him, and now he wants to see you."

John wanted to know what had occurred between the XO and Boats for this would tell him what kind of mood Pebbles was in. "Okay, Boats. What happened? I guess I'm to get an ass chewing, too."

"Well sir, I went home with that old hooker you saw me dancing with a while back. Before I got drunk, I asked her if she had an alarm clock. Of course she said yes and being a dumb ass, I believed her. So I told her to be sure to set the mother for 0400 in the morning and not to forget to wind the damn thing. When I woke up this morning, it was 0900 and she was snoring louder that a chief boatswain's mate. If I hadn't had to piss, I would still be over there sleeping. That damn whore didn't even have an alarm clock."

"What did the XO say?"

"Oh hell, Mr. Yorktown, I should have lied to him. He doesn't mind you lying so he won't have to put you on report. But I've always been told that he who tells the truth would be rewarded. That's what my old spinster aunt used to say before she departed for better things. So I told him the truth and got an oar up my ass. I think you have to die to get the reward my aunt was talking about since she didn't get a damn thing on earth, not even a good fuck."

"What excusable thing could you have told him?"

"Oh, I don't know, something like I saved a life, and it took longer than I expected it."

"Are you restricted?" asked John.

"No sir, at least not here. The XO said he didn't want to restrict me in such a swell liberty port. Instead he's going to have me stand a CO's mast back in Yoko where the liberty isn't as good. It has something to do with me deserving a reward for doing such a good job on Yankee Station."

"Yankee Station?" John could not remember him doing anything noteworthy.

"Oh, that's in the South China Sea where all the action is.

That's where captains make admirals and sailors bust their asses." Boats forgot that John had already spent enough time on Yankee Station to memorize the coordinates.

"Boats, I glory in you not getting restricted in Hong Kong where boot ensigns and seaman deuces need your professional advice on the beach. A man who risks restriction in Hong Kong rather than tell a lie is worth a great deal. By the way, do you know why the XO wants to see me?"

"No sir, he wouldn't say. His tongue, however, was darting in and out just like a snake's. That means he's nervous and out to get someone's ass. Sure sign. That's why some of the fellows call him 'Snake' rather than 'Pebbles.'"

"Well, wish me luck. All I need is to get restricted, and then I will have had a perfect time in Hong Kong. I have to admit that there is one advantage to restriction, no one can ask you to buy them a lady cocktail," John said in a serious tone.

As John walked toward the XO's stateroom, his stomachache increased. He had just finished a pure syrup Pepsi. During his conversation with Boats, his stomach supplied the other ingredients necessary for an excellent case of pre-diarrhea.

The straightest direction to the XO's stateroom was blocked by a swabbie who refused to open the access hatch. "The wax ain't dry and footprints will just fuck her up, sir. I haven't yet buffed her down, and it will take fifteen more minutes for dryin'."

For a brief moment, John thought about telling him that he was an officer and he would be fucking up the deck in the line of duty. However, the few months aboard had taught him several things. Like the fact that the XO was in charge of the ship's general appearance, hence the importance of buffed decks. Because of this, he yielded and ended up making a very laborious journey up and down ladders.

Upon reaching the XO's stateroom, he found the ship's yeoman typing at his desk with his usual two-finger style. "Reed, where's the XO? I hear he wants to see me." Reed didn't answer but continued to look for the q on the typewriter. "Reed, damn it, where the hell is the XO?"

"Oh, excuse me, sir. I'm trying to type, and it demands all of my attention. I guess I shouldn't have cross-rated from boatswain's mate. Hell, I was happier as a deck ape. Back then, I had ten swabs under me. I didn't take no bullshit off any of them either."

"Reed, I'm sure that before retiring from this man's Navy, you'll learn to find the alphabet on the typewriter. In the meantime, where the hell is the XO?"

"Sir, he is up in radio."

From the XO's stateroom, John took the ladder straight up to the radio shack. Since it was a secure space, he had to knock on the door for a visual check before the sailor inside released the electronic lock. John pounded on the door three times before it finally opened. "Malicote, where's the XO? Reed said he was supposed to be here?"

"Yes sir, he is back in crypto." The words reverberated on the crest of a large coffee-laden burb.

When he entered the crypto room, John found the XO seated at his desk. This was the first time that the XO had entered

John's small office. The thought occurred to him that he was going to catch hell for all the "Playmate of the Month" pinups he had hung on the walls. "XO, I'll take down all the pinups and get my record player and lawn chair out of here," John volunteered uneasily.

"Mr. Yorktown, that's not what I am here to talk to you about. I'll take up the matter of crypto looking like the foyer of a brothel with you at a later date. What I want to know is what these safe combinations are doing written on the bulkhead."

In the school for prospective communications officers they were told never to write the combinations down. Instead, they were to memorize the series of numbers. It was already difficult for John to remember the combination to his one bicycle lock in high school, much less the five safes under his control now, so he naturally wrote the numbers down in various locations such as on the bulkhead and under the drawer of his desk.

"Sir, I'm not sure those are combinations. I tried a few of them in different locations, such as on the bridge and not one of them opened a safe. Now what I think happened was that Decker had a few on the beach, or someone with the mentality of Decker, and then came back aboard and wrote down the phone numbers of all his girlfriends right on the bulkheads." Luckily, John had not put a dash in the series of numbers. "I heard him say that he couldn't remember a thing unless he wrote it down. He even has some girl's name and address tattooed on his arm."

"Mr. Yorktown, I don't have to tell you how serious such a security violation could be or the consequences to your Navy career," Pebbles said, his tongue darting in and out.

"No sir, you sure don't," responded John.

With this comment, the XO left. He knew they were the combinations to the safes, but all he really wanted was an excuse not to put John on report. To place an officer on report would occupy days of filling out forms and he could spend that time ashore. No one in his right mind would want to miss Hong Kong. John had counted on that fact to save himself.

John started to tear the March Playmate down, but just couldn't do it. He knew there were weeks at sea coming up and he would need something to look at instead of haze-gray metal walls. Instead he spent the afternoon erasing the combinations he had written on the bulkheads; only smudge marks remained.

Prior to liberty call, John searched for his suit coat. One of his fellow officers had the habit of borrowing his clothes, especially when the weather was cool. Fred was from a wealthy family, but he never seemed to have any cash. He continually sought to borrow money and would act offended when asked for it back on payday. *I'll kick that fucker in the ass if I catch him on the beach with my coat on,* John thought. Instead he put his overcoat on and buttoned it at the top so he appeared to be wearing a suit coat underneath.

The quarterdeck was cold. A strong wind blew across the deforested mountains of China and kicked up a light spray in the harbor. "Hey Pete, too bad you have the quarterdeck watch. My, look at that, here comes the bam-bam boat and this time I don't have to wait all evening. By the way, if you see Fred, kick his ass for me. That bastard has gone off wearing my suit coat," said John with irritation in his voice.

"Come on, Yorktown, are you suffering from that complex wherein you think that people are wearing your clothes? I hear that you marked all your uniforms on the outside with a big Y for identification," Pete said, laughing. "I'll have to remember to ask Regrets if he can find a label for that particular mental illness."

"Think what you want, but just see if Fred isn't wearing my black suit coat tonight."

"Oh my Lord, John, look! It's Boats returning in the boat. That fucker managed to get early liberty again today."

"How in the world did he do that?" asked John.

"Oh shit, you know, he's earned "vampire liberty." Donate a pint, get off early. I bet he has given four pints of blood in the last four days. Those British nurses plan on draining the crew for the whole week. They sent new nurses over; they don't notice or care who they suck."

"Wait a minute, Boats," Pete shouted, "what do you have in your hand?" Boats began to fall back into the bam-bam boat but some of the less intoxicated sailors behind him managed to support his wiry frame.

"Well, you have to let me inspect it. The XO has been chewing ass about sailors bringing booze aboard," said Pete after noticing the size and shape of the package in his hand.

Boats flung out his arm, and the box went sailing into the air, landing with a mighty splash and quickly sinking from view. "Oh hell, them new shoes didn't fit no how," said Boats.

John knew from experience that it was not good to expect too much too soon. This afternoon, he was going to be just a plain tourist; a civilian visiting the Orient. The entrances to the shops would be his gateway to excitement but only from the chin up. One thing he was certain of was that there would be no more "Janes" for him.

During his brief stopover in Yokohama, his intentions had been similar. After walking for several blocks along Yokohama's heaving congested sidewalks, he found himself having to use the restroom. Something in his conscience would not let him use a private head without making a purchase. In the States, John would always buy gum or a piece of candy in a filling station. In the section of Yokohama where he had weeks earlier found himself, there were no filling stations. So the only thing he could do was enter a bar and order a beer. This way the bartender was happy, and he was happy to be able to go to the restroom. The only trouble was that a few blocks later, he had to go again. Before the day ended, he was already drunk.

This time John was going to be smarter. He wouldn't buy a beer or even a Coke. Water fountains, if he could find one, would be his only source of hydration. There would be no staggering along the streets of Hong Kong in search of restrooms. At least not this time.

John walked three blocks to where the trams began their journey to the central part of the city. He boarded one without any knowledge of its destination. Through the windows, he observed a new view of Hong Kong. The streets were crowded with people of all descriptions and dress. The traditional Chinese walked the streets side by side with youths dressed in Western clothing. Everyone seemed to be in a hurry. John was also in a hurry even though he didn't know where he was going, or for what reason he was going there. Occasionally his eyes would be attracted to firm hips or bouncing breasts, but soon everything blended into a kaleidoscope of colors.

The tramway ended up in a remote area of Hong Kong. There were no Westerners in the area, and he felt not only conspicuous but alone. One thing, however, was familiar to him: he had to go to the restroom. His thoughts were filled with his immediate problem. *Where can I find a head? Every sign is in Chinese, and these people don't look very friendly. Someone may try to steal my camera,* thought John, experiencing a mild form of panic. He was carrying the ten-year-old Keystone Capri 8mm windup movie camera that his parents had given him in the eighth grade. The camera was worth about fifteen dollars in a pawnshop, but he feared it would look like gold to the poor people around him.

As he walked along the street that he hoped would lead back into the European section of Hong Kong, he glanced into the shops. The people were frantically busy with their own tasks. Butchers did not walk with pieces of meat, instead they ran about, pitching the cuts onto the countertops. He thought about how the flies must be exhausted from trying to catch rides on the fast-moving carcasses.

John passed a dark entrance with a familiar smell to it. *A bar, a restroom, hallelujah!* He entered the darkened foyer and noticed the great depth of the room. This was a Chinese bar. There was no loud American music necessary in bars frequented by American sailors. It was also different in the sense that no hostess approached him demanding drinks and yet he could sense their presence.

He sat down at the counter and waited on the bartender. John had the uneasy feeling that he had made a mistake. He could feel piercing eyes watch his every move through the darkness. A bartender appeared out of the smoke-filled murkiness and spoke to him in rapid Chinese. John pointed towards a display that featured Tiger Beer. After studying John's selection, he sucked air through his teeth and gave him a glass with a huge ice cube in it. John looked at the yellowish ice cube and felt compelled to hold the glass up to the dim light for intense inspection. *You've got to be kidding*, he thought. *This cube is loaded with last night's insects.* John looked towards the bartender whose smile quickly turned into a frown. He thought about refusing the beer, but he was too aware of the position he was in and decided to simply smile and wait for the beer. He gulped the warm beer frantically, hoping that the ice would not have the chance to melt and release its petri dish of bacteria.

After finishing the beer, John remembered his reason for being in the bar. There were no doors inside except for the entrance. There was, however, a small staircase that appeared to be suspended from a black void. John became afraid to go to the restroom since the only place a head could be located was up the small flight of stairs. After one brief moment of consideration, he decided to leave.

After only two blocks, it began to happen. Green beer had been mentioned on the ship. It was known to work faster than prune juice. His stomach began to cramp quickly. His only thought was, *Oh no, oh no, this just can't happen to me. Not here in this section of Hong Kong!*

At first, he tried to walk very swiftly, but the pace proved unsatisfactory. Soon he found it necessary to trot, and finally he broke into a run. His 8mm camera swung from his shoulder like a ship's pennant in a high wind.

"The bastard, I bet he knew that bottle contained green beer. He's probably back there laughing," John said to himself as he gulped air.

There, there's a bowling alley! At least I hope it is a bowling alley! He ran into the entrance and headed straight for what he thought was the restroom.

"Jeez!" he muttered. Written above the door, in both Chinese and English, was the too familiar and very dreaded sign: OUT-OF-ORDER. *How the hell can a hole in the ground be out of order?*

John then trotted out of the front door and headed down the street at a gallop. He found it necessary to run in the street along with the flow of congested traffic since the sidewalks were far too crowded for anything but slow walking.

There! There! It's a hotel ... Man, it's not only a hotel but the fucking Hong Kong Grand Baron. He approached the main entrance without breaking his stride. Luckily a doorman opened the door just in time to save the glass. He tried to say, "Thank you," but could only mutter incomprehensible sounds for he was choking on his own breath after having run for more than two miles.

John ran up the escalator to the front desk where a British-looking clerk at first attempted to not notice him. He knew that hotel clerks always appear to be very busy when you first approach them. Finally his brief patience became even shorter. "Have you got a room? I'll take anything you got—even if it's the honeymoon suite."

Not only did he have to go the restroom but his stomach felt like a virus had launched an attack in it. It was apparent that a bathroom would not be enough. The way he felt, it would be impossible to try to make it back to the ship. He needed to lie down for a few hours.

"Yes, sir. Would you like a room with a view of the harbor? We have some U.S. Navy ships in port that certainly add to the view. You know they have their holiday lights rigged, and it is quite lovely at night."

"I would prefer a view of a brick wall, but I'll take it."

"Let's see. The room will be sixty-five U.S. dollars. Please sign our guest register. The bellboy will be here in a minute to help you with your luggage. By the way, where is your luggage? Remember, sir, there's a law in Hong Kong against having unaccompanied ladies invited to your room. Now if you would like to pay for double occupancy, that'll be another matter. In fact, if you don't have a young lady, I can recommend one that is especially nice."

Without responding, John grabbed the key from his hand and ran for a flight of stairs.

Behind him, he heard the clerk say, "Man, she must really be something. I've never seen a Yank run so hard in my bloody life."

The stairway led to an escalator that in turn led to an elevator. He pushed the button for the tenth floor and instead of going up, the machine went down. The elevator hit the bottom floor where a heavily intoxicated fellow, whom the bar had just asked to leave, attempted to board the elevator. After he struggled to gain forward momentum for a second try, John mashed the DOOR

CLOSE button. The last thing he heard from the bar reject was, "You, you damn son of a—"

The elevator finally arrived on the tenth floor. "There, down the hall is my room!" John muttered. He ran towards his mecca. His only concern now was that the toilet didn't have an OUT OF ORDER sign on it.

John virtually had to twist the key off before he could get the door to open. He entered the room with a great leap towards the head. Immediately he placed himself upon the toilet bowl. His heart was pounding in his ears.

"Damn it! Damn it!" He couldn't go.

CHAPTER FOURTEEN

Aiding the Affluent

WATTS: SHOTGUN SQUADS PATROL DISTRICT
—*Herald Examiner*, March 16, 1966

The smoke-filled wardroom made breathing difficult. It was a mixture of cigar, cigarette, and pipe—blended with burned coffee. The cadre was waiting for liberty call to sound in fifteen minutes.

John passed the time looking at several articles on the war. Many of the correspondents predicted an eventual settlement that could be speeded up if the U.S. continued to bomb the hell out of the enemy.

Some career types, who waited with John, liked to reminisce about how the ship would shell a location and then receive counter battery from the beach. The Old Man, in response, would immediately radio a carrier for an air strike. John remembered how the jets pulverized the beach for twenty to thirty minutes. Then *Hyman* would move back in to continue shelling. The counter battery would then open fire once more. It seemed as if the North Vietnamese enjoyed a state of continuous resurrection. Their army had become the legendary phoenix.

John looked towards Frisbee who, still restricted to the ship, arrived for a donut and a cup of coffee. "Are you planning on eventually going over? Oh, I forgot you prefer to stay on board and fix the radar. I hear it hasn't been working very well since we left Taiwan."

"Fucking boot!"

Tom also took advantage of the opportunity. "Frisbee, is the view really good from the top of the antenna? While you were up there, I was lying in my rack thinking about you enjoying all that beautiful seascape."

"Shit ass!" hissed from Frisbee's mouth.

"Well Frisbee, I'll try and have enough liberty for the two of us," said Tom with a laugh.

John looked again at Frisbee. "You should see what some of the girls look like. Boats told me about one carrier that pulled in here a few years back and couldn't get underway. Half of the crew had deserted and the other half had VD."

"Bullshit!" said Frisbee.

"Frisbee, be happy." Tom smiled. "I'm already worried about the clap. Let's see, we've been in port just a couple of days, and I have screwed six broads. That means I am six times more likely to have VD than you."

"Fucker!" said Frisbee quietly since the XO had just entered his stateroom nearby.

"Tom, not to change the subject," John said, "but Mark told me he received a pamphlet on an orphanage here in Hong Kong. I thought I might go over and visit it. You know, it would be good to see something that's okay for a change. Something you wouldn't mind telling folks back home about. What scares me is that I am beginning to believe my own cynicism. Maybe if I see something good in people, I'll feel more like risking my own neck for others in some third world toilet," said John in a serious fashion.

"Yorktown, are you just going out there to look at them or what?"

"Fuller, damn it, I'm being serious here. I plan on stopping by the China Fleet Club to buy some gifts. From the looks of Hong Kong, orphans can use just about anything."

"Yorktown, with all the beer and bar girls in Hong Kong, you expect me to visit some orphanage? You've got to be kidding." Tom picked up an eight-month-old *Readers Digest* and flipped through its pages for about two minutes. "Oh jeez, I guess I might as well go with you. The bars don't start swinging until 2200; I figure you'll be sick of orphans by then. Besides, there might even be a good looking one."

"If you want to go out there and get laid, then forget it," said John.

They stopped by the China Fleet Club and purchased an assortment of games, stuffed animals, and dolls that they thought children would enjoy. Unfortunately, everything at the Club was intended for

English, Australian, or American servicemen and their families.

"What the hell? All the dolls look like Marilyn Monroe and Paul Newman. If I were an orphan, I would be glad to get a toy that looked like LBJ instead of nothing at all," said John. He handed the taxi driver the address of the orphanage.

Tom leaned towards John. "No wonder they need an orphanage here. Their parents were killed by taxi drivers." He was thrown against the back of the driver's seat as the driver accelerated and then braked in an attempt to miss a pedestrian. "Damn it, watch where you're going! Jeez, you nearly ran over some old mother back there!" Tom shouted. His loud protestations then weakened. "I better stop cursing or I'll end up in purgatory. Shit, I haven't been to confession in a year or two. I just can't seem to get up in the morning. Sleep or church? No contest there."

"What do you mean, purgatory? Anyone thinking to visit an orphanage in order to get laid isn't going to purgatory, but straight to a less desirable spot."

"You mean like Yankee Station?" Tom laughed.

"No, I was thinking more of an eternal bridge watch on a tin can," replied John.

Suddenly they stopped in front of an eclectic church. The building was very clean and elaborate in its plainness. It glistened white in the sun and contrasted savagely with the dilapidated buildings and tenements around it.

John and Tom unloaded their packages from the taxi and handed the driver a rather large bill. He smiled at them for the first time. Instead of giving change for the bill, he stuck it in his pocket and sped off.

"That son of a bitch! I wanted the change back! I'll get his fucking number and turn his ass in," said John, realizing he didn't have that much money left to spend in bars. He would have to sell his new super 8mm movie projector in order to go to the beach.

"Oh get off of it, Yorktown. He'll just claim that you tipped him for a tour of the slum area."

They followed a path alongside the church that led to a very comfortable modern home. "Jeez, John, it looks like California."

John knocked on the door; a well-dressed, attractive, young Chinese woman opened it. "Good day. Can I help you gentlemen?" Her accent reflected her birth in the States.

Tom answered, "Yes, ma'am, you sure can. We brought some gifts for the orphans." It was apparent that Tom was using the introduction as an excuse to eye her from head to foot.

"Oh, that's very nice. Why don't you come in?" She called for her husband to join them. After shaking their hands, he sat down in a large leather chair and began to light his pipe. An uncomfortable silence, an indication that he could not speak English, ensued that was broken by Tom's whisper: "Yorktown, he has as much luck smoking a pipe as the CO does. He looks like he's smoking a box of matches instead of tobacco, too."

His wife then left them alone. John was anxious to see the orphans, especially since Tom wanted to get back to the bars before 2200. As John spoke, he attempted to act out his words. "Sir, may we see the orphans?"

After playing charades, he answered John with a Los Angeles accent, "Of course you can, please follow me."

They left the house and followed a pathway between the

buildings until they came upon a small courtyard surrounded by wooden barracks in great need of paint. Tom smiled at John. "Yorktown, if I ever want to be crooked, remind me to buy an orphanage."

John opened the door of one of the nearby frame buildings and expected to see farm equipment. He was immediately greeted by very cold, damp air. On long rows of cots were small children no more than one or two years old, perhaps even younger.

"Tom, if I stay in here too long, I'm going to catch a cold." John had no sooner spoken when they heard loud coughing from one of the darkened rooms. They walked towards the source of the noise. The minister stayed outside in the dying warmth of the sun.

On a small cot was a child swaddled in layers of soiled clothing. He appeared to be more cloth than a little boy. John shouted to the minister who had just entered the building, "What's wrong with him?"

"Gentlemen, this poor child only has a cold. We've been giving him the best medicine, Tiger Balm. He'll be well soon."

John looked towards Tom and whispered loudly enough to be overheard, "A cold! Hell, this child has pneumonia. Listen to the rattle as he breathes." John then looked towards the host. "Look, I know orphanages have limited funds, but can't you afford to heat this damn building?"

"We can only give what God provides us. Please refrain from cursing."

"Why? Are these children bilingual?" uttered John sarcastically.

"One thing, though," Tom said loudly, his voice filled with

anger, "apparently God has provided you with a nice-looking church and home, but forgot about the children."

"You two Americans are not used to the ways of China. I am Chinese, but I was educated at UCLA. I'm as American as you two are, therefore, I'm used to American standards. However, the poor people in Hong Kong have never had anything, and that is especially true of these orphans. These children have it better than they will ever have."

"Well, it's like my old hometown minister used to say, 'The ways of the Lord are strange to mortal men,'" John said without smiling.

Their guide looked confused by his statement and forced out a smile to acknowledge the justice of God's odd behavior.

The three of them walked back towards the house. When they entered the door, the minister's three children greeted them with joy-filled expressions as they held up the toys for the orphanage. It was all too apparent who was going to benefit from their gifts.

John looked towards Tom. "Let's get out of this place. At least in bars the people are what they appear to be. There a thief is a thief and not a pantomime saint."

They walked away and ventured once more into the noisy streets of Hong Kong. "That's the last orphanage for me in WestPac," Tom said, conveying an unusually strong emotion in his anger-filled words. "To think I spent all of that money on a bunch of toys for a crook's children. It would have been wiser to buy 'lady cocktails.'

They say that giving is a pleasure, but the strange thing is I don't feel any damn bit better."

"Well, we both learned something today," replied John.

"John, let's go to Kam Fong. Boats said it's just like the Fuck and Suck Hotel back in Yokosuka."

"Come on, Fuller, where did they get a name like that?"

"Sorry, Yorktown, I forget you aren't a China sailor yet. Well, its real name is the Fukasuka Hotel. There you can get a handjob for about five dollars along with a fine massage, or you can get a blowjob for ten and they throw in the rub down. The rest of what you can get depends upon your ability to negotiate with a hostess."

"Fuller, that sounds like where a loser would end up on an early Sunday morning."

"Come on, Yorktown, we haven't anything to do for a couple of hours."

"You pay for the taxi," replied John.

"It's a deal."

Obtaining a taxi was not as difficult as it usually was. As they sped through the filling streets, the lights of Hong Kong began to turn on. They masked the ugliness of the pavements' contents and turned even the most depressing of tenement buildings into a carnival with lights and myriad people sitting on the balconies. The noise of chatter was incessant.

"John, I never thought about it before, but buildings are like people. Some of them look better under artificial light."

The cab halted in front of Kam Fong Hotel from which loud laughter erupted. It was a European-style brick building that resembled the exterior architecture of the New Orleans French Quarter.

An all too familiar voice spoke loudly from inside. "Hey, look who's comin'. If it ain't Mr. Fuller and Mr. Yorktown. I'll be damned, just look at those two saints. It's 1900 and both of them can still walk a straight line. Shit, they must have had themselves one hell of an afternoon visiting orphans."

John looked towards Tom. "Of all the people in Hong Kong, why did we have to run into Boats again? I'm surprised he wasn't at the orphanage, too. How come he's always where we are?"

"It's simple, John. Boats has been in and out of here since the end of the big war. Hell, he's probably the father of some of the broads he's been fucking. He wouldn't know and, if he did, it wouldn't bother him. As he says, 'Pussy is pussy.' He's the one who recommended these facilities, and naturally he frequents them himself."

Boats approached and placed his arms on their shoulders as he stood between them. He said confidentially, "I want to introduce you to Donna and Beth. Of course they ain't lookers, but what the hell—any old port in a storm. The reason I want to introduce you to them myself is to ensure that they don't steal your watch and billfold while you're soaking in the tub. A few of these broads ain't too honest, but I figure if they know you're my personal friends, they'll treat you as VIPs."

In a louder voice, he said, "Beth, Donna, I want you to meet two of the nicest third classes you will ever meet. These are my drinking buddies, so I want you to treat them just as you would treat me, with the respect comin' to a China sailor." Both girls were short and heavily pockmarked. Neither Donna nor Beth appeared to understand a word of what Boats said.

Boats maintained his equilibrium for as long as he could. After finishing the introduction, he stumbled back to the wall and melted down it until he came in line with an empty fifth of Old Crow. "I'll see you two fellows later." These were the last words he spoke before the morning hours found him.

"John, I hate to pull rank, but I feel that Beth is the girl for me. I know that Donna is no looker, but they say that the ugly ones try harder. They are kind of like Avis."

The two girls led them down a dimly lit hallway. After coming to a small door, Beth led Tom into a room. John followed Donna a few feet more until they too entered a confined space that felt like a hothouse. Without speaking a word, she handed John a basket to put his clothes in. He bashfully undressed and waited.

"You want hand- or blowjob?" Donna said.

"Uh?" John did not expect such a blatant question. It was apparent that this was not going to be a romantic evening of polite conversation. "What is the price difference between a handjob and blowjob?" he asked.

"Oh, handjob ten American dollar. A blowjob twenty."

"Those aren't the costs that Boats told Fuller," John said with some agitation.

"Boats no good liar. He always too drunk to know truth."

"How much is a plain bath. No bubbles, nothin'?"

"It cost two dollar and a dollar for the towel."

"If it won't ruin your evening or deprive your children and old grandmother of a meal, I'll just take a plain bath," John replied with a smile.

Donna's expression conveyed her disappointment. "You get in water. I be right back." When she returned after about ten minutes, she too was smiling.

"You pink! You look like boiled lobster."

"Yah, I feel cooked about medium." John's brief sentiment apparently served as a cue for the door to fling open. Two large Chinese men entered the vapor-filled room and walked over to the basket that contained his possessions. "Hey, what are you doing with my clothing?"

Both men ignored him and busied themselves in emptying the contents of his billfold into the hot-sea bath except for the bills that they neatly folded and placed into their own pockets. After getting thirty dollars in cash, they left. John splashed about in the water trying to find his credit cards that did not float. Some of the other cards trailed ink as they bled. "Just wait till I get out of this tub and call the police!"

Donna could suddenly speak near perfect English: "Sit down, fool! This place off-limits to American serviceman. You call police, they put you in jail. You best forget everything, or I call the manager. He cut your balls off."

"Okay, okay, don't get so pissed off. I'm not going to call anybody. I'll be happy just to get the hell out of here."

"No! You can't go until you get the bath you paid for."

"What are you talking about? I just got robbed and you want me to finish my bath?"

"It's either bath or balls."

"Your words sound like a slogan," said John in disbelief. "Well, bath away." She then proceeded to rub John down as though nothing had happened. She even hummed as she scrubbed. He was very thankful that he had only wanted a bath; he was not physically able for anything more athletic. He knew that his failure to get an erection would have been a personal and unforgivable insult.

John dressed quickly and hurried down the hall to the main waiting room filled with the sound of Boat's snoring. After John had stood in the foyer shaking for about three minutes, Tom appeared with a big smile on his face. "Yorktown, I've got to hand it to Madam Kam Fong, they know how to treat a man. That Beth is one swell girl."

CHAPTER FIFTEEN

The Searcher

The previous day's encounters with the orphanage and the bath had left John in a state of confusion and disillusionment. After a rather tasteless meal on the ship, he turned down several invitations from Boats and Fuller to go on the beach to "get a little." Instead he finally decided to start acting according to his deeply buried convictions.

The ship's lay leader had a list of churches located in the Hong Kong area. John selected a church close to Fenwick Pier. As usual, the bam-bam boat was late getting to the ship. He had planned on going over very early in the morning in order to meet the priest. However, the late arrival of the boat meant that he would be pressed to even locate the church by the time the services began.

From the pier, he took the first taxi he could find. "Let's see, oh here it is, yah, church on Queen Victoria Road. Let's see … that's 811 Victoria, I think." He could not read his own handwriting.

They sped up the mountain through crowded, winding streets. After a silent prayer for a safe journey, John thought, *At least if I die now, I should have a better chance of going to heaven than I would have had last night.* Soon the driver stopped in front of a very old building whose brick walls were covered in peeling stucco.

In the States, this particular structure would have been on its way to becoming a parking lot. The driver turned towards John and struck out his hand.

"How much?" John asked nervously.

The driver looked at him with disgust. He had obviously expected a large bill with no request for any change back. He replied in broken English, "Twenty Hong Kong dollar."

John's conscience protested, *I'll be damned. On a Sunday trying to do the Lord's business, and here I am being cheated by an illiterate taxi driver.* He reached into his billfold and gave him exactly twenty dollars—which was the money he was going to contribute to the church. He still had some money left over, but he planned on eating a big meal later.

In front of the building was a small sign that had been turned into a graffiti wall. Written on the poorly cut wooden slats that composed the sign were the words THE LORD'S CHURCH IN GOD OF THE HOLY TRINITY. John figured that title would cover just about everything. Many other words surrounded the inscription, but they were in Chinese. *They are probably the equivalent of KILROY WAS HERE,* thought John.

The small hallway leading into the heart of the building was dimly lit and smelled of coal smoke. As he walked down the passageway, the noise of a small child crying sounded from within the dimness. Then singing joined the cries of the child. It was a mixture of English and Chinese. *At last,* he thought, *this must be the sanctuary of the church.*

He opened an unmarked door and found a small congregation singing in the nearly empty building. They looked at him in wonder and fear. Their surprised expressions made John somewhat afraid himself. At the head of the congregation was an old Englishman with a worn suit that shone in the dim light. His voice was hoarse and weak, strained by age and the fervor of his calling.

The singing soon dwindled, which had an unnerving affect on John. The priest stared at him, then said with a strained voice, "Welcome, sir, to God's people."

"Thank you, sir," replied John.

"It is not often that an American visits with us here in Hong Kong. We have need of your donations and your voice in our service."

John smiled and went to find a pew in the back. He noticed that even in Hong Kong the entire congregation was seated on the rows furthest from the deliverer of the message. He had to push his way past the legs of a member near the aisle who clung tenaciously to the armrest. It was all too apparent that the thoughts of the congregation had drifted away from God to John.

"Now turn to hymn number 124," said the minister in a serious tone before translating it in fluent Chinese. The old English gentleman fumbled in his pocket for a small metallic instrument designed to produce the right pitch for a song leader to begin with.

As in the churches of his youth, the song leader did not start on the note provided by the pitch pipe. It was an old hymn, "Walking in Sunlight." As the congregation attempted to sing, John looked around the small room. The assembled were very old and appeared to be very cold. Only a few children were present, and they were accompanied by their grandmothers or elderly aunts. The ages of the congregation were so close that he imagined the whole group journeying to heaven at the same time.

An older lady in front of John turned completely around and stared. Her gaze was very intense and maybe with some justification. The hymnal was printed in both Chinese and English. John had attempted to sing in English that contrasted strongly with the harmony of those seated about him. He looked at her in return just long enough to notice that she was keeping time to the music with the chewing of her snuff. Not once during the song did she turn her eyes from him.

To keep from becoming overly conscious, John returned to looking about the room. The walls were soiled with age and coal smoke. There were a few of the usual religious pictures on the wall, including the Last Supper in which the Lord appeared to be wearing an oversized heart around his neck. Christ, in one of the pictures, looked very much like a Chinaman with an Italian noise.

John's hips began to ache. The bench he was sitting on felt harder than a stone. Its appearance was that of a piece of unpolished driftwood bearing the scars of many encounters with people. It had been carved upon at different times in the past. This meant that it had probably been used as a park or storefront bench in its youth.

"Brethren, I speak to you not as a man but as a voice of God." The congregation shifted uneasily in their seats. No one appeared to be comfortable in John's presence. It was also apparent that the vicar was going to preach in English for John's benefit. It was also obvious that the congregation would not understand a word.

The minister went on to emphasize many portions of his sermon not only with his voice but with his entire body. "When our death comes, we should look at it not with the fear of sinners but with the conviction of saved and worthy *Christians*," he said, standing on his toes to accentuate the last word. "*Christians* know they are joining hands with the eternal God."

He then clasped his own hands. "It is only the sinner who fears death." He made a waving motion with his hands to encompass his glassy-eyed audience.

"Is it not reasonable for death to be good? Did God not make us to die? How could the fields yield their flowers or the trees wear their new garments of leaves if death did not occur? Life is built upon death. It is the soil beneath the oak that nourishes it." It was apparent that the vicar was referring to the English countryside.

"No man's death diminishes me for it is God's plan that new life should spring from the winter; and from the decay of leaves, flowers are born."

Sadness came over John. Here in the suffering and poverty of Hong Kong, to die would be a release. He thought of all of the beauty in the world and how it conflicted so greatly with the barrenness of the sanctuary. *Is it possible for two worlds to exist in one?*

Which world is true? This old man shows greater contentment than I have known, but his peacefulness frightens me. Tonight I will probably be in some bar with Tom and Boats, while this man looks towards the crest of the mountain and beyond.

"Brethren, be not afraid! Take the hand of Christ," he said, extending his own hand towards the audience, "and walk gently with him. He has prepared a place for you where there is neither hunger nor cold. In his bosom, you will be comforted like a small child pressed against the breast of his mother.

"Come now if your hearts are heavy and take my outstretched hand. Together we will begin our walk towards the mountain whose summit yields to everlasting life."

The audience understood the outstretched hand as a cue to stand and sing. It was obviously the invitation portion of the sermon and, as was typical in most services that John had seen, no one responded.

Once the service had officially ended, the vicar approached John and took his hand. "My son, in Hong Kong there is much suffering and sadness, but in the hearts of Christians, there is much comfort and happiness. Here you feel the presence of God in the needs of these people. The time is so short for when brethren can be together. Come back when you can, and together we will worship our God who is our only hope."

John looked intently into his eyes. "Why did you preach on such a sad subject today?"

"I am an old man who is nearing the summit. I spoke to myself, for to be honest, even I am afraid at times. To me, even the heartbreak of Hong Kong is preferable to death, but as a Christian I must conceal this. There are times in one's life, as all men know, when death does not seem so alien. I understand our conflict as mortals who are a part of the earth and a part of the heavens."

"Thank you, I will come back next time we are in port." John then walked out of the small sanctuary into the nondescript hall that funneled towards the street. It was warm outside and the brilliant clear sky accented the beauty of the day. He looked back towards the dark entrance and then toward the blue sky. *It's good to be alive. I want to live.* The thought that he was alive and healthy made him feel good and complete. *Surely religion is more than just waiting for death.* At that moment, he looked back once more towards the entrance of the church and saw the vicar emerge. He too seemed rejuvenated by the light as he looked towards the blue sky.

CHAPTER SIXTEEN

Never Again, or at Least Until Tomorrow

"Hey Yorktown, let's go over tonight. I'm ready for a big, fat, bloody steak and some Tiger Beer. In fact why don't we leave now? No way am I eating wardroom food." Tom punctuated his sentences with long puffs from a new shore-bought Swisher Sweets cigar. With each suction, he looked at the ever-growing ash and watched the smoke curl to the wardroom overhead.

"Tom, I'm not going over tonight. No way. I've seen enough of this place to last me a long time. I have finally made a firm commitment to myself. Tomorrow I am going to buy an Atari tape recorder and a Minolta camera and leave the streets to suckers like you. I might even buy myself a new tailor-made suit, that is if I can think of why I need one."

"Come on, John. I've heard that bullshit before. Just the other night you made the same comment and ended up getting a handjob at the Kam Fong Hotel."

"Man, all I got was a mugging followed by a rubdown that I did not want. You didn't see me wearing a shit-eating grin like you had on your face when I came out."

Wan Chai was brightly lit. The lights on the bar fronts were once more glowing fingers that pointed into dark doorways. As they approached each bar, strong smells of bourbon and cigarette smoke greeted them like a pair of ambitious hostesses. The outward appearance of each bar was very much the same: flickering neon signs that promised heaven but too often yielded only regret.

Just inside the doors were the older women who kept hoping that a drunk sailor, unable to clearly see them or oblivious to their looks, would enter. The younger girls worked the interior, busily moving from the tables to the bar in order to obtain the tokens for the drinks that they hustled to their customers. Like in Japan, each girl carried a ring upon which they placed their tokens. John and Tom could easily pick the most beautiful girl by noting the number of coins she carried about her tiny wrist.

"Yorktown, I'm more hungry than horny right now. I say let's eat," Tom said.

"Yep, I'm with you. I had just as soon spend my money on steaks as on a stranger's drinks.

There before them was a corner bar. BAR G. I. JOE was written across the entrance in large red letters. Under the marquee appeared:

> *Fine American Food.*
> *Direct from Mom's Kitchen.*
> *Beautiful Hostesses to Cut Your Steaks.*
> *Tonight's Special only $1.50 U.S.*

"Tom, I hope this isn't what I think it is. If those waitresses are carrying tokens, I'm getting my skinny ass out."

"Come on, the special is only $1.50? Hell, a handjob would cost you five. All you can get for $1.50 is a meal."

The entrance of the bar led to a large dance floor that was skirted by booths. There was a jukebox in the far corner of the dance floor. Its lights were flashing as no one was paying to play it. Business was certainly not booming—a fact that made John afraid of the quality of the food.

"Welcome, American sailors," an old madam of Russian and Chinese mix said. "Right this way." They followed her command as though she were their Captain.

"Tom, how did she know we are sailors?"

"Are you nuts? Who else would eat here?" he replied.

The room narrowed sharply towards the back, giving the bar the appearance of a large skillet whose handle disappeared into darkness. "Excuse me," John mumbled as he bumped into a waitress who was in the process of taking drinks to a table.

"Watch where you go sailor!" she said angrily, then managed a smile.

"Well, I'm sorry. It's so dark in here; I didn't see you. I hope you didn't spill anything."

Just then, their greeter stopped abruptly which caused John to slam into the waitress a second time. This time, she simply laughed. As they stood, she began to rub his fly.

John said loudly to the waitress, "My primary body need at the moment is to eat." He turned towards Tom. "Well, you've done it again. To think that I followed you on the beach to get a steak, and now I'll be having crab instead."

"Boy, I hope you're right. Who wants to eat steak? When we first came in, I saw a broad that I would give twenty U.S. dollars for. Yah, twenty and even throw in the hotel room," said Tom loudly as though he wanted to be overheard.

They seated themselves after scraping their hips over cut vinyl and spilled drinks. The old madam vanished and they found themselves alone for several minutes. Their eyes gradually adjusted to the shadows. The only light in the room was provided by a clock with a soft drink for a background. John could feel eyes staring at him from a group of B-girls seated along an aisle seat. They had interrupted their card game to stare.

"Hi boy-sons," two plump, elderly career girls shouted at them. It was apparent that seniority determined who would approach first. Without being asked, they seated themselves on the edge of their booth seats, shoving their hips against Tom and John in order to make room for themselves.

"My name Susie and her name Alice." Like Americans, they offered their hands, which John and Tom shook as if they had just signed contracts with them. "What your name? What ship you off?" Every bar girl in the Orient asked the same questions.

Without giving them time to answer, the madam appeared

on cue. "What you want to order?"

"I'll have a steak and beer. Make it a small beer. I don't want any blood showing on the steak. Uh, and I'll have a little coleslaw, too," Tom said. It was obvious that Susie was rubbing his leg. "And a cocktail for the lady!" he added with enthusiasm.

"Might as well make it two," said John. He expected Alice to rub his leg too, but she proceeded to rummage in her purse for a cigarette instead.

After lighting up, Alice kissed John lightly on the lips. Her breath was strong, her mouth discharging the combined odors of bourbon and cigarette.

As they talked, both girls kept their hands on their captives' knees. Whenever they wanted another cocktail, they rubbed the men's legs briskly. John decided that it would be better to continue ordering cocktails for Alice to keep her from rubbing his leg raw. It was obvious that the exercise was intended to increase their passion, which in turn would increase the number of lady cocktails ordered. The only passion rising in John was the acute and demanding desire to eat.

Looking around at the other tables, he noticed a girl who had just walked up to the bar from a dark booth. Her back was well shaped with long, straight, black hair hanging down to her well-formed hips. She appeared so different from the rest of the girls that he couldn't resist staring at her. She seemed to sense his stare and turned towards him. Her face was young with very large, piercing but friendly eyes.

"Hey, look over there." John pointed with his chin.

"Where?" asked Tom.

"There!" said John, pointing with his finger.

"Yeah, now that's what I call good," Tom said, smiling.

"She no good girl. She called Firefly," Alice said with conviction.

"Firefly?" asked John.

"Sailor call her 'Firefly.' She go from one table to next getting drinks. Soon as she stop at table, she bum cigarette. Lights up like Firefly on August night."

"What's wrong with that? Don't all of you bum cigarettes and hustle drinks?" asked John.

"Sure, but we put out too, and she doesn't. She damn virgin. Sailors buy her many drinks and give her gifts. Nice girl screw. Not Firefly, she say she get married someday, and she must be virgin to get rich Chinese husband."

"A real virgin?" asked John.

"Now come on, Yorktown. A real virgin? You don't believe all that crap, do you? Hell, Boats is probably shacking with her," said Tom with a sarcastic laugh.

As Firefly continued to stare at John, he felt a strong sensation enter his body and cascade down his chest and legs. John had never believed that a look could capture a person's entire persona before. She then suddenly vanished into the darkness of a nearby booth. "Tom, tell me the next time you see her. I'm going to have a date with her," John whispered across the table.

"You've got to be kidding. A date? I thought you just wanted to eat."

"Alice, I hate to do this, but I would rather eat my steak alone tonight if it ever arrives. I'm just about broke," said John.

During their discussion about Firefly, the two girls had been silent except for an occasional comment in Chinese.

The silence was broken by Alice. "You no good butterfly!" With that statement of condemnation, both girls got up and stormed off, the darkness devouring them. From where they were sitting, the bar area appeared to be a stage on which the characters ascended, performed, and then exited with profit. The steaks arrived topped with raw eggs.

Tom picked up a knife and attempted to cut the meat. "Yorktown, I don't know about your steak, but mine is like a rock on which a bird had dropped an egg." From out of the darkness, Firefly appeared together with another girl.

"Relieve the watch." Tom laughed. "The pumping is about to start anew."

Firefly introduced her friend. "Smiley Ho-Chan, number one Wan Chai girl, she not worn-out like Alice."

"Well, you two might as well join us. But let's get something straight first: Tom and I don't have much money, so make the drinks last," said John, smiling.

Firefly sat down next to John, and Smiley placed her body against Tom. Smiley was not very attractive. She was short, stocky, and—like many young women in Hong Kong—pockmarked. John was certain that he had met several Smiley Ho-Chans since arriving in Hong Kong.

"Firefly, how much do you go home for?" Tom asked. He took her reported virginity as a challenge.

Smiley answered, "She virgin. She no go home with sailor."

"Don't tell me you're a virgin too." Tom smiled.

"Me no virgin. I go home with nice man," blurted Smiley.

"Firefly is as much of a virgin as my Irish mother." Tom laughed.

"Me a virgin!" Firefly shouted, defending her honor.

The old Russian madam appeared at their table with a round of drinks. She sat two large lady cocktails in front of Firefly and Smiley. The madam had assumed that Tom and John were officers and therefore had abundant money to spend. It was widely known that officers were more reluctant to part with their money, but in the end they were fools like everyone else.

"What ship you sailors off?" the madam asked.

"*Hyman*, ma'am," replied John. He suddenly remembered the part in the manual expressly stating: *Do not reveal the name of your ship or the next port of call.* His hands began to feel clammy.

"*Hyman*? Big carrier?"

"No, ma'am. You're thinking of the *Yorktown* that is in port now." John was being courteous for it was common knowledge that the madams of the Orient knew far in advance what ships would be arriving. If a sailor wanted to know when his vessel would depart, a madam could tell him not only the day, but the hour as well as her next port of call.

"I don't like carrier sailor. They smartass," said the madam, rising to go to a nearby table to reenact her short play with other sailors.

With her exit, John became keenly aware of Firefly's presence. Days at sea had made him more forward than he would have been otherwise. He touched her hand that was on the seat beside him, then placed his hand on her leg. She gently picked up his hand and placed it back on the seat while still holding it. Her hand was strong yet soft. Desire surged in him like a tide that can be held in check only so long before breaking down all restrictive barriers. "Let's go to your place. I'll pay ten American dollars," said John, trying not to be heard by the others.

Tom overheard him. "Ten, hell! I'll pay fifteen."

"Your mother! I'll give twenty," said John sternly. The auction continued until they got to fifty American dollars.

"I'll go!" blurted Smiley with tremendous enthusiasm.

"Dream on, Smiley. I'll give you five Hong Kong dollars," Tom chuckled.

"You typical sailor. I not go home with you for one hundred dollar U.S.," said the offended Smiley.

Firefly joined in: "I not go home for one hundred dollar U.S. either."

"Well, that deals me out," John spoke dejectedly. "I can buy an acre of land in Texas for a hundred dollars and that includes mineral rights."

Smiley examined John's head closely. "You are starting to get bald."

"Wow, you noticed," replied John.

Firefly looked towards John. "My father was bald. He ran junk from Canton to Hong Kong."

Tom smiled at John. "Wow, he had his own command."

"Yeah, something you will never get," replied John with a smile.

"I want to dance," Firefly said, getting up. She did not invite John to be her partner and didn't look back as she walked to the dance floor. John quickly followed her for fear that some other sailor might notice her. She turned towards him as he placed his arms gently around her small waist.

"The End of the World" sung by Skeeter Davis flowed from the jukebox. He had never heard the words before. Softly Firefly sung the last verses:

> Why do these eyes of mine cry?
> Don't they know it's the end of the world?
> It ended when you said goodbye.
>
> Why does my heart go on beating?
> Why do these eyes of mine cry?
> Don't they know it's the end of the world?
> It ended when you said goodbye.

The song was slow. Tender emotions arose within him yet there was no time to truly care. As they danced, he pulled her closer to him. "Are you really a virgin?"

"Me virgin. You no believe me?"

It was strange but he did believe her, perhaps he wanted to. The dance ended and they walked back to their booth.

"John, Smiley is going to take us to a rooftop crap game. It'll cost us ten U.S. dollars apiece to get these two girls out. To be honest, Smiley is giving me a bargain, you know, throwing something extra in." His words implied that John was being shortchanged on any deal he had concluded with Firefly.

The ride was fast, furious, and without event. Firefly and Smiley talked to each other and ignored their companions.

"Tom, I sure hope this is worth ten dollars. So far watching a movie in the wardroom seems more thrilling than this."

Smiley and Firefly talked excitedly since they were going to have an opportunity to spend both officers' money. The taxi stopped in front of an old brick building. John overpaid the driver to avoid any argument over whether they had experienced a tour or simply had taken a ride.

In the semi-dark hall, John tripped over a human form. "Excuse me," he said quietly as if afraid that his words rather than his kick might disturb the person. The reply came back in the form of groans.

"He opium head," Smiley said loudly.

"Thank goodness. I kicked him pretty hard." Before them was a narrow stairway that ascended steeply up into a black void. "Now I see why he's at the bottom of the ladder." Strong smells oozed out of the walls and spilled onto the floor. Sounds greeted them from every doorway, giving John the feeling that the building itself was alive. "Tom, I guess you known that rooftops are off-limits?" said John, not bothering to conceal his concern.

"Come on, John, why do you think we're up here? The way to increase your business in Hong Kong is to get placed off-limits. You too looked at the off-limits list that was handed out at the brow. Well hell, so did all the other sailors. Now what do you think is off-limits? Gambling and women. And what does a sailor want?"

"Okay, okay, gambling and women," replied John.

"Right. This is the way these places get free publicity. I've written down the name of a few of the off-limits places that sound pretty good. That Sailor Chan's Massage Parlor over in the New Territories seems like a good joint if we strike out on the beach."

Finally, they reached the top of the stairs. They were breathing hard when Smiley pushed open an unmarked door. John immediately began to sneeze and cough for the scene that greeted them was the opposite of Shangri-La. Sprawled on the edges of the room were old men and women smoking opium. Encamped in the center of the room were younger bargirls playing cards and shouting at one another. Each girl held money in her left hand as though she was bear-baiting her opponent.

So focused were the players that their presence was not acknowledged at first. Without any hesitation, Smiley shoved her way into the competing circle and made some remarks to the girls who glanced up at the newly arrived group and briefly examined their new competitors before returning their concentration to the game. They did move over to make a place for Tom. John and Firefly were left to stand and watch.

Tom leaped at the spot made available to him. He seemed anxious to give some of his money to them. It really didn't matter—John was sure that Smiley would have most of his money by morning anyway. The girls finally made space for John when one of them left, but he declined the invitation. He didn't know how to play anything except Chinese checkers. Firefly smiled at his reluctance, an expression of understanding on her face.

John watched the excitement of the card game, then his eyes followed the periphery of the room where old people lay in disarray as though cast like fortune sticks tossed by a teller. The smell of drugs floated about them. It was obvious that his world was not theirs; they were content with their illusions.

"Let's go, Firefly," said John in a serious tone. Without a word, she took his hand and led him across the room to the door. Outside it was very late. The streets were empty and a dampness from the harbor crept upon the mountain like a lioness stalking its prey. The foghorns of distant ships sounded clearly. Despite Firefly's presence, he felt very much alone.

They walked slowly through the unpunctuated quietness. "Let's go to your place." John's words sounded like sacrilege. Perhaps it was the silence of the street that gave the moment a religious ambience.

"No, can't go."

"Why not? I won't tell Tom or Smiley." John was still not totally convinced that she was a virgin. *In all probability,* he reasoned, *she is shacking with some English sailor off a British frigate. That must be the reason why she won't take me to her place."*

"Can't take man home. I have to go now." It was apparent from her tone that John had offended her.

Oh, what the hell, he thought. *We are only in port a couple of weeks. I paid ten dollars just to let her go home early. There's no point in insisting. It's late and I'm tired.*

The ride in the bam-bam boat was cold. Then an uncomfortable thought occurred to him: *I bet Tom is scoring right now while I am sitting on this dumbass bam-bam boat. This is the last time I'm going to pick a beautiful girl. From now on, I'm going after hogs, at least they know how to treat a man. Alice was right about Firefly—no damn good!*

CHAPTER SEVENTEEN

Lost Horizons

The Captain was later than usual in his arrival for dinner. The rumor was that he had become overly intoxicated in Kowloon and that some of the sailors had to help him back aboard. Since no one had seen the Old Man during the day, it gave credibility to the rumor that he was sleeping off last night's adventure.

"Did you get any?" Tom said, smiling and winking at John.

"You bet I did. Man, that girl wore me out," John said, winking back.

"Oh come on, Yorktown, tell the truth," persisted Tom.

"You're right. It was just my luck to pick a prostitute that's a virgin. I bet she's shacking right this moment with some sailor off HMS *Viceroy*. By the way, how was Smiley in bed?" asked John.

"The truth is, we played cards until four this morning. The

more I looked at Smiley, the less horny I got. I ended up with a rub down at the hotel. Man, you should see the girls they got working between four and five in the morning. From now on, I'm going to find me a herd of sheep."

"It seems like you don't have many nice things to say about Smiley," John said with a laugh.

"That's not half of what I could say about Smiley. She got forty-five U.S. off of me. With this hangover, I can't remember if she won or stole it."

The Captain finally arrived very blurry-eyed and holding his head. He looked at John. "Mr. Yorktown, what flick have we got on board tonight?"

"Sir, it's *Tom Jones*. I had my men go over to the newly arrived oiler and trade films. I had to trade them three 'fly' movies to get it."

"What do you mean, 'fly' movies?"

"One was *Curse of the Fly*. The others were *The Fly* and something like the *Teenage Fly*. To be truthful, I feel that we got a real bargain."

"Did they have any Bing Crosby flicks?" asked the Old Man.

"No sir, but I did remember to ask."

The Captain left as soon as the steward placed a large bowl of oyster stew in front of him.

"Come on, John, and let's find us some action. Boats said he wanted to go along with us."

"Oh God!" uttered John.

As the three of them walked along the brightly lit and noisy street, Boats stared into each bar. He was apparently getting more excited with each step. He was also gifted with keen observation. "Man, look at those tits. Look at that ass. Could you handle that piece, Mr. Fuller? Eh? What's wrong with this bar? Eh?"

Through the process of elimination, they found themselves once more at Bar G.I. Joe. Tom and John now considered Firefly as a challenge. Upon their entrance, three girls approached them. One of them was Smiley but even in the darkness, the other two forms did not appear to be Firefly.

"Where's Firefly?" asked John.

"Firefly not here tonight. She sick," responded the unknown hostess.

"Sick? What's the matter?" asked John.

"Come now, Mr. Yorktown," Boats said, gently nudging John's ribs with his elbow. "It's one of two things—either it's her time of the month or she's shackin'. I bet two weeks' pay it's the latter."

Smiley's face came alive with anger. "You son of a bitch! Firefly sick. Not shackin'! You typical sailor. She have bad blood that makes her cold and ache. Doctor say something in blood not right."

As John spoke to Smiley, two girls approached Tom and Boats and immediately took them to a nearby booth. Laughter soon came from the conclave that indicated that they had established an effective beachhead. Boats shouted towards John, "Hey, Mr. Yorktown, come here." Boats was obviously tickling one of the girls as John neared the booth.

"This here is Cherry Sally. How much?" Boats asked her with an exaggerated wink.

"More than an old boatswain have," Cherry Sally replied.

"Come on now, Cherry, how much?" pleaded Boats.

"I go for twenty U.S. I best lookin' girl in bar. My friend go for fifteen."

Tom didn't think he was getting a bargain. "What do you mean, for fifteen? I'll give you ten and you throw in the drinks."

"Smiley," said John, "these two idiots might as well hand over their wallets now. Do you know where Firefly lives?"

"She live in Wan Chai with her family."

"Yah, I know, but where in Wan Chai?"

Boats smiled. "Mr. Yorktown, if you don't mind me saying so, you are going to fuck up some chief's evening with Firefly, and I bet he paid through the ass to get her. Come and join us. She'll be here tomorrow just as cherry as ever. Hell, I bet Cherry Sally can line you up with one fine looking *virgin*."

"I tell you where she lives," Smiley replied with apparent agitation. "It near harbor, across from Fong's grocery. Many junks tie up nearby. Apartment #1210 on twelfth floor. I wouldn't tell anyone else where she lives but you. She likes you. She say you good to her and not typical sailor like Boats."

Fong's was a dilapidated food store on the fringe of Wan Chai. Fruit was placed outside the entrance while Peking ducks dangled from the overhangs and dripped their tallow onto the sidewalk. Avoiding the drips, John decided to surprise Firefly with some vegetables and meat. Since she was weak, food would be needed. As he entered the store, a variety of strong Far Eastern cooking odors met and held him momentarily. It was difficult for him to know what to buy since he had done very little grocery shopping in civilian life. The clerk swiped at the beads of the abacus as he rapidly totaled the bill.

As John reentered the street world, he noticed the tall building across from Fong's. It appeared to be at least fifteen stories high. It was a large, poorly built structure. Bamboo framing still enforced the lower four floors.

The entrance to the building was dim, partially illuminated by light escaping from various apartment doors that faced a long hall. John walked cautiously to a narrow staircase, and then climbed to the second floor since he could not locate an elevator shaft on the first floor. He looked at the aged elevator and decided to walk the remaining steps to the twelfth floor.

Around the stairwell of her floor, there were the entrances to four apartments. John knocked on the first door. It opened quickly, then was slammed immediately, allowing a strong drug odor to burst from the apartment. John knocked gently on the second door. It opened slowly. A small child looked up at him with an expression of fear and curiosity.

"Does Firefly live here?" John said in a hushed tone. The child turned towards the darkness of the apartment and spoke in Cantonese. After a brief moment, the door opened wider, and Firefly stood before him. She was wearing a light green gown that touched the floor. Partially concealing the flimsiness of the gown was an old cotton housecoat. She was silent as she looked up at him. John could not help but notice the small beads of sweat on her forehead.

"I brought you some meat and vegetables from over at Fong's. Smiley said you were sick. At first she didn't want to give me your address, but I talked her into it. I thought that since you felt bad, I might be of some help."

Firefly stepped back and allowed him to enter. She had not yet managed a smile. As his eyes adjusted to the semidarkness of the room, he noticed other people seated in various locations; a few were standing. Some sat erect while others slouched in cushioned chairs. A small incense burner gave the base light for the room. As the flame vanished into smoke, some of the other figures disappeared also.

"My aunties, brothers, and sisters live with me. Just a second, I cut on light." Suddenly the room was filled with dim 60-watt illumination. "This my aunt, Donna Hochan."

"Hello, Donna." John extended his hand which she took and shook vigorously. So this is the Donna Hochan that Boats had told him about. The Donna Hochan that had been working the bars of Wan Chai since the end of World War II. She showed her age, and it was obvious that those years had been difficult ones.

"Aunties, brothers, sisters, come meet Ensign Yorktown. He United States Navy officer off ship in harbor. He good man. Bring food." Gradually the family oozed from behind the few doors that led from the living room. Various shapes and sizes approached John, all with their heads bowed as though humbled before him. It was as though they were using a homing device to locate him.

Firefly looked towards John and sensed his curiosity. "I make money for family. Send brothers and sisters to school. In Hong

Kong, it costs to go to school. Costs much money. This is Yu. He smart brother. He speaks English better than me. He even read English. Someday he will be able to write letter for me."

"Hi, Yu," said John in a soft voice. Yu appeared small and frail. His eyes were sensitive and questioning. His hair was cut very close, almost a burr. The frames of his glasses were too large for his small face.

"Hello, Yorktown." With those two words, Yu stepped back into the dimness as though waiting for further instructions.

"Firefly, since this many people live here, how many rooms do you have?" asked John.

"We have two rooms. I have bedroom that I share with my two sisters. Brothers and aunties sleep in living room on floor and couch."

My Lord! thought John. *Can this many people live in just two rooms? How do they sleep, bathe, dress?*

"Firefly, I didn't mean to bother you or your family. I just wanted to give you some food."

"Yorktown, you good. Stay with me awhile. I don't feel okay and that makes me afraid. I am cold. Whenever I get cold, I get scared." She took his hand and placed it in hers. He was surprised at how chilly her hand actually felt. She then led him to the one bedroom. Even though he must have appeared to her family to possess saintly qualities, his heart still raced. He thought, "No, it can't be. Not with all of her relatives here."

The bedroom was very small, with bunk beds and one miniature dresser. There were no closets. Through her window, he could see the lights of the crowded anchorage filled with junks and, beyond that, the harbor of Hong Kong. The masthead lights of his destroyer were visible in the cold, crisp night. He looked towards her. "I have met all of your relatives except your parents."

"My father, he dead with cancer. He boat skipper. He run junk from Hong Kong to Canton. I grew up on family junk. When he got sick, I had to do the work of a man. My brothers and sisters were too small to help."

"What about your mother? Didn't she help out or was she separated from your father?"

"My mother alive. She helped my father some, but she was sick too. Opium made her very weak."

"How in the world did you end up a Wan Chai girl?" John asked softly.

"Before my father die, he told me I would have to go to bar. It only way for Chinese girl from very poor family to make money quick to pay hospital debts. So he sold me to the bar. Father make me promise that I not become like Donna. I must remain virgin."

"Tell me more about your mother?"

"She alive. Mother live in Kowloon. She take dope too much. I don't want my brothers and sisters around her."

"You mean you're the sole support for all of these people?" asked John.

"Yes, I have much responsibility for a young girl."

"How old are you?"

"Me seventeen this month. How old you?"

"I just turned twenty-two." Desire swept from him as he contrasted her life with his own. "Life is often not kind nor is it fair."

"What you mean, Yorktown?"

"I just feel that life is good to some and very bad to others. However, even to the ones that have a good life, their existence must end cruelly and pointlessly. I guess that life is indifferent, and that's what scares me. I had rather it be cruel and that cruelty have direction and purpose. I am afraid of nothingness just as you are afraid of the cold."

"You don't make sense to me. You drink something?" she asked in a serious tone.

"No, Firefly, I didn't drink anything." John noticed her frail body sitting on the lower bunk that sagged under her light weight. Despite the hopelessness in her surroundings, she was beautiful and young, her beauty highlighted by the desolation of the room and the full moon just rising above the bay to furnish light to the small chamber.

John moved closer to her on the bed, but as he did so, the bed threatened to give way. She responded with a warmth alien to him. She took his hand and placed it on her lap. To hold another's hand had never meant so much to him. However, her gesture awakened in John a heretofore unknown desire. A desire not to make love but to love. The sound from the nearby rooms and the unending harbor noises vanished with this emotion. It was a feeling that he sensed but could not understand. He realized that he was falling in love with a stranger.

CHAPTER EIGHTEEN

Ascension

The day aboard the *Hyman* seemed agonizingly slow. As soon as liberty call sounded, John found himself standing in front of Bar G. I. Joe. It was apparent that something strange was happening. A struggle existed within him over whether to even go into the bar. He knew that if he went in, a commitment would be made. Outside were bar smells as sailors opened the decorated glass doors and freed the strong odors held captive within.

No, I won't go in and get involved. She might even be telling the truth about being a virgin, and I could end up spending a lot of money for nothing. In war, there is no time for love. Just as his thoughts came to a conclusion, Firefly opened the door.

"Yorktown, what you doing on sidewalk? I expect you to come early and buy me out of bar. I wait very long time for you."

"I thought you were sick, or at least you were last night."

"I go to clinic this morning and get blood. Now I feel great," she said with a smile.

"I am very thankful that you are better. Let's get out of Wan Chai tonight. I'm tired of blinking lights, beer, and the sounds of the traffic. What I need is a beach or maybe a mountain. I want us to be together and far away from all of this."

"You give me ten dollar bill, and I pay mamasan."

Without a word, John searched through his wallet for a ten-dollar bill. He knew better than to give a twenty and expect change. The thought of fleeing entered his head again, but her business transaction was over in less than a minute.

"What matter with you tonight? You seem sad. You not even like Wan Chai," she said in a teasing voice.

"I only enjoy it here because you are a part of it. To me, you are Wan Chai with its contradictions. It is dedicated to pleasure, but at the same time, it conceals a deep pain within."

"Yorktown, you nuts. If you want mountain, then we go to top of Victoria Peak."

"Great, but how do we get there?"

She stepped into the street, waved, and shouted, "Taxi!"

A taxi swerved towards her but did not slow down. "You motherfucker! He no good! Try to kill me!" she screamed towards John who had remained on the sidewalk.

Firefly was not to be outdone by a mere attempt on her life. She stepped boldly into the street again. After a second close call, she once more screamed, "Taxi!" This time one swerved towards her and stopped.

The road to the top of Victoria Peak wound like the spiral of a drill in ever narrowing bands. The physical sensations of Wan Chai faded below them as the taxi swerved along the tight streets where small hovels shouldered the road's edge. John found it difficult to imagine that people lived in dwellings of cardboard, plywood, and tin.

Hong Kong was a movie set whose façade, as seen from the harbor, was beautiful. Yet behind the backdrop, John found debris of people whose existence revolved around a never-ending search for food and warmth. At that moment, he regretted the new knowledge that had been cast upon him.

The taxi halted at the peak's summit just as the cog train had earlier. They stepped out into another existence as a strong sea wind blew across their cheeks and moved Firefly's clothing like a jip sail. Far below them lay the harbor with its moving lights. A harbor whose shoreline glowed with neons. It was godlike on the peak where suffering and fear were hidden by the darkness. John felt as though they had ascended above reality.

He looked at Firefly who appeared to be studying Wan Chai from her heavenly view. "Yorktown, the city and harbor look beautiful from here. Nothing seems cold and I not afraid. I wish you and me stay here always. No sail away."

"I wish that could also be. I don't want to go back to the war. If it were within my power to stay on this peak with you forever, I would. Damn my responsibilities and the future! Have you ever loved anyone?" John asked as he too looked at the harbor.

"No, I never love anyone but my family. Sailor not want love. He want to have sex. You first sailor who want to talk. Sometime I think you too strange."

"I feel different around you," replied John. "Maybe you're not good for me. You cause me to think and as you said before, it's not safe to think. By the way, what are those two people saying about us?" Nearby were two elderly Chinese women who appeared to be enjoying the opportunity to observe them. Every now and then one would point towards John and Firefly and then talk loudly. They appeared like choragi in a Greek play.

"They say I lucky girl to be with rich American officer," she replied without revealing their true conversation.

The moon rose over China and cast its glow upon them. John embraced Firefly and then kissed her tenderly. He knew that love must not be a part of their relationship and yet he could not fight it in her presence. He felt the urge to protect her, to make the cold go away, to remain forever upon the mountain.

CHAPTER NINETEEN

Repulse Bay

The mamasan of Bar G.I. Joe grew to like John in the few days that his ship remained in port. It was no longer necessary for him to ask her how much it would cost to buy Firefly out of the bar. She would merely put her hand out and John would obediently place a ten-dollar bill on it.

Despite his growing love for Firefly, he felt that he was buying only her time with no guarantee attached. If he eventually made it to bed with Firefly, that would be his good fortune; if she only wanted to talk, that too would be enough. He found himself torn between desire and love, a vacuum that must be filled.

During the afternoon, John read about Repulse Bay from a travel guide someone had left in the wardroom. The bay was located on the opposite side of the mountain from Wan Chai. After purchasing her time, he mentioned Repulse Bay to Firefly who seemed almost as enthusiastic about it as he did.

The car ride was beautiful as they drove along the shoulder of the mountain and then down the winding slopes to the bay. John felt that he had left the present in Hong Kong for a different time period that now existed only for them. The cab was like a time capsule, violating the quietness of the previous centuries. Even though he was thinking about the striking contrast as well as Firefly's beauty, he never forgot about the cab meter's incessant click.

After he had searched through two pockets for the fare, they stepped from the taxi. Firefly led the way down a wooden walkway that creaked under their weight. The sand at the bottom felt hard as though packed by heavy rain.

"A typhoon must have passed by here not too long ago. There is so much debris on the sand," said John.

"Yorktown, you good observer. Make fine lookout. Storm hit just south of here about two months ago. It killed many people on the mainland."

"Are you afraid of typhoons?"

"All people afraid of storms in Hong Kong. Buildings collapse and wash down sides of mountains. Storms are cruel. They hurt the poor who cling to the sides of Victoria Peak. They live in houses built of discarded wood and cardboard. Rich people do not get hurt, but storms cost them money." She looked at him as he wrapped his arms around her frail body. "Cold. I never warm enough. Bar is so cold. Mamasan never put fuel in heater unless pipes about to break."

"You can say that again." John had noticed how cold the bar was but he figured that the heating system was not working properly. It was so uncomfortable that patrons were forced to dance to avoid freezing. It was said of Bar G. I. Joe that no man could go to sleep there and wake up well.

"Firefly, you mentioned several times about being cold, is something wrong with you physically? Smiley said you have bad blood. You also mentioned that you had to have a transfusion in order to feel better. I know the bar is an ice box, but I have noticed that even under the warm sun, you wrap your arms around yourself."

"Doctor say my blood no good."

"I'm sorry. I guess you are anemic," replied John.

"No be sorry for me, I'm alive. Many die here, but I not die. Me live to be very old woman."

"Being alive is beautiful," John said, looking into her eyes. "We do have days like this one. Look at that sky—completely clear and even the ocean sparkles beneath it. You look so beautiful and young in the sun's light. There is something eternal about you that time cannot alter. I have the same feeling when I see a person in a painting that never can change."

"You nice sailor. You horny?"

"To be honest, I am. But even if I strike out, I'll think of you and this day as good. After all, the mamasan did not guarantee anything for ten dollars."

"You not get anything in Hong Kong for ten dollar, not even handjob at Won Chow Hotel." They both laughed, and as they laughed, John thought about how true her statement was.

"To think, Firefly, that tomorrow night is Christmas. It will be my first Christmas away from Texas. God, at times I do get homesick. I can remember the smell of the Christmas tree when my father brought it home—freshly cut from the side of a dirt road. Of course, it was just a cedar tree. Spiced tea would flow from hot large kettles while we all wait for Santa Claus. My great aunt Ruby would pound the piano, playing it by ear. I couldn't wait for Santa Claus to arrive."

"You wait for Santa Claus? You be dumbass."

"No, I'm talking about waiting for my father. He would go out in the yard and yell, 'Ho, ho, ho!' It's the cue for the young children to go into the bedroom and give the older ones a chance to bring out the toys."

"Christmas night is good business in the bar. Sailors like to get real drunk and talk about home. Even old ladies get boyfriends."

"I guess that's what Christmas means now to most of us. Boats was saying the other day that the best present he ever received was sex on Christmas night in Sasebo. He bought this hog out of the Black Rose and ..."

"What you mean 'hog'? Is that what you call me later? She working girl just like me. We too have feelings. Boats is a no-good crummy sailor. Smiley say he worse she ever have."

"You've got to be kidding. Smiley? I can't believe she let Boats get to her. Oh wow, that's the best I've heard yet."

"You and Boats two of the same kind."

"I'm sorry. I apologize for what I just said. It's that I'm around that type of language all day on the ship. It's hard to turn some things off." John caught sight of a shell as it reflected the sun's rays. It was intricately carved as though a small creature had taken great pains to sculpt it well. "Look at that shell!" he said.

"That China shell."

"It's beautiful. Why do you call it 'China shell'?"

"Long time ago in Northern China, Dutch ship wreck. Sailor survived. He fell in love with beautiful Chinese girl. He had nothing to give to her so he picked up a beautiful shell on the beach and placed it in her hand. He soon taken home by passing ship but before he left, he promise to come back. He no come back. Gods look down on her and change her into loveliest shell of all."

"That's a moving story. It seems sad that when so beautiful a shell is made, the artist must die and leave his work to be buried by sand. His sculpture is on display for such a short time, and then the sea's indifference covers it. I'm sorry for anyone that is left after a promise is made."

"You not happy now?" Firefly asked.

"Yes, I'm still happy. I imagine that your story of the Chinese girl happens very frequently in Hong Kong. I bet it is especially true in Wan Chai."

"It not happen to me. I never fall in love with sailor."

"Love, I'm afraid, is a destiny that cannot be controlled."

"Yorktown, you wait and see. Firefly no fool."

As they strolled along the beach, John noticed how far apart they now walked. "People are alone too often and even when they are together, they walk apart. I have never believed it improper for one person to hold another's hand." John took her small, frail hand that felt very cold in his. "We touch so infrequently. In America with all its movies and television, we really never know each other. Here in a few days, I have grown to know you better than anyone I have spent many days and nights with. I feel that we are not two separate people, but one as we look upon the same sun and winter-touched mountains. Do you understand what I am saying?"

A smile was her only response as she looked away.

"I was talking about how two people can become like one individual," John said, looking at her lips.

"You crazy American. Buy me beer." As she spoke, she pointed towards an old wooden structure that resembled fractured driftwood that had resurrected itself into a concession stand.

"Let's keep walking past. Look, several people are sitting there anyway. I would feel like a member of a convention and besides, this sand feels good to my feet."

"Buy me beer! Only stingy son of a bitch not buy his girl something to drink."

"Oh shit, might as well." The bench was hard and gritty as though seashells had been partially ground upon its surface. The various odors of the sea were replaced by the cooking aroma emitted by large pots of boiling seafood.

Still feeling horny, John noticed a middle-aged woman who sat with her legs apart while drinking a malt-like beverage. She was the only occupant in the small island of driftwood who smiled at him. The rest of the crowd ignored them.

"Firefly, it's strange that I am sitting here with you having a beer and in just a few days, I'll be helping to kill people I don't even know in a country far away. How foolish that there is a war. Just think how easy it would be to love instead of hate."

"Japanese war no good. Uncle killed in bombing of Hong Kong. He left wife and children to starve," she said. "Why you fight, Johnnie Yorktown?"

"I don't know, and I really mean that. I was told that what I am doing is right. I guess it is. Just think, if not for Vietnam, there would be no business in Wan Chai."

"You Hong Kong bet ya! Business good. I like that. Smiley say that if you and the Brits have more wars, business get even better. I soon be rich girl."

"Well, one thing is sure, your business will always be a good one. If it's not Vietnam, then it will be Cambodia, Burma, or maybe even Thailand."

"Navy officer say Cambodia next. I be rich girl soon. Two front war very profitable. Smiley say it take twice as many carriers."

"Boats said that the Navy uses two types of fuel: Bunker Charlie oil and whiskey. We can get our black oil at sea, but there's no place like Hong Kong for topping off on corn mash," said John. "I wish that broad over there would close her legs."

"What wrong with you? She nice lady."

"I feel that if I look towards you, she'll think I'm looking up her dress. Her probable anger doesn't bother me, but look at that block with her. He looks like he could chop wood with his hands."

No matter how hard John tried, he kept finding himself looking towards the lady who had since stopped smiling, but refused to close her legs. The more he tried to resist temptation, the more small beads of sweat began to break out on top of his head. Since his hair was thinning, it did not require close scrutiny to tell that he was becoming overheated. The more effort he put into relaxing, the more the flow of moisture increased.

"What matter with you, Yorktown? Your head is wet."

John reasoned that if Firefly could see the sweat, the Block could as well. He probably would take the perspiration as an indication of rising desire.

"Yorktown, you worry too much. You must never have known anything bad. You too concerned with things that aren't important. You kind of dumb."

"Thanks for telling me," John said, laughing.

"Lady name Tiger Lee. That her bar name."

"Oh, come on. Don't tell me she works in Wan Chai? No American sailor could get that drunk."

"No. Tiger Lee retired lady. She used to own one of the biggest bars in Wan Chai. Some say she work for Japanese during war. That mean she pretty important person."

"Yah, that's what I would want on my resume."

"What is 'resume'?"

"Firefly, I don't think you will ever have to worry about a resume. That is where you write down all the lies about yourself. In a sense, it is a dream sheet of what you should have been." John paused. "So, she helped the Japanese?"

"She no fool. She charged Japanese top dollar."

"Now what in the world could she tell anyone that would bring more than a few cents?"

"She once real pretty. Important officers off ships her clients. She get them drunk and soon they start talking about home. When they talk about home, they curse Navy and tell how it ruined their marriage. Tiger Lee agree with them and this makes them talk more. Before long, she know where ships are going and when they will arrive. Some say that she even had charts with ship movements on them. She sell charts to Japanese agents. Her friends called her Admiral Lee then. Dumb sailors never figure out why until after war. English get damn mad when Japanese prisoners tell about Tiger Lee. She tell English that Japanese are lying dumbasses. She say no Japanese ever tell truth. English don't believe her."

"What did they do to her?"

"They put her bar off-limits to sailors. Government also make her pay lot of fines. All these problems make her eat. The more problems she had, the bigger she got. Today, she one of biggest women in Hong Kong. There no way she can keep legs together, she too fat."

Tiger Lee smiled again towards John, then moved her enlarged neck to confer with her gentleman friend. After a brief conversation, both of them smiled at each other. To John's great displeasure, her muscular friend got up from his chair and walked towards him.

"Hello, Firefly. How Smiley?" he said loudly.

"Hello, Sam Chan. This my boyfriend, Ensign Yorktown. He wealthy American rancher from Texas. His ranch bigger than Hong Kong."

"Hello, Ensign Yorktown. You lucky man. She prettiest virgin in Hong Kong."

"Well, eh, Sam. I appreciate your congratulations." A moment of silence followed as the two men examined each other. Sam was a large man with exaggerated muscles. He was either extremely large or he bought very small shirts and pants for his garments were stretched like canvas before a gale.

Sam looked at John as an intimate friend might. "I know Firefly virgin. I thought you being sailor must be very horny. My girlfriend, Tiger Lee, she no virgin." At this statement of apparent fact, that John had never once considered to be a theory, they both laughed.

"Sam, you are a fortunate man."

Sam Chan's eyes squinted as a physical manifestation of thinking. "What you mean, fortunate man?"

"Eh, I mean that it is nice to have a girlfriend that's not a virgin." John didn't know why he told Sam how fortunate he was except it was his nature to compliment people that he met, especially if they were a threat. Everyone, he reasoned, needed to feel good and a compliment was totally without expense.

"You like Tiger?" Sam asked.

"Sure, she looks like a nice mature lady. *Oh my lord*, thought John. *Surely he doesn't mean what I think he means.*

"She yours twenty minutes for twenty dollar American."

"Now, really, uh, I would like very much to take you up. She does look nice, but I'm with Firefly, and I don't think it would be polite. Besides, I don't want her reaching for her butterfly knife," stuttered John.

Firefly smiled. "I don't mind. Tiger my friend. You score with her Yorktown, then you not be so horny." There appeared a mischievous spark in Firefly's eyes. It was obvious that no man could desire Tiger once they saw her during the day. It was also obvious that Firefly was enjoying the game. "Yorktown, you no like my friend, then you no like me. Sometime Sam take it personal if a sailor not believe Tiger attractive."

While they discussed Tiger, she smiled in their direction. Her cheery expression looked as though it had been created by animation.

"Sam, I have two problems. One of my biggest difficulties is that I am running out of money, and the other problem is of a technical nature, like where am I supposed to take Tiger? You did say I had only twenty minutes?"

"Old British ambulance back of restaurant still have stretcher in it. Firefly say you big wealthy Texan. Did you tell her lie?" He provided the appropriate physical emphasis by flexing his huge muscles, making them ripple like shallow water over sand.

"No, I didn't lie. You see wealthy people never carry money with them."

Sam's breath began to be expelled from his body like steam from a straining locomotive. "What you mean, rich people never carry money?"

"People who have money use charge cards. That's why a man is real dumb to rob a rich man on the street. Only poor people carry cash."

"You carry charge cards. That okay. You give credit card to me, and I take to friend. He take Texaco card. Other friend, he take Mobil card. He write Tiger up as 'gas' and 'lube job.'"

This can't be happening to me, thought John. *Look at Firefly over there smiling. What on earth can I do to get out of this one? If I were in a lifeboat for a hundred days, I couldn't get it up for Tiger. And he gives me twenty minutes! That would require a miracle, and you can't put those on credit cards. Another problem is how to know that he will* only write up the 'gas' and 'lube' job? He might also write up an oil change, a tune up, and maybe even a set of tires. *This just can't happen to me!*

Firefly looked towards John with sparkling eyes. "Hurry up Yorktown, I not spend all day waiting on you." Firefly then leaned towards John as an indication that her next words would demand privacy. "It not polite to refuse Sam. He loves Tiger very much. Besides, he bigger than you."

John drew Firefly closer to him. "It's not the twenty dollars I'm worried about. It's the fact that I can't get sexually excited about her. No way! I remember a friend of mine who got into a similar situation down in TJ. He couldn't get an erection. That infuriated the girl. Just about cost him his life. Look at that ape over there, he could bend me into."

"Yorktown, you got no choice, honor involved now."

"Shit!" John then turned towards Sam and Tiger with a smile on his face. The smile concealed the fact that his hands were sweating and that his head felt dizzy. "Okay, here's my credit card."

John leaned towards Firefly. "Pray that I can do it." Her reply was laughter that followed him all the way to Tiger.

Tiger took his sweating hand in a vice-like grip and led him as an overweight majorette would lead a band. With each stride, her grip grew tighter and his legs grew weaker. He did not need to turn around to see if Sam was watching. He could feel his stare stabbing his back.

The wrecked ambulance was a 1938 black Packard that had suffered a head-on collision several years prior to his ship's arrival. It had probably been wrecked carrying a patient to the infirmary. Two head prints added a sculptured effect to the front windshield, while a cracked chrome swan swooned on the curled hood.

Tiger looked at John and grinned. "Not Hong Kong Hilton but fine for short time."

"Now look, Tiger, I'm really not in any mood for making love. I am worn out, and the last few days in port have cost a lot. Now you know I am sort of wealthy, but my inheritance doesn't become effective for a few more months."

As he spoke, Tiger clawed at his pants. "Hey, you are ripping my new shirt! The material is caught in the fly." Now he was not only afraid, but disgusted that his cheap new shirt, bought at the Navy Exchange in Yokosuka, had been shredded by his own zipper. It was also evident that he would never be able to zip up his pants again. "Wait a minute!"

Instead of pulling his worn out boxer shorts down in the appropriate manner, she was trying to rip them off in an animal-like fashion of primitive lust.

"Hurry up, Yorktown. Tiger very busy and important lady. Haven't got all day to fuck in ambulance."

"Okay, okay." Soon his ripped and frayed clothing lay in a pile on the Packard's dust and oil-soaked floorboard.

"Hey, Sam!" Tiger called. "He smaller than you."

John felt the blood surge in his head. "Come on, Tiger, you don't have to shout about it."

"We gonna have to get thing larger," she said, laughing.

"Watch it! Hey there. That hurts. What in hell? This isn't going to work."

"You no good! What wrong with you? You queer?"

"Hell, no. I'm just a damn fool."

"You only candy ass on ship."

"Hey, go easy on that thing. Don't tell me you've serviced the entire *Hyman*."

"I work harbor for many year. Not many sailor not know Tiger Lee. Me start out painting sides of ships with Sally. See, it does work. Hey Sam!"

"You call Tiger?" Sam replied.

"He alive now."

"That the way Tiger," he reassured her.

The simulated lust lasted for only a moment. "Yorktown, you one hell of a sailor. You best lay Tiger have in many year. Never before have sailor excited Tiger so much. You even better than Boats."

John walked back to where Firefly and Sam were waiting. Both of them looked at him and smiled. It was strange, but he believed that Sam's smile contained a degree of admiration.

Firefly laughed. "See, Yorktown? You no longer horny. I never tell you wrong."

His sense of responsibility returned. "Sam, don't lose that credit card and be sure and return it to Firefly. Remember, we agreed only to a 'gas and lube job.'"

"I no forget."

As quickly as they had appeared into his world, Sam and Tiger vanished. Tiger had accomplished her mission and could go home and rest from her labors, and Sam could manipulate John's credit card.

"Firefly, I tell you, I've had it for today. You go back to the bar. I'm heading back to the ship and hit the rack." It was odd that Firefly did not protest as she would on other occasions. It might have been the fact that a new carrier had just pulled into port early that afternoon. Money would soon be flowing through the streets. No smart B-girl would want to be anywhere else but in Wan Chai that night

For the first time since John had been aboard the ship, she was truly a welcoming sight. It was mostly because he was fatigued, but also because he wanted a hot shower. Fuller had told him that the first thing a sailor should do after getting laid was to "dip his wick in some wine and then race to a hot shower." That way he would never catch anything but the crabs, and he had bedded some real animals.

John threw his shorts and shirt on the stateroom deck and made a beeline for the shower. To his horror, the only water working was the hot water that would more properly be called live steam. He found it relieving to curse his environment. "This fucking Navy is alright! This fucking Navy is alright!" he shouted as he danced in the cloud of super-heated moisture.

"Hey Yorktown, are you talking to the pipes?" Tom had entered the head just in time to hear his curses.

"Tom, I tell you, I've had one afternoon that is too bad to be true. A fat whore called Tiger Lee raped me in a junked '38 black Packard ambulance."

"You're shittin' me? Not Tiger! Oh man, I can't believe this. Come on, don't tell me you got to Tiger, or did she get to you? I thought you were with Firefly. Now don't tell me, Firefly took you to an old shack over on Repulse Bay?"

"Yah, that's right."

"Shit man, being baptized by Tiger is the first step in becoming a real China sailor."

"How did you hear of Tiger?"

"Yorktown, am I a China sailor or not?"

"Tom, you are. How else could you have sunk so low morally?"

"You see, it's a romantic story. Tiger was a real beauty back when Boats was a teenager. He claims that Tiger got his cherry. Anyway, after a few decades her beauty failed her and by that time the British had closed her bar for helping the Japanese."

"A few decades, hell! Let's say more like half a century," said John without smiling.

Tom continued, "She finally found a new job at China East Bar. One of the bartenders named Sam Fong fell in love with her, but he never stood a chance until she got fat and became pockmarked after catching smallpox. Then the bar fired her since not even a drunk sailor could mistake her for a beauty. Well, when she left the bar, Sam left with her. They moved out to Repulse Bay."

"Firefly's version is that she owned one of the largest bars in Hong Kong."

"Which story is better to tell a loser—hers or mine?" asked Tom.

"Okay, that explains their geographical location, but why did Firefly take me to that old shack? What has she got in it? Surely she doesn't expect a three-way cut on a 'gas and lube job.'"

"You got a gas and lube job? I got a tire fixed," said Tom, laughing.

"Are you shittin' me?" asked John.

"No kidding! The girls in Wan Chai are a compassionate lot. Compassionate with each other, that is. Tiger has no income except what the girls can hustle for her. I'd go as far as to say that no sailor has ever been to the Bay without getting laid by Tiger Lee. You followed in the footsteps of thousands."

"Surely someone must have refused her?" asked John.

"Are you kidding? One fellow tried and nearly succeeded, but I think he regretted his attempt. He just flat told her no and then made a remark about how she looked. Then she screams out that he pinched her. Lo and behold, the next thing he remembers is being hit by something like a blackjack. Sam had obviously defended her honor. Can you guess what the sailor did next? Well, he got up and apologized for having pinched Tiger, and you bet he ended up in the old Packard, after all."

"Tom, tell me again—does washing off help you to not get VD?"

"Well, Yorktown, it would have been pretty effective had you worn a Sheik, but the best thing to do now is to cut the damn thing off."

"Wiseass! Do you know what happened to the water on this fucking ship? A while ago it was scalding my ass and now only a small amount of hot water is oozing from the showerhead."

"Yorktown, on a ship there is either no hot water, no cold water, or no water at all. Just dip what remains of it in a bottle of rubbing alcohol and call it quits. They have plenty of alcohol in sickbay."

"You know, Fuller, every now and then you come up with a good idea, but I bet sickbay is closed."

"Don't worry, just go to the CDO and ask him for the key. By the way, don't forget to soak your balls. Man, once the crabs get to them, you have a problem."

"Yah, I kind of know." John found the CDO asleep in his bunk. Smitty was nearly always hyper when fully awake so it came as no surprise when, upon being awakened, he shouted, "What? What? Where am I? How bad is it?"

"Smitty, it's Ensign Yorktown. I need to get the key to the sickbay."

"Oh, you. What the hell do you need the key for? Can't it wait?"

"No, sir. I think I'm about to come down with one of the most itching rashes imaginable. Fuller was telling me that he had one like it when he was in the Philippines. The doctor told him that the only thing to do was to soak the irritation in rubbing alcohol before it spread to the crew."

"Yorktown, my Lord, just go get the corpsman to let you in. We have enough crud on this ship as it is!"

"Who's the duty corpsman?"

"Oh shit. I don't know. Just take my fucking key and get the hell out of here so I can sleep. One thing though," he added with a yawn, "don't unlock anything else in there. One misplaced Band-Aid, and we'll have to inventory the whole damn place."

John slid the key into the lock, but the door wouldn't budge. The key would turn the lock halfway and no more. He pushed and strained, but the door only persisted the more in not moving.

"Mr. Yorktown, you need some assistance?" Boat's words rode the crest of a hangover's breath.

"Yah, the damn door won't open!"

"Sir, you got to lift up and turn to the left, but do it in two jerks. There you go." Instead of standing to one side and letting John enter after the completion of his magic trick, Boats blocked the doorway with his belly. "Sir, you didn't catch any social disease? I heard about one ship where a junior officer slipped into sickbay in order to give himself a shot of penicillin, at least he claimed it was penicillin, if you know what I mean. If you got something, I know a drugstore over in Kowloon that will fix you up just fine."

"There's one thing I'll never do and that is give myself a shot of anything. But I'll be happy to stick a needle up your ass, that is, if you develop any social disease," said John without concealing his anger.

"Now, no point in getting sore, sir. I was just joking. Everybody I've talked to today has gotten mad. The whole damn world has been fortin' on me." Boats then left sickbay and slowly walked down the passageway, careful not to spill his freshly poured, steaming coffee on the deck.

As John closed the door, he heard Boats say, "Abato, you fucker, watch where you're going."

To John's surprise, it was not difficult to find the bottle of rubbing alcohol. It was one of the few containers that was clearly labeled. He decided that in order for him to douse himself properly, it was necessary to lean over the sink. "If any crab can survive rubbing alcohol, well, power to him."

John positioned himself over the lavatory and began to pour. At first the liquid felt good and cold, but suddenly—

"Ah e-e-eoh!" Such agony he had never experienced before. It felt like he was wearing a jockstrap made of jellyfish tentacles. It was impossible for him not to scream again, "Ah e-e-eoh!"

He couldn't stand still. Out of instinct he began to dance in a small circle. Suddenly outside the sickbay, he could hear people running and shouting, "It sounds like we've been boarded!"

Another voice shouted, "Did you hear the chemical alarm?"

A reply came back, "Hell no, I was in the shower and someone said we were being attacked!"

John raced to splash water upon himself and get his pants up. The water eased some of the pain but certainly not all of it. He finished zipping up just as the door to the sickbay burst open.

"Did you hear anything?" the CDO said between gasps of air. "I think we've been boarded!"

"Yes sir. I heard a scream. It sounded like it came from the weather deck. My Lord, do you think they got one of our sentries?" asked John.

"Keep me informed, Mr. Yorktown. Why in the world did the Captain pick this evening to go shopping?" Smitty vanished from the sickbay while cursing his luck and the communists.

In less than a minute after the CDO's hasty departure, the word was passed over the 1MC: "Away the In-port Emergency Team."

Another voice was then heard faintly over the 1MC: "Damn it, I said away the In-port Boarding Team."

A private but very public argument then ensured.

"Sir, that ain't right."

"Damn it, just pass it the way I told you to."

The quartermaster's voice sounded throughout the ship. "Yes sir! Now hear this, away the Boarding and Assistance Team. Conduct a search of the ship for suspected boarders. Report same to the bridge." It was followed by a faint reply from Smitty: "Shit!"

As John listened to the confrontation between the quartermaster and Smitty, it became clear that Tom had played a prank on him. He couldn't believe he had fallen for it. But, in his own defense, how could he have known that rubbing alcohol would feel like acid on his genitals?

John heard the door to the sickbay opening and just as he turned, he saw Fuller emerge through the hatch. "Yorktown, I wanted to check out the space and make sure that no boarders were in here with you."

"Go to hell, fucker!"

"What's the matter, John? The ship is under attack and you're telling your best friend to go to hell? Come to think of it, you don't look too well. Maybe that's it. You're not responsible for what you are saying. As a matter of fact, you even have sweat on top your head. Sure sign of crab-antis."

"Are you kidding? I'm sweating all over. I bet you'd be perspiring too if you had just stuck your damn balls in acid."

"No, John, I didn't say it wouldn't hurt. All I said was that it would irritate the crabs."

"I'm going back to Wan Chai. At least my guard's up there," said John.

"Yeah, there's no place safer than the beach. That is, if you can stay out of Packards. By the way, you might want to stop by the drugstore over in Kowloon, you know, the one that Boats uses."

CHAPTER TWENTY

Tiger Balm Garden

The early signs of evening were settling upon Hong Kong as John arrived outside Bar G. I. Joe. It was that dim and indistinct period between the sun's illumination and the time of glowing neon lights. Even Wan Chai seemed quieter and lonelier at this time. The *Hyman* had been in port several days and not many of the sailors could afford to leave the ship before late evening. Already the rumor concerning how broke *Hyman* sailors were had spread throughout Wan Chai. On the returning bam-bam boats, some of the sailors mentioned how the girls showed little interest in them while the early afternoon cabarets consumed the eager crew of the newly arrived carrier.

After entering Bar G. I. Joe, John took a few minutes for his eyes to adjust to the dim light. Shapes appeared gradually. Near the bar, Firefly was leaning over an English sailor. It was apparent that she had been successful in obtaining several tokens for her effort. John could not help but feel a small amount of jealousy. Somehow he had hoped that she would instinctively sense his presence. It was not long before reason ruled. After all, this was how she made a living. It did, however, seem like an eternity, measured in lady cocktails, before she noticed him.

"Hello, Yorktown. I thought you go to ship for evening. You typical sailor. Can't stay away from Wan Chai." He could not deny that fact; it was true that Wan Chai appealed to him. *What is it about the lights, the sounds, and the girls with slit dresses?* he asked himself only to reply: *Oh I know, the girls with slit dresses.*

"What you drink?" asked Firefly.

"Oh no, not this early. Let me sit awhile and build up my thirst. I drank a Pepsi before I left the ship."

"You son of a bitch, the mamasan throw you out. If she not kick your ass, Firefly do it herself."

"Make it a tall beer, and I mean a tall beer." At least suds would last a long time, and it didn't cost as much as the other poisons. He looked around the bar and noticed a lot of new faces. Already the younger sailors from the carrier were being pumped dry of their money and made drunk at the same time. He watched one beginner reach into his pocket and bring forth a large wad of bills that he didn't bother to count. Without any hesitation, he placed them into Firefly's hand. She merely smiled and disappeared behind the bar to count the money. From John's angle, he watched her sort the bills and add five red tokens to her ring. *Wow, that fool just bought her five lady cocktails. He'll be lucky if he even gets a beer in return.*

In less than a minutes after Firefly left with her booty, the sailor placed his head on the table and went to sleep. He was only asleep ten minutes when the shore patrol took him off. *Poor fellow,* thought John. *He must not have known it was illegal to sleep in a Wan Chai bar."*

The beer tasted bad, but John forced himself to drink it. He was beginning to learn the trick about timing your drink. Some China sailors could make one beer last three hours. That is, when they were about to go broke. Of course, the girls never looked at them, but maybe it was enough to sit in the dark and remember when you had all the money in the world and every B-girl thought you the most handsome swabbie in Wan Chai.

Before long, John needed to make a head call. The head smelled of vomit and beer that was unusual for so early in the evening. As he excused himself, he read the want ad section above the urinal: IF YOU NEED BLOW JOB, TAP YOUR FOOT. Just as he was reading the advertisement, someone began tapping his foot. At first the tap was soft, and then it grew louder. John became so self-conscious that he couldn't urinate which made it appear that he was either an exhibitionist, a narcissist sailor, a voyeur, or a homosexual. In order to exit gracefully, he flushed the urinal and left with his zipper snagged on the cloth of his trousers.

After taking a few fast gulps of his beer, he watched the bathroom door to see who would appear, but no one exited. He knew it was necessary for him to stop thinking about needing to go, but it was very difficult to do so while drinking beer. He knew better than to leave the bar in order to urinate. They always removed your bottle the moment you left, and the mother had cost him a buck fifty.

"Yorktown, you not drink beer. You sick?" asked Firefly in a caring manner.

"Listen, Firefly, there's a guy in the head tapping his foot."

"So what?"

"Oh, you don't read bathroom walls? Well, he wants a blow job and his tapping is an invitation."

"What you want me to do about it? He customer too!"

"I don't want you to do anything about it. I just wanted you to understand why I am not drinking very fast."

"You go in private ladies' room. It used only by hostesses. No one tap foot in there."

"Oh sure. Thanks a lot. That ought to get me a General Discharge. What I really want you to do is hurry your ass up. Let's get out of here so I can go to the bathroom before I explode."

"You cross your legs. This busy time in Wan Chai. Not often carrier come in right after payday. Sailors not have time to send money back to States. I work to nine and then we go."

"2100? Hell, that's another hour," said John, frustrated.

"You go get coffee at Neptune Café. It only cost you fifteen cents. Don't talk to waitress name Donna. She no good. She whore."

"I guess it's a novel approach to work the restaurants now," said John.

"She gets to keep everything. She work for old dumbass. She lay him once a month."

"Wow, there's a girl with business savvy."

The Neptune Café was located above a candle and butcher shop. As John approached the entrance, a blend of raw meat and scented candles greeted him. From the street, the stairway was dimly lit. He would not have gone up except for the noise. The main attraction was that many of the sounds were women's voices.

As he stood waiting to be seated, he noticed the view of the harbor. It was easy to recognize the Star Ferry boats by the rapid motion of their lights as they steamed back and forth across the harbor on their way to Kowloon. It was a chilly night, and he thought about how good the warmth of the café felt. *A warm fire, a girl, a cold beer, and a warm bed—wow, that's what liberty should be!*

The Neptune Café was certainly a lower-class restaurant, but situated right in the middle of the floor was a bilingual sign: WAIT FOR WAITRESS. He thought this was simply another ruse for someone to get a tip. He knew, however, that it was necessary to play the game if he expected to get a menu during the evening.

Fortunately, his waiting was shorter than he had expected. A young girl in her late teens started to approach him when, all of a sudden, she dropped her pack of cigarettes. As she knelt down to pick it up, the center slit—a novelty in Hong Kong—in her dress opened to reveal her beautiful legs and a portion of her black panties. The cigarettes had rolled into different directions that forced her to readjust her position several times. After she had finished her task, she looked up at John and smiled. A smile that made his throat go completely dry.

"Hello sailor, you want table by window? Beautiful view of harbor. Very romantic spot for you and girlfriend."

"Oh no, I'm alone," replied John.

"Handsome sailor should not be alone in Wan Chai."

"Yah, well, I just got into port today, off one of the carriers. Yesterday was payday. I shouldn't have left the ship tonight before sending my allotment check back to my old lady in Texas."

"Why not?" Her eyes narrowed.

"Oh, I spend every damn cent I make. Can't control myself," said John who could hear his heart beating in his ears.

"I'm very glad to meet you." Her eyes opened wide and her voice was cheery. It was as though they had been hoping to run into each other for several days. "My name Donna."

"Donna, that's a very attractive name." John looked her anatomy over as he spoke in order to convey a visual compliment. Her breasts and body appeared to be so firm that one would swear she was wearing armor under her garment.

"What you want?" asked Donna.

John had to pause a moment before answering, "Oh, let's start out with a tall beer. I mean a tall beer."

"Beer not good for you. You start with cocktail. It got class. You need class."

"Yah, well, make it a big cocktail." It was obvious that he was speaking to a lady that demanded good taste in her men. She then bent over the table and began to clean it with a soiled-looking rag.

It was strange but in the dim light, the surface of the table appeared to be spotless. As she scrubbed its cleanliness, the opening of her blouse exposed her large breasts, which also seemed to be buffing the table top as they shuffled back and forth in her loose bra. "Eh, Donna, make that a double. I'm getting awfully dry." She looked at him and smiled.

The hour that John had been assigned to wait for Firefly passed by too swiftly. Donna managed to spill her cigarettes two more times, but each occasion was for the benefit of swabs who were handsome and obviously officer material. John felt that he had been chosen as a member of a very elite corps. He felt disappointed when 2100 arrived, for he would have enjoyed seeing which one of them finally won the dubious honor of paying for a night's worth of her pleasure. He felt that he was surely in the lead since he had mentioned his problem of not being able to control his spending habit.

John decided to take his time arriving at Bar G. I. Joe. From his experience, he knew that Firefly would be late in leaving the bar. "God, how lonely the streets can be," he said out loud to himself. Time hung patiently by on each street corner. If he ever decided to prolong his life, he would take up loitering on streets and in parks for then it would have seemed that he had lived forever. Finally his path along the circumference of the earth led him back to the bar.

There he found Firefly's friend, Molly Hochan, still adding more tokens to her tab. He walked over to her and interrupted her passage from one table to the cash register.

"Where is Firefly?" he asked.

"She sick," Molly replied.

"She was just fine when I left an hour ago," replied John.

"Firefly not well. She did not want you to know. She want you to be happy and not worry about her."

"Not worry about her? How in the world could I not be?"

"She tell me to be your friend tonight. She will be better tomorrow, Firefly said to tell you."

John did not know what to think. He knew she was sick often, but should he believe her tonight?

"Okay, Molly, so it's your turn to entertain me." John did not really want to be with Molly. Even though he found her attractive, he longed for Firefly's company that evening. As Molly moved from table to table, he could not help but admire her ability to hustle drinks.

She felt him staring at her. "You not rush me! It good night. I have plenty money when night over."

"Jeez, come on now! I've drunk coffee, beer, and two two-dollar-and-fifty-cent cocktails while waiting for Firefly. I even turned down a fine piece just to be with her. Man, I must be out of my mind."

"You mean Donna pull cigarette trick on you?" asked Molly.

"Now wait a minute. That wasn't any trick. She just happened to spill a few cigarettes on the floor."

She laughed. "Firefly say you sure not China sailor yet. Donna think all young officers are wealthy. You too stingy to be wealthy."

"Thanks a lot. I'm not tipping you tonight, and that will cook your ass."

"You go be nice creep and have another beer. I get off at midnight and then I do like Firefly say, entertain you."

"Just hang it on the wall if you think I'm going to wait. At least Donna puts out. Hey, that's an idea! So far the only action I've gotten from being around Firefly is getting raped by a female wrestler in the backseat of an old wrecked ambulance."

Molly looked at him sternly. "Donna no good whore! You

buy me out of bar—give me twenty-five dollar extra and I go now."

"Wow, what a bargain. One thing is certain: I'll be screwed at least once tonight."

Her eyes flashed. "You not want me. You go to Donna!"

"Okay, okay. If I strike out tonight, I swear I'm going to invest all my money in a brothel and give up on you B-girls. At least there you don't wait hundreds of hours and hear the same Patty Page or Skeeter Davis record over and over. Oh, I forgot, I have also heard 'Auld Lang Syne' played around seventy-five times. What is it with that song? Does anyone know what it means?"

"Yorktown, you just dumb enough to go to whorehouse. I scared to screw you. You probably already fuck girls there. You know Boats, he stupid once just like you before he became true China sailor. He give up Wan Chai bars and go to whorehouse. I remember sitting in Bar G. I. Joe one Sunday afternoon. No carrier in port, quiet like Wan Chai get when no heavies anchor. Anyway, I hear moan in men's room. I no remember anyone in bar."

"Oh hell, I bet it was a rat with the clap. I remember the first night I ate here, I saw a rat the size of a waiter walk, not run, by."

"No, I serious. Mamasan kill old rat anyway."

"One thing that bothers me is how the hell did anyone get past your radar? You seem to be able to ping off dollar bills like a sub does off the bottom." John laughed.

"I sleep in booth." She smiled at John's admiration of her money-making capabilities. "I couldn't figure out why man groan so loud so I go look."

"That figures," said John.

"When I open door, I see Boats holding onto water pipe

with one hand and trying to hit the water with other. I then hear cussing like no China sailor ever say before."

"Well, what was wrong?"

"You not know symptoms of the shanks?"

"Stop being clinical. What the hell was wrong?"

"He got what Boats later called 'Luther Rot.'"

"Only a damn Catholic uses the word 'Luther' when referring to his equipment. I didn't know Boats was religious."

"What you mean?"

"Oh never mind, just get on with the 'Luther Rot.'"

"He get it bad," she said in a serious tone.

"I take it that the moral of this story is, don't dip the wick in the local hoses."

"You Hong Kong bet ya!" She laughed.

"Now this had been a story with a moral. Just think of all the pain that you have saved me from. That could have been me holding on to a pipe with one hand and Luther with the other. Wow, I bet that does sting. I'll have to ask Boats if there are ever any flare-ups. You have to be careful about seconds."

The night air felt good outside the bar. Molly did not speak to John as they waited for the cabs that would not stop. John assumed that they were waiting to see which one of them would have the courage to step out in front of a taxi. As they waited, she hummed "Hush, Hush, Sweet Charlotte." Something in the way she hummed indicated that she was really pissed off.

John looked at her. "You got your money, what's wrong now?" He was worried that he would not get anything after paying for her to get out of the bar.

"Tonight is good night in bar," she replied without taking her eyes off the approaching cars. "I should not have left with you."

"What do you mean a 'good night'? Shit! The traffic had really slowed when I was walking back from Neptune Café—and I might add that is the place where I should be right now. It was almost safe to run across the street."

"You got no sense. British soldiers come when American sailors not on liberty. They know how to treat a lady. They not have lot of money to spend, but they show respect."

"Bullshit! All I can say is that they must be another group of dumbasses." John started to add more comments, but Molly turned to him and lightly rubbed her hip against his fly while laughing. "Forgive me, sometimes I take out my frustrations on the wrong person."

"I forgive if you be good now," said Molly.

"Say let's go someplace different tonight. A place that no tourist has gone before."

Molly's only reply was a smile as she stepped in front of a speeding taxi.

The drive was a short one. Sometimes he liked it when taxi drivers took their time even if it was at his expense. He found himself often journeying to places that were not worth going to, much less hurrying for. Tonight, however, he was glad that the excursion had not been a lengthy one.

"What's this?" John asked, staring at two large gargoyle-like statues. He looked at her and said in amazement, "I never thought hell was at the end of a flight of concrete steps."

"It Tiger Balm Garden. One of most beautiful sites in Hong Kong."

"Well, maybe it looks better up close." It was true that in the Orient, evil spirits were often discouraged from entering a beautiful place by planting grotesque gods at the entrance. "Why are you all looking at me?" Then it dawned on John that he hadn't paid the driver yet. "Yah, just a second, let me find my money." He had to take out his credit cards and a picture of his parents in order to find a ten-dollar bill that he had neatly folded for emergencies.

Small beads of sweat began to magnify on his forehead. *He'll never have change for a ten*, he thought. "Here you are, sir. I hope you have change for ten." Molly took over before the driver reached for the money. She spoke harshly to the driver who immediately agreed with her. He searched in his pants pockets and handed her a roll of uncounted bills. She took the roll from his hand and held the money up to the light provided by a nearby shop window.

She then exchanged words with the taxi driver which resulted in another extensive search of his pants pockets. A compromise was finally reached and the driver sped off after Molly and John had disembarked from the cab. It was apparent that Molly preferred that the bulk of John's money be spent on her and not on a greedy taxi driver.

John was wrong about the guardian gods being only at the entrance. The designer of this dream intended that no evil spirits should be found in any area of the garden.

"Remind me never to come here when I'm depressed," John said with a degree of sincerity.

"You not sensitive to art. Rich Chinaman built garden many years ago."

"Where did he get the money?" asked John, looking at the statues.

"He sell Tiger Balm medicine. It cure anything. You got bile problem, it clean your liver."

"Well, my bile has been acting up lately. Is there any alcohol in the stuff? We can get it on the ship as a medicine. Remind me to check on the regs when I get back. I could clear up the ship's bile problems if there's enough alcohol."

"Chinaman help many people, he not bootlegger."

"I bet he helped them just like my uncle did back in Hugo, Oklahoma. He made a small fortune selling Mo-I-Can to the Negros and Indians. One swig of Mo-I-Can and you raced to the privy. Back then if a medicine worked, it did two things: it made you tippy and it gave you diarrhea. If it didn't do either, it didn't sell. Mo-I-Can could do both. I remember my uncle telling me about the time he visited Broken Bow, Oklahoma to resupply his customers. He was walking past this old ladies' house when a thunderous voice sounded from the privy, 'If I ever gets outta here, I'm gonna hit you upside the head. You hear me, Mr. Percy? Upside de head is what I says.'

"'What ails you there, Mabel?' my uncle shouted back with a voice so loud that the chickens around the outhouse scattered.

"'I'm out here when my man gets up in the morning and when he goes to bed, I's still out here.' You know Molly, a week later my uncle sold Mabel another bottle of Mo-I-Can."

"Did your uncle own big medicine company like rich

Chinaman?"

"I don't know what your standards of wealth are, but he did own a big cast-iron pot that sat in the middle of his backyard. That was the Mo-I-Can Company, or as you might say, the kettle of the enterprise."

A horn honked, bringing John's mind back to Tiger Balm Garden. "I hate to say it, but this place has the same effect on me as work does. Now don't get me wrong, I appreciate the fine art, but you have to admit that it was designed to lead to repentance rather than to rejoicing. I've had my share of repentance ever since I joined this man's Navy, and now I'm ready for my share of rejoicing."

"Johnnie, you good man. You awfully nice to Firefly. I give you little tonight." Her eyes looked more mischievous than lustful. She continued, "You leave this week. I not want fine American sailor to leave Hong Kong without good memory."

John took her small hand in his and led her to where he hoped to find a taxi. "I could never ask Firefly to lose her virginity to me after she had saved it for so long," John confided.

Molly looked up at him. "I too planned on being virgin when I marry, but that not important now. What is important is that I make you happy. I not give myself to anyone else on *Hyman*. Not to Boats, that fucker, not to Mr. Fuller."

"Hey, look over there. Well, I'll be damned, if it isn't a parked taxi," said John in amazement.

"See? You have good night already. Not have to look all over city for ride."

John opened the door so fast that he startled the sleeping driver who immediately assumed a defensive position as though he were used to being hit. "Tell him that all we want is a ride and not his wallet. Talk about a guilty conscience, just look at that face."

Molly leaned towards him and reassured the driver that all they wanted was a ride. His fearful expression broke into a smile that only the thought of a profit could have induced. The driver did not wait for any explanation but floorboarded the taxi. John instantly recalled that most drivers would travel in a straight line just as fast as they could go while he attempted to explain his desired destination. If he was slow in explaining his intention, his bill would soon be very high.

Tom remembered his search for the Imperial Palace in Tokyo. No matter what he did, the driver could not figure out what emperor he was talking about. In other words, John had learned never to give directions while underway.

"Say, shouldn't we have told him where we are going? He looks like he's on a course for China, and I'm paying the fare."

"Oh, I sorry. I forgot. I tell him now." She leaned over the seat and carried on a rapid conversation with the driver. The taxi squealed to a halt in the street, then shot into an alley and burned off in the direction that they had just passed through.

"I'll be a son of a gun, we're heading back to where we started." John's voice carried a tone of frustration.

"Johnnie, you not get mad. It my fault. He nice driver," assured Molly.

"Come on, how in the world do you know he's a nice driver?"

"He friend of Smiley Hochan."

Wow, that's a great recommendation, John thought.

"Johnnie, look! There is a jewelry store open. Let's stop."

Without any further discussion, she shouted to Smiley's friend. The taxi plowed to a halt, sending those walking in the road scurrying away.

"Now wait a minute, at least tell him to cut his meter off while you look around... I mean, 'window-shop.'"

"Not allowed to cut meter off. Strong union in Hong Kong."

"Jeez, here we go again. Tell Uncle Ho to keep the buggy close by because we won't be long."

"You no worry. He understand."

They entered the store without any preliminary warm-up in front of the display windows. The store was as brilliantly lit as an operating table and as clean. The beauty of the individual gemstones was lost in the massive collection of the displays. As John leaned over the glass cases and noticed the prices, his enthusiasm about the evening weakened. Every three or four paces produced a cue for her to say, "Umm, isn't that lovely?"

She pointed towards a beautiful necklace that suddenly lost its anonymity in the delicate hands of the clerk. Molly quickly put it on and admired the necklace.

"Wow, ummm, isn't that lovely," said John after a very brief glance.

"Johnnie, it's so pretty. This is necklace that Firefly wanted me to tell you about. She never be happy until she get it. No other girl in bar have so good a necklace. They think Firefly very special if you buy it for her."

"Well, maybe that is something I can put five dollars away each month for." Despair crept back into him for he had the feeling that the logic of Benjamin Franklin concerning the saving of a penny a day was not going to work in Kim Fac's Jewelry.

"You do not understand. Necklace have no meaning unless lover give it to you. Even whore at Bar Neptune was bought ring. Firefly lose face if you no buy."

"Molly, exactly how much does that cost?"

"Oh, in American dollar, maybe ninety, no, maybe ninety dollar and ninety-nine cents with tax."

"Now wait a minute. I haven't got anything like that on me. I don't suppose they'll take a check from the Bank of Canton, Texas?"

"You real dumbass. They take Mobil credit card."

"Oh come on, not again."

"Either you buy, or Firefly find someone that will. Fuller, he better looking than you. He not stingy ass either."

John was, for a brief moment, tempted to tell her to get Tom to buy the necklace for Firefly. The memory of how much he had already invested in her bothered him. He thought of all the lady cocktails and beer he had purchased, not to mention the number of times he had bought her out of the bar.

John knew that the ship was leaving soon for Yankee Station in the South China Sea and that he might never again get a chance like this one. The decision-making conflict continued. He would need the money for graduate school if he ever managed to get admitted to a good one. For that brief moment, however, graduate school did not seem as important as his desire for Firefly. "Okay, I'll tell you what I'll do. I'll buy it for her on the way back. How about that?"

"What you mean, buy it for her on the way back? You think

I haven't learned anything in Wan Chai? Sailor never buy girl anything after he finish with her."

"Okay, here's the credit card."

"Okay," she said, smiling at her victory.

"Now that you have the prize, I'm curious about one thing. Is the jeweler a relative of Firefly?

"Oh, no. He no relative. Never seen him before in my life."

Outside it began to rain. At first the drops were small and scattered but before long turned into a downpour. People ran for shelter. The street odors hid from the rain and even Hong Kong smelled clean. They were both soaking by the time he successfully hailed a taxi. The cab's wipers beat a sleepy rhythm and for a moment John remembered slumbering in the backseat of his family's 1948 black Packard on long trips during which it never failed to rain.

The road they took was a familiar one that led over the mountain to the fishing village of Aberdeen. Unfortunately, its odors had not retreated from the rain. The taxi pulled up before a deteriorating wooden pier. A fishing hut sat precariously on the edge of the wharf. It was a small wooden frame structure that had never known paint.

"Molly, I hate to say it, but I had rather be in a Holiday Inn with a view of the pool. It's not exactly warm this evening."

"This my father's house. We live here when I was young. This house lived in by my family for many years before typhoon. I haven't been back since the storm. I wanted to see if still here. Firefly want you to spend money on me and not on expensive hotel room."

"You are right, it does look like a typhoon hit here. I mean, like the living room was the eye of the storm." Luckily the rain had stopped and overhead moonlight suddenly appeared through the breaking clouds.

"I thought we were going to make love. Well, eh, at least that is what I thought before I saw this place. You know, you are right. My gift to Firefly is beautiful when seen by moonlight," said John to Molly who continued to model the necklace.

"I lost my cherry in ancestral home."

How can this be an ancestral home when it's probably built out of shipping crates? John had thought about making love in the Hong Kong Hilton on clean, softened 100-count sheets after a nice soaking bath, the water oozing with the fragrance of an expensive bath oil. At the present moment, the cold dampness was supplying him with a nice case of the itch, and it sounded as though the mosquitoes that had been spelunking had now found the ear cavern.

"First thing lover do is relax. You all tense. I read book by Jacqueline Susann. She wrote *Valley of the Dolls*. She know how it is done."

Without another word, she put her arms around his neck and pulled him close. Her breast felt like metal cups against his chest. He wondered if it was some support bra she had on. At first he tried to maintain a long kiss by bending over, but the kiss was longer than he had planned and his back began to hurt. He then pulled her thin body up to him in order to ease the strain. As he held her, a very large mosquito lit on the entrance of his ear and began to bore in.

"Wait, wait just a moment. There's a mosquito in my ear." With one hand, John held her tightly and with the other he hit the side of his own head. "Man, I think I got it."

She pulled him down to what was left of an old couch. While still completely dressed, he found himself in the subservient position with her on top. It was only a brief moment until he had absorbed most of the moisture in the couch. "Maybe it would be better if we stood up and made love. I bet Susann talked about making love in the vertical position in her book."

"Shut up and pull your pants down. It look like rain overhead again." She was not in error for soon there was a dim flash of light in the room produced by distant lightning.

"Wait, first let me get my suit coat off. The cleaners will never be able to get the press back in this thing."

She released her dominant position for a moment as he searched for a place to hang his coat and vest. Finally he found a peg on the edge of the porch that hung precariously over the water and he hung his wet coat and vest on that pedestal. Suddenly he heard a loud noise in the room.

"What's that?" he questioned.

"It's wharf rat."

"Oh my God. Do they bite?" John shouted.

"Only dead stuff. If you don't make love quick, you find rat attracted to you."

John obeyed her command promptly. He pulled off his pants and boxer shorts and hung those upon the board, too.

She smiled. "I think we now informal enough for you to pull your tie off."

John proceeded to take his tie off, but ended up with a fisherman's knot at the end of it. The more he pulled on his tie, the tighter the knot became. "Hey, help me before I throttle myself."

Molly walked towards him, her silhouette illuminated by the lightning. "Your tie clasp caught in tie make knot very fast." She was referring to his destroyer tie clasp that he greatly treasured. "Go hang your tie and shirt on peg and come here. I very disappointed in your size. Very small for American."

"What kind of authority are you on size anyway? I thought you were a novice."

"No novice to handjobs." Her statement disappointed him because she had seemed so innocent at first but giving handjobs for money must have made an interesting occupation. Thinking and only paying faint attention to his surroundings, he managed to hit his knee on a large wooden chair. He recoiled and backed into the wall, sending a section of boards toppling followed by a very loud splash.

"Oh no! Shit!"

"What matter now?"

"My suit and pants fell into the bay with the damn peg! That's what happened! Jeez, help me quick before they go out to sea!" He lunged forward and managed to hit the chair one more time. "That fucker!"

The house was built on pilings that had broken glass and fragmented rocks at their base. "How am I going to get to my wallet? Quick, get my shoes. I'm going to leap." Molly ran back into the house, and John could hear her moving furniture in search of his shoes. Just then another bolt of lightning flashed nearby and revealed a bay void of any signs of clothing.

"Hurry, my credit cards are in those pants! Jeez, someone will find those things and I'll never get out of debt." In spite of the cold, rivulets of sweat ran down John's face and pooled around his eyes, causing them to blur and burn.

"Here, I find!" Panting, she handed him his shoes and socks. Out of habit, he began putting his socks on.

"What am I doing with these socks?" He then hurled them against the porch rail in frustration. The rain had soaked the laces that caused the shoes not to loosen and he had great difficulty in putting them on. "Damn these things, I'm going to split these fuckers' seams!"

"Shoo, shoo, you wake up people."

"Forget the damn people!" John whispered since he was nude except for his black regulation shoes. He did not, however, want to meet any neighbors. Then, without looking down for height always frightened him, he leaped. No sooner was he in the air than he realized that he had made a mistake. It was further down than he had thought. After what seemed like a long descent, he hit solid pollution. "Yah!"

John attempted to make a proper jump with the intention of keeping his legs bent so that the shock would be absorbed properly. Instead he landed on his toes while most of the impact was absorbed in his knees. During the plunge, however, he hit his upper body against one of the pilings. "God, I think I broke it."

"What, what?" Molly shouted as though calling from the heavens.

"My arm, my arm. Jeez, it's killing me." He had obviously

fractured his wrist. "Wait, wait, it's beginning to get numb. I can take the pain, I think. Look close and see if you can spot my pants."

"It no good, tide running out."

"Oh no, oh no, that can't happen! If that Mobil card gets loose in Hong Kong, I will have to end my life." He splashed in the shallow water, trying to search in an ever-widening arc but to no avail. "Damn it!"

"What wrong now?" Molly was beginning to laugh. She tried to control it but the more she restrained herself, the louder were her bursts of laughter.

"Shoo, shut up! I just walked into a submerged log. I give up. I mean I give up! How the hell do I get back up the piling?"

"You crawl up." It was no longer possible for her to contain her laughter.

"What? I got a bum wrist. Never mind, I'll crawl up a piling." Climbing up a slimy wooden pole was an experience that not even the marines had practiced for. It was certainly not recommended to try it in the nude with a fractured wrist.

Cut, bleeding, and his joints stiffening, he reached the pinnacle. A deep feeling of self-pity flowed over him. "What am I going to do? Every card I have is in the ocean along with my ID. I don't have any money for the taxi back to Hong Kong."

"You not even have any clothes!" Molly looked him over and laughed.

"At least don't laugh. Damn it, this is serious! What can I do about getting some clothes, or am I just to plan on coming out at night from now on?" His cuts, saturated with cold salt water, were beginning to itch and burn.

"Say, I got idea. I go get some clothes," Molly said, enthusiastic about helping him.

"Where? I guess they have a Salvation Army dump down the block?" John said sarcastically.

"No, I have some money. Firefly like you. She will pay me back." Molly quickly vanished around the corner of the shack. No sooner had she left than John felt something licking his lower leg. "No, no, shit, what!" He was caught completely off guard by a very large mongrel that was trying to be friendly. He felt as bad as the dog smelled. "Hello boy, how you doing? I'm surprised you haven't bitten me yet. Why don't you leave and come back after someone has bathed you?"

John heard footsteps coming around the building.

"You still here?" she asked.

"No, I left a while ago. Did you get me anything to put on?" John could make out a bundle of material in her hand. For the first time in more than an hour, he felt hopeful of surviving the evening.

"I found robe on neighbor's clothesline." She held it out for him to admire. The robe was illuminated by another flash. It appeared to be dark in color with a very large dragon on the back. John had seen one like it back at his grandmother's house. His uncle had brought it home for his mother. As he examined the material more closely, it began to rain hard.

"How do we get back to Hong Kong?"

"You not want to make love?" Her voice had a tease in it. The yellow dress made her figure stand out in the intermittent lightning. Even though all his worldly rights to credit had just been consumed by the bay, his sexual urges had not been affected. He resented his own body for not being more aware of his plight.

"Uh, yah, that would be great."

She took his hand and led him back into the old dwelling. Molly's passion seemed to be on a rapid time schedule. Quickly, his financial worries vanished and the most important event on earth was her touch. He then turned her about and tried to unzip her dress. As usual, the zipper got snagged on the frayed label and wouldn't budge.

"Never mind dress, I pull it up," she said mockingly. She raised it so quickly that it seemed she had been rehearsing the event for weeks. John then knelt down and lowered her panties. She leaned back on top of him.

As the athletic event that had cost him so much time and money ended, his wallet and suit came back to mind as well as the problem of his current logistical situation.

John felt exhausted but was quickly revived by the myriad of large raindrops that splattered on the roof. He released her small breasts, which he had used like handles to move her body back and forth.

"You stay inside while I get taxi." She raised her panties and lowered her dress as untouched by the experience as though it had been but a urine break.

"You're right to get the taxi by yourself." Even John knew that no one would stop for an American standing in the rain in a kimono bathrobe and Navy regulation shoes. "Some virgin and some evening. I'll probably get VD now. What does it matter if I wasn't the first?" He continued to stand still, letting the blowing rain slap him in the face. It wasn't long before he heard Molly shouting at the sound of an approaching automobile. Suddenly he heard a taxi speed away.

"Molly! Molly!" he said, his voice containing the sound of pain. Silence answered him back.

The walk was a long one. Two dogs attempted to bite him, but he never broke his pace while ascending the flank of Victoria Peak. His fear of the Captain's wrath provided the needed incentive. When he reached the squatters' huts that stood guard over the city, he thought, *Three hours before liberty expires. My God, it's still miles before I can get to the landing.* The thought produced immediate beads of sweat on his cold forehead and forced him to break into a trot. His shoes felt like two pieces of sharp iron bolted to his feet. It was not long before his running brought forth more dogs that, by nature and breeding, enjoyed a good chase. The animals seemed to be particularly attracted to his flowing robe. A particularly large dog clamped its teeth on the garment's hem and held on. It was not long before the cur and John were engaged in a tug of war.

"Stop, you son of a bitch!" John cursed and the dog growled. It dawned on him that he was not going to win. His muscles were no match against a dog's. Instead, he decided to respond with submission rather than combat. Once John stopped pulling, the beast became disappointed quickly and released its grip, but waited for the contest to begin again. Instead John raised his kimono beyond the reach of the dog and began running. It followed him for a short time, barking. Soon they passed another dog and his pursuer's attention went into sniffing its fellow beast.

John did not know what he would do once he reached Fenwick Pier. Without money, he would not be able to get a bam-bam boat to take him to the destroyer. There, however, to his amazement was Boats sleeping on one of the landing's benches. John grabbed him forcefully by the shoulder. "Come on, Boats, it's me, Yorktown."

"Uh, what, yah?" His breath reached John before his words. It was the typical coffee, cigarette, whisky, beer, failure-to-brush breath. "Well, I'll be a motherfucker. If it ain't Mr. Yorktown. What in hell happened to you?"

"I spent the night with a virgin."

"Jeez, you made it! I'll be damned."

"Yah, Boats, I made it. It was one fine piece of ass. Why do you think I'm sweating? She damn well wore Luther off."

"My Yorktown, I am proud of you. You finally made it. I have to admit that there were times when I was worried about you. But now I have to hand it to you. You're one hell of a China sailor.

CHAPTER TWENTY-ONE

Moment of Regret

IS GOD DEAD?
—*Time: The Weekly Magazine,*
April 8, 1966

It did not bother John that he lied to Boats about his conquest of a virgin. Nor did he feel compelled to tell him it was Molly Wong, not Firefly that he had spent the evening with.

He laid in his bunk thinking about how close he had come to missing muster on the *Hyman*. For an officer, that would have been an unforgivable sin. After showering and putting on fresh civilian clothes, he waited patiently for the bam-bam boat to appear. In the distance he could see the smoke being emitted from her two-cycle gasoline engine.

"Well, Mr. Yorktown, it's the last night in port. What ya

going to do?" asked Boats.

"I thought I would go to the G.I. Joe and say goodbye to Firefly. Even though I have tried not to fall for her, I have even failed at that. I should never have followed you and Mr. Fuller ashore. I should have stayed here and practiced on the maneuvering board or learned flashing light or some other worthless experience."

"Now Mr. Yorktown, you don't need to be so down on yourself. What would your men have thought of you if you had stayed aboard in such a swell liberty port as Hong Kong? They would have thought that you were some kind of fairy or somethin'."

"I guess I risked my life and spent nearly all of my money so I could uphold the standards of the officer corps. Damn, I sure am glad I didn't slip up."

"That's the spirit, sir. Now that you're a China sailor you have standards to live up to. If you were enlisted, I'd tell you to get a tattoo. You know, have CHINA SAILOR inked on your chest, nipple to nipple."

"Damn Boats, I might just do that. That would really make an impression on any girl that I dated back in the States."

At that moment Tom rested his hand on John's shoulder. "Last night in port, boot. Man, I hate to leave this place, odor and all. I was really getting used to the girls. Did I hear right that you finally scored with Firefly?"

"Tom, I'm just going to leave my affair with Firefly to your imagination. Each time that you think about it, it will only get better."

They saluted the OOD and then the in-port ensign as they departed the ship. The harbor was choppy with spray being cast upon the enlisted who rode in the bow of the boat.

When they landed on Fenwick Pier, dusk was settling in on the island. Streetcars were filled with office personnel riding home while rickshaws and taxis competed. The rich smells of food cooking on the verandas above them added to the cauldron of odors.

John walked into Bar G. I. Joe followed by both Tom and Boats. "What are you creeps following me for? There is only one Firefly."

"Mr. Yorktown, I needed to verify that you did indeed earn the title of China sailor," said Boats with a wink.

"My salty friend, how are you supposed to do that?" asked John.

"I'm going to ask Molly. All the girls tell one another about their men. Firefly would have told her the truth."

"Now wait a minute, I'm an officer, far superior to you in every way, and I expect you to take my word for it."

"Sir, I trust you but the code of fellow China sailors requires verification."

As they entered the bar, the smell of beer and cigarettes greeted them. Out of the darkness, Susie approached them. "Mr. Yorktown, you looking for Firefly?"

"Yes, Susie, I am," replied John.

"I bet your friends are broke. Been in port too long to be interesting," she said, smiling at Tom and Boats.

Boats looked at Susie. "May I buy you a drink? I have a little money left. No point in exchanging Hong Kong dollar for U.S."

John felt Firefly's hand take his. "John, I am so happy you have returned. Molly told me what happened."

"How are you feeling now? I really didn't want to be with Molly last night. I am glad she told you what happened."

"I did not want you to go to bed with her. I wanted her only to make you happy. It was my idea for her to take you to Tiger Balm Garden. I did not want her to take you to Aberdeen."

"Are you mad at her?" asked John.

"Yes," Firefly replied.

"Are you mad at me?" asked John.

"No, not really. I can't blame you for my being sickly. Not your fault. I am glad that your pants fall in water," she said, laughing.

"Thanks for having someone return my wallet this morning or I would never have been able to get off the ship. As you know, I couldn't see in the dark. Just lucky for me that they landed on a support before they hit the bay. Whoever found them was very honest."

"I sent my cousin to look for them very early this morning. It was he that happened to see them. Not too easy to spot."

John reached into his wallet and handed Firefly five dollars. "Here, please give this to your cousin. He saved my last night in port."

"Last night in port? I didn't realize that!"

"I'm not supposed to mention ship movements, but it will be pretty obvious that we are gone when you see us getting underway from the anchorage."

"I don't want you to leave! Even though you butterfly, I still like you very much."

"Let's go somewhere, anywhere to be together."

"My aunt has friend that owns a small restaurant on rooftop. He owned famous rooftop restaurant in Cebu. Great view of the harbor and Victoria Peak. Of course, all we will soon see will be the lights. Twilight not last too long in winter."

"*Hyman* pulled into Cebu not that long ago. Tom dined at one of the rooftop restaurants. He said it was some of the best food in P.I. While he was in Cebu, several of them went over to Lapu-Lapu to see where Magellan was killed. He said the place had not changed since the explorer was murdered there," said John.

"Owner been in Hong Kong several years. He may be related to man who owned restaurant in Cebu. We will ask him. Is it okay if we go?" she asked quietly.

"That is fine with me. How much to buy you out of the bar?" John asked.

"Mamasan say it is okay. I have already asked her. You have been very good customer. She hope that you return again."

The ride to the restaurant took longer than John had expected. The taxi driver continued to honk his horn and swerve between cars. John felt a little uneasy since the drive took them into what was officially known as an off-limits area. The buildings were older while their occupants sat on the various porches that rose above the streets. The building itself was located much higher than the rest of the city. He, however, did not question either Firefly or the driver.

In the distance, he could see the *Hyman* and several other

small boys from navies around the world. Due to its immense size, the *Yorktown* dominated the harbor. The most active vessels were the Star Ferry boats that busily crossed the harbor back and forth between Kowloon and the island of Hong Kong. The sound of the wind as well as the call of sea birds could be heard.

"Here we are," she said, looking up towards the top of the building.

There was a small elevator in the main entryway that took them slowly to the rooftop. Several tables were placed outside even though the majority of customers wanted to be served inside.

An unusually tall man approached Firefly and took her hand. First words were exchanged in Cantonese and then English.

"Hello Firefly. It is very nice to see you. Who is your friend?"

"Emanuel, this is my friend, Ensign Johnnie Yorktown. He off big destroyer. He say that his friend loved rooftop restaurant in Cebu City. Very good food."

Emanuel acknowledged John with a smile and a nod of his head. "Welcome. Firefly very nice lady."

John could not help but notice how beautiful Firefly was. The red dress, her long black hair, and soft voice intoxicated him. When he looked into her eyes, he forfeited all reasoning and his own identity. His body responded without his conscious control. At that moment, he knew he had fallen in love with Firefly.

Emanuel handed them menus that were written in three languages—Cantonese, Mandarin, and Spanish.

"Firefly, please order for me. There is no use in my pretending to read languages that I'm not familiar with."

"Do you trust me?" she asked, smiling.

He realized that her question involved much more than ordering a meal. "I trust you with my love," he replied.

Firefly did not respond but only ordered from the menu. As they ate, John touched her hand, and then held it. When they finished eating, they both rose and walked out to the veranda that overlooked the city and the harbor. The lights of the ferries traced the width of the harbor. He took her in his arms and held her tightly, shielding her from the strong cold wind that blew from the mountains and the distant ocean. Softly he kissed her.

She looked inquisitively at him. "You can't love Chinese girl. Navy will forbid it. Besides, you very foolish. How can you love a girl that you have known only two weeks?"

John looked intently into her eyes. "You are correct in everything that you have said. I can't explain it to you. I cannot understand myself. You are the first person I have ever loved. Before 'love' was only a word I used to get what I wanted from a girl. Now I know what it means. I also believe that a man only loves once just like a dove."

Upon returning to Fenwick Pier, they waited for the small boat to take him back to his ship.

"John, will you come back for me?" she asked, looking up at him. The strong cold wind of the harbor blew through her long black hair.

"No man can stop me from returning. I promise you."

"Then I wait." She paused. "I scared that you not come back for me. Sailors promise many things to Wan Chai girls. I am only

Chinese girl and you will soon be far away."

"I will return for you," he replied as he released her. "I promise. I will come back!"

Firefly paused. John noticed that new tears were forming in her eyes. "Johnnie, I must be truthful to you. Yesterday I go to hospital to see doctor. My biopsy report came back." She looked away towards the harbor. John could barely breathe. "I have leukemia. The doctor said that I may not live until I be old woman. I am so sorry that I allowed you to love me. Please know that I will love you forever even if you not come back for me."

"Come on, Firefly, that can't be true. It can't be! I would know if that were true. I would feel it in my heart."

"No, it is the truth. You do not want to understand."

"If what you say is true, we will fight it together. There is always hope. Somewhere there is an answer. The next time that we are in port in Hong Kong, we will go to the doctor together."

"I not have money to pay doctor. Free doctor no good in Hong Kong."

John hesitated for a moment. "I will pay for it! I swear I will! I have no place in heaven if I do not keep my word."

"Johnnie, don't say that. I know you mean it but don't say it. Sometimes bad things happen, and you cannot help them. I only want you to be happy." Firefly paused and then held John tightly. "Come back for me!" she said, tears filling her eyes.

"Hey Mr. Yorktown, the bam-bam boat is ready to depart for *Hyman*. Come on or we will miss muster," shouted Boats above the roar of the engine.

He embraced and kissed her, then let go of her frail body.

CHAPTER TWENTY-TWO

The Enemy Is Exhaustion

THE GENERATION THAT FORGOT GOD
   (among other images, the execution of a Vietcong prisoner, Tet Offensive, 1968)
                      —*Time Magazine*, April 5, 1993

The ship rode the darkening swells as the crew looked at the increasingly distant silhouetted shoreline of Hong Kong. The crew, dissipated by their evenings in Hong Kong, manned the bridge as the underway watch relieved the sea and anchor detail. Eyes still blurry from lack of sleep, voices hoarse from whiskey, and cigarettes exchanged looks and comments. All hands stared towards the dark sea as the small islands of the bay disappeared astern. A weather front consisting of lightning and rain presented itself off to port as the head of the ship swung past 180 degrees as she steadied her course for Yankee Station. Each man knew that the earliest he could return to land was not less than thirty days, which more than likely would extend to sixty.

John looked towards Tom. "Well, no more liberty for a while. I guess it's the gun line for us. I sure hope we don't pull north SAR again. I hate having to look at the scope, trying not to run up the ass of the can in front of us."

"Boot, what are you complaining about? You need the practice. When you have the conn, a man can't get any sleep. No telling what you will hit out here."

The routine of a small boy underway in the tropics slowly drained the endurance and judgment of the crew. Medicated by cigarettes and coffee, the sailors of the *Hyman* went about their shipboard duties—a routine published in the ship's official plan of the day. The scheduled events seldom happened in the order in which the mimeographed document had promised them.

The weeks, then months, went by slowly since the ship had departed Hong Kong. The letters from Firefly became less and less frequent until by mid-August they stopped. Since Firefly could not write, it was apparent that Yu had written them for her, polite letters void of any passion. He continued to write her but no one responded, not even Yu.

In her letters, she never referred to her illness. John wanted to know, but at the same time, he was afraid of the truth. It was as though her disease did not exist. There were rumors that the ship would return to Hong Kong, but they remained only rumors, scuttlebutt generated by loneliness and desire.

Due to lack of sleep and the unending watches, the potential for shipboard accidents haunted the crew. It did not take a shell from the enemy to destroy a ship or alter the lives of her crew. The morning of October 26, 1966 would prove to be no exception.

As the *Hyman* steamed towards her new H&I assignment along the coast of South Vietnam, John was on his way to the bridge when he saw smoke rising on the distant horizon of the Gulf of Tonkin. He immediately wondered what could be producing the billowing white smoke that appeared off the port bow at a considerable range from the ship.

John was approached by Tom who was to assume the watch with him. "Hey, what is taking place over there? There shouldn't be that much smoke even if the carrier is blowing her tubes," said John.

"All I know is that the Commodore has ordered us to plane guard the *Oriskany* for a couple of days before releasing us for H&I. Something to do with one of her small boys having a boiler problem. The *Philips* can't keep up with the bird farm," said Tom, staring at the plume of smoke.

Boats approached the two officers. "Shit man, not another problem?" he said as he squinted in the direction of the rising white vapor.

"We don't know what to make of it," replied John. "I guess we'll find out when we relieve the watch."

Suddenly, word was passed over the 1MC: "Now hear this! Now hear this! The ship will commence search and rescue operations in 15 minutes."

John and Tom ran quickly up the ladder to the bridge. There they found the Captain and the Executive Officer standing with the OPS boss. The mood on the bridge seemed very somber.

"Say Bernie, what is going on?" Tom asked the OOD.

"We have a problem. This morning we were assigned to plane guard the *Oriskany* (CVA-34). On the way to assuming our plane guard station astern of the carrier, a loud explosion occurred on the *Oriskany*. We don't know what hit her or if she exploded internally. There were several explosions, one right after another. She is attempting to keep the smoke from engulfing the ship. We were told to stand by to search for survivors."

"Bernie, why aren't we closer to the ship?" asked Tom.

"We have not officially relieved the *Philips*. Seems like Flag wants us to stay back since, as you know, a carrier can't stop on a dime. We are now just about where the *Oriskany* was when she caught fire. Survivors would have abandoned the ship at this spot. I figure that some may have been blown off the flight deck or jumped from the hangar deck."

"All hands man the rail. Maintain a look out for survivors. Report any sightings to the bridge immediately." Soon all hands not on engineering watch were leaning on the rails to search for signs of movement in the water. Then Signals, located directly above the bridge and using the large mounted big eyes, spotted a sailor splashing in the water off the port bow. Word was immediately passed down to the bridge.

"This is the Captain, I have the conn. Ahead flank, steer course 089." The *Hyman* quickly responded to the new commands. The hull vibrated with the surge of sudden speed. Soon she was cutting smoothly through the glasslike sea.

"This is the Captain, man the sling for a close aboard shipboard rescue."

Soon the man in the water had a face. He had lost his shirt but his khaki pants identified him as an officer. He was swiftly lifted aboard by the sling. He stood for a moment leaning against a stanchion. "I am Lt. Osborne, VAH-4." The lieutenant spoke as though he was mustering on station rather than just having been fished out of the Gulf of Tonkin. "When she caught fire, I couldn't see a damn thing. The smoke was choking me. I asked a sailor which way to the flight deck, and he pointed towards an open hatch. The only problem was that there was nothing beneath the hatch. I must have fallen seventy feet into the ocean."

Around the *Hyman* appeared half-sunken rubber life rafts. It was apparent that even though they had been deployed, the majority had failed to inflate properly.

Lt. Osborne turned towards the crew who had congregated around him and smiled. "Thanks to you swabbies, an airedale lives to fly another day." He raised his hand as though offering a toast. "Drinks are on me."

The corpsman took him to the sickbay. It was apparent that the lieutenant was about to go in shock. Unknown to everyone on the main deck, the polyester pants that the airedale wore had melted into his flesh.

Since the *Oriskany* was heavily damaged, the *Hyman* was no longer needed to assume plane guard duties. *Oriskany* was to depart Yankee Station and seek temporary repairs in Subic Bay. From there, she was to journey to the San Francisco Navy Shipyard.

Lt. Osborne was the only man that the *Hyman* rescued that day. She was relieved at 1900 and changed course and speed. Towards the coast of Vietnam she traveled and for the unknown that awaited in the coastal waters of a nation growing increasingly hostile. The crew was silent as the smoke from the *Oriskany* vanished over the horizon.

Later, John learned that forty-four officers and men died that day when the sky was free of clouds and the sea was smooth. She had been the victim of a careless accident, or so it would seem. Those aboard the *Hyman* needed few reminders that there were more dangers present than the Viet Cong or their allies, North Vietnam. Just as it had been onboard the *Oriskany,* exhaustion was to be their enemy.

Boats leaned on the rail. "Mr. Yorktown, I figure we are now headed for one of those damn SEATO exercises. At least that's the scuttlebutt I hear. All we need to keep us busy is to work with one of those carrier types where you can't understand what the hell they are saying. You would think that those Australian assholes would learn to speak English," added Boats, whose breath indicated he had consumed more than just one San Miguel in Olongapo where the ship had stopped for a short port visit, or perhaps had smuggled a cool one onboard.

"Something bothers me," said Boats with his usual

philosophical wisdom. "You noticed that weather front as we left the bay islands? Not a good sign. You know that when you've been out here as long as I have. You look for signs and shit. Maybe it's just a tooth that's bothering you or a shoulder that aches but you always look for signs. That storm was not a good one. The ship didn't roll right or something. I feel that we are going to have some problems this time. Shit, I just hope that it don't slow us down from getting back to Yoko."

John heard someone stepping quickly up the ship's ladder. Decker approached from the shadow of the bridge hatch. "Mr. Yorktown, we just got this." He handed the message board to John for his initials. Both John and Tom saw the concern on Decker's face.

"Mr. Yorktown," said Tom with junior officer authority, "who do you think is driving this motherfucker right now? You or me? If it involves a course change, let me take a look at the message board first. The Old Man likes someone to explain his messages and then he reads it to you word for word in order to correct what you just said. Kind of instructional, you know. It is Navy policy that only skippers can understand flag shit."

Tom reached out for the message board, John hovering near his shoulder. "Oh no, our luck just got worse. Before we join the SEATO exercise, we have been ordered to provide cover fire for a marine landing just south of the DMZ. That means we'll be hauling ass again. No sleep."

"I guess I should look on the bright side, at least I can save some money. Considering what I spent in Hong Kong and later in Olongapo, I can use a break from the bar scene. Now I have to wake the Captain. I doubt he'll be very happy about the news," said Tom, staring at the sea.

Just as the messenger departed, Decker returned to the bridge. As before, John took the message board, initialed it, then handed it to Tom. "Proceed to the waters of Song Doc. Provide H&I fire as shown in Enclosure 1." The enclosure provided the coordinates for the harassment and interdiction fire.

Tom looked towards John. "Good thing I didn't have to wake the Old Man twice. That would have really pissed him off."

The ship proceeded in the darkness of the hot, humid, and still night. In the distance, flares could be seen falling over what appeared to be a fishing village but they could not be sure. "Someone is having a party over there," said Boats, squinting in the direction of the falling light. "Glad we were not invited."

John looked towards Tom and said sarcastically, "Why can't we cut on our running lights, light the smoking lamp, and play 'Born Loser'? You know they're very aware of our presence."

"Yah, you probably told every hooker in Olongapo where we were going. But we have to do it by the book. Even if we go to hell in a handbasket, we need to do it right."

"The only ones we're harassing are ourselves. We're the ones that get no sleep," said John.

"Now hear this, now hear this, darken ship," said Boats over the 1MC. "Close all outside hatches and doorways. The smoking lamp is out throughout the ship. The ship expects to go to General Quarters at 2100."

At 2100 the alarm sounded. "General Quarters, General Quarter." The shrill bosun's pipe had been omitted.

The ship entered the waters of the bay at 2130 and then proceeded to the mouth of what was known as the "River of Dreams." John and Tom studied the navigation charts using their red-filtered flashlights. John then went to the radarscope and passed information on their bearings, ensuring that the ship stayed in the middle of the dark, wide river. The speed of the ship had not been decreased, resulting in a confined rooster tail that slapped against the ever-narrowing riverbanks. It was impossible to tell from the scope if any fishing boats were present. If they were there, they were simply too small or close aboard to appear on the scope.

The river's birth was in the mountains where she was nurtured by multiple tributaries. The silhouettes of large trees that crowded the riverbanks were framed by the moon. When rigged for silent running, John was surprised at how quiet the *Hyman* could operate. Despite the speed of the ship, only the muted sounds of the bow wave and the stern wake sounded in the night. Soon Vietnamese voices could be heard coming from the surface of the river, seemingly very close aboard.

The Captain appeared on the wing of the bridge. Facing the unidentified voices, he hurled a percussion grenade over the side. There was a large explosion as fresh water bathed the superstructure of the vessel. He then ran to the opposite wing of the bridge and tossed another percussion grenade. The Captain quickly ordered the fifty-caliber machine gun to fire a few bursts into the inkwell of the night.

Then all was quiet on the river. There were no voices to be heard. The Captain spoke over the squawk box to gun control. "Fire for effect. Both batteries are released." The gunfire was rapid and accurate that night. The enemies were but coordinates on a map, nothing more.

Suddenly the order was given to come about as the mounts continued to respond to his command. After completing a 180-degree turn which necessitated the reversing of one engine, "All ahead flank" was commanded by the Captain who had once again assumed the conn. The ship shook with the new speed as she steamed towards the bay with Mount 52 continuing to fire at the coordinates given by CIC.

It was apparent that once their presence was known, the Captain did not want to be trapped in a narrowing river where handheld missiles would make a quick work of her. Once into the heart of the river, he ordered, "All ahead, standard."

Once at sea, the mood of the vessel changed. There was a more relaxed feeling for no deepwater sailor feels comfortable being so close to the shore. Each member of the crew hoped that the night would settle back into the well-established routine of a vessel at sea.

Once again the messenger of the watch reappeared on the bridge. He handed the message board to John for his initials.

Tom approached John. "Let's see what it says. Damn it!" he moaned. "I knew it was going to be a bad watch. We're going to work with some Aussie bird farm at Yankee Station. Seems like they want to practice colliding with us."

Tom continued, "Boats, better check the alarm systems. I imagine that we are going to need them. And by the way, let's have at least one inflatable that floats. I remember when the *Oriskany* caught fire, half of their inflatables sunk. You must have been Chief Boats on her at one time."

The days on Yankee Station passed without incident or concern as the ship waited for the SEATO exercise to commence. Hours of watches and drills, followed by the ship movie and then the sleep that only a small boy underway can give, a mixture of sound and rhythmic motion.

John, however, found it increasingly difficult to sleep. Thoughts of Firefly continued to haunt his waking moments and his dreams. He knew there was no cure for her type of cancer, the slow wasting away of life. Time was both her enemy and his. John realized that he needed to be with her, to help her fight the disease as best he could. He also sensed the fear she was experiencing.

John knew he was in love with her. He was desperate to call her yet he could not. He wanted to send her money, but he had none to spare after spending everything that he possessed in Hong Kong. Postal mail, which took weeks if not months, was the only way he could communicate with her. His letters had to first travel across the Pacific to the Fleet Post Office in San Francisco before being rerouted to Hong Kong and arriving weeks later.

John, Tom, and Boats had the mid-watch at the very moment that the quartermaster had predicted they would rendezvous with the carrier task force. A flurry of messages had preceded the event the previous day. OP plans were helloed to the destroyer. John had spent that day looking for the necessary pubs and found all of them save for the usual missing one. He always felt that there was some unwritten rule in the universe dedicated to his being able to find 4 out of 5 items or 9 out of 10, always one short regardless of the number of possibilities. The rule, like the cycle of tides, had never changed throughout his life.

What in the world did Frisbee do with it? thought John. *Can't he ever page-check a pub before signing off on it?* John ignored his own problem of depending on others to page-check for him. *Oh no, what if the exercise was in one of the pubs that we burned yesterday?* Moisture appeared on his forehead.

Mid rats were disappointing since the steward had locked the reefer and left two stiffened donuts on a tray. The bug juice tasted of metal and water. The ice had long since left the metal pitcher for the tropic night.

I'll have Decker get some coffee when it's my time to relieve, thought John. He sank down into the donated seat in the wardroom as he watched a picture of the Medal of Honor recipient after whom the ship was named, now liberated from its glue, slowly rotate with the rolling of the ship.

Time passed faster than any law of physics could allow before a watch was relieved. The hands on the bulkhead chronometer chased one another across its face.

The air on the wings of the bridge smelt of the sea air. The warm tropical night enhanced the light mist over the ocean's surface. The encoded voice traffic from the approaching task force became increasingly audible over the bridge speaker. The bird farm and her escorts were arriving on time at the rendezvous point.

"Ensign Yorktown, give me a course and speed for the rendezvous point," Tom commanded. His formality indicated that he was very nervous.

John spoke softly into his headset. "Hey fellow boot, Mr. Fuller wants a course and speed to the rendezvous point." John immediately attempted to work out a solution on the paper maneuvering board that required the use of parallel rulers, dividers, and an eraser for any mistakes he made. Luckily, before John could determine a totally incorrect course and speed, CIC reported a solution.

"Mr. Yorktown, CIC recommends a speed of 14 knots, course 270."

John replied loudly to the bridge team, "I recommend a speed of 14 knots, course 270."

Tom smiled. "What's with the 'I' part? I hope to golly that your partner Frisbee got it right. Yorktown, have you ever worked a maneuvering board solution in your life? I would hate for us to be sailing to China instead of to the rendezvous."

Having reached the rendezvous point just south of Point Yankee, the *Hyman* joined the formation of the bird farm and her three small boys. Everything seemed to be in Navy fashion except for the uneasiness that Tom felt; perhaps it was Boats' premonition that caused his tension. Close order formations of 1500 yards traveling at 18 knots left little room for error or hesitation especially if they were ordered to make a turn or, God forbid, a reorientation of the screen. He knew he was entrusted with the lives of everyone on board. When he considered his backups, John and Frisbee, he felt genuine concern.

Tom was, however, happy that the Old Man had not recorded in the night order book that he had to be awakened at the rendezvous point. It was apparent that the skipper had forgotten to write one of the most common Navy commands. The signal bridges of both ships exchanged communications since the first classes knew each other after having shared the same bar girl back in Yoko. They liked to refer to themselves as "Fore" and "Aft."

"Top Flight, this is Cactus, Bravo Tango Alpha."

In response to the transmission, John and Abato raced to pull the signal pub from the metal shelf and flipped hastily through the pages to decode the signal. John dropped the signal book on the grated deck plate and had to start looking for the signal again. Abato could not immediately locate ATP Volume II since it was placed in the wrong location. He also paused to look at a cover of *Playboy* that was stashed where the pub should have been.

Moments passed before the signal could be deciphered as the ships paralleled each other only 1500 yards apart. John finally decoded the signal.

"Let's see, Bravo Tango Alpha, it means ... oh my God, it's a screen reorientation! The fucking carrier is making a 90-degree course change to port!" John shouted across the bridge to Tom.

The bridge speaker blurted the carrier's command, "I repeat,

Bravo Tango Alpha, standby, execute."

Tom, who was on the starboard wing of the bridge, yelled to Yorktown, "John, what did you say? They're warming up a jet engine on the bird farm and I can't hear a damn thing."

"Tom, it's a screen reorientation. The fucker is making a 90-degree turn to port! The signal has already been executed!" Tom noticed that the running lights of the carrier were changing orientation. It was apparent that she was turning, but his first impression was that she was turning to starboard, away from the tin can, and not to port that could result in crossing the T.

It then became apparent to Tom that she must be in a port turn since he could now make out her starboard running light. "My God, my God!" Tom shouted. "Sound the collision alarm!"

John froze for a moment as he processed the information. The quartermaster of the watch pulled the collision alarm, sending a loud, repetitive clang throughout the ship. The Captain arrived on the bridge in his skivvies just as the two ships were closing on a collision course.

"I have the conn!" shouted the skipper. At that moment, a shattering sound of metal against metal, electrical wires sizzling, and screams from the signal bridge filled the night air and carried over a calm sea. Suddenly, the carrier's port anchor passed over the bridge as the ship received its fatal blow, forcing it to sharply list to port under the pressure of the carrier as it sliced its way through the bulkheads.

Immediately the bow section began to settle. Tom and John fell backwards into the water where CIC had been just moments before. The bow rose as those cast into sea attempted to avoid the impending suction. The stem rose high, stopped, and then the bow rolled over to port and floated as though designed for such a purpose. Screams sounded from the forward half of the ship as seawater flooded the passageways and raced down the escape ladders. The passageways had been blocked by twisted metal illuminated by the ship's red battle lanterns.

John knew that Frisbee was lost as well as the CIC watch team. Tom swam towards a moaning sailor he did not know whose arm was entangled in metal wiring. He attempted to free the sailor, but only managed to entangle himself too as the bow shifted angles. John swam to their aid in the darkness, guided by the sailor's moans and Tom's curses and pleas for help.

The bow, after having been stable for a moment, began to rise once more as the entrapped air made its way forward. It stayed suspended for a moment and began its descent to the bottom of the Gulf of Tonkin. Tom and the unknown sailor were entangled with the ship, inseparable despite John's efforts.

John looked upon the water blackened by fuel oil and illuminated by the searchlights of another destroyer that had raced to provide assistance. The ship, his friends, and his youth suddenly slipped into the dark sea. Young, boastful men silenced before age could steal their dreams.

In the Gulf of Tonkin, the *Hyman* lies silent at the 100-fathom curve. At night, tiger sharks visit her like the recurring dreams of Professor Yorktown.

"Hey, you alright?" asked the taxi driver with his Mid-Eastern accent. "You been standing there looking at the water ever since I arrived. Didn't you hear me honk?"

The professor turned towards the driver. "I'm sorry, my mind was elsewhere. Just remembering." He looked down at the rising tide and then at the empty pier. A seagull called as the present reemerged in his thoughts and the dream awaited him in the night. John now realized that the greatest loss had been that of innocence.

ABOUT THE AUTHOR

Franklin Lafayette King, a combat veteran, served as an officer aboard a destroyer homeported in the Far East during the Vietnam conflict. The storyline of the book is taken from his journal written during a time of social change, undeclared war, and potential global conflict. In addition to *China Sailor: The Shooting of Whales*, he is the author of ten books that include both novels and works of poetry.

www.ingramcontent.com/pod-product-compliance
Lightning Source LLC
Chambersburg PA
CBHW030135170426
43199CB00008B/71